YES, LORD, I KNOW THE ROAD

Yes, Lord,
I KNOW THE ROAD

A DOCUMENTARY HISTORY OF
AFRICAN AMERICANS IN
SOUTH CAROLINA
1526–2008

Edited by J. BRENT MORRIS

THE UNIVERSITY OF SOUTH CAROLINA PRESS

Published by the University of South Carolina Press
Columbia, South Carolina 29208

www.sc.edu/uscpress

Manufactured in the United States of America

26 25 24 23 22 21 20 19 18 17
10 9 8 7 6 5 4 3 2 1

Library of Congress Cataloging-in-Publication Data
Names: Morris, J. Brent, editor.
Title: Yes, Lord, I know the road : a documentary history of African
Americans in South Carolina, 1526–2008 / edited by J. Brent Morris.
Description: Columbia, South Carolina : University of South Carolina Press,
[2017] | Includes bibliographical references and index.
Identifiers: LCCN 2016047778 (print) | LCCN 2016049459 (ebook) |
ISBN 9781611177305 (hardcover : alk. paper) | ISBN 9781611177312
(pbk. : alk. paper) | ISBN 9781611177329 (ebook)
Subjects: LCSH: African Americans—South Carolina—History—Sources.
Classification: LCC E185.93.S7 Y47 2017 (print) | LCC E185.93.S7
(ebook) | DDC 975.7/00496073—dc23
LC record available at https://lccn.loc.gov/2016047778

"Sheep, sheep, do you know the road?
Yes, Lord, I know the road.
Sheep, sheep, do you know the road?
Yes my Lord, I know the road . . ."

Sea Islands spiritual

CONTENTS

LIST OF ILLUSTRATIONS

FOREWORD

This documentary narrative of African Americans in South Carolina covers the broad sweep of the state's history from early Spanish explorations to the modern political and social activities of people of African descent. It promises to be a boon for students, teachers, and the general public interested in the unique background of a small, complex, and fascinating region. The documents are extraordinary and well chosen. They reveal, for example, that less than thirty-five years after Christopher Columbus's first voyage, Spanish explorers incited here perhaps the earliest rebellion of enslaved Africans on the North American coast and one of the earliest anywhere in the New World. They contradict any notion that armed resistance was practically unknown among peoples brought unwillingly to labor for Europeans in North America (in contrast to what is conceded for enslaved Africans elsewhere in America) or that the northern mainland was in any way exempt from the prevailing cultural, political, and social currents that affected the meeting of black and white people everywhere during their settlement in America and during and after the development of plantation economies. There was cooperation and conflict, personal affection and abiding antagonism. No other time or place offers better examples of these commonalities than South Carolina, particularly during the colonial period. Here captive south-central Africans staged the largest slave rebellion in England's continental colonies, featuring a prominent ethnic dimension, and here planters evinced a more open toleration for interracial dalliance than is often acknowledged for the English main. But the intriguing features of this province did not end when it rejected British hegemony. Whether in religion or revolution, this small state offers extraordinary illustrations of African American agency (to evoke a convenient term too easily used) that discredits the idea that African peoples lacked intelligence or initiative and leads to the suggestion that those in South Carolina may have had a disproportionate influence on American society and culture in relationship to the size of the region where they lived. The state was distinctive in the dimension of its African population and in the nature of its African-influenced culture. Moreover, these features extended beyond the colonial period and continue to affect Carolina culture and society in the modern age. There are examples here of the context within which

African Americans operated as well as the communities they formed and the activities they adopted to overcome their obstacles.

Professor Morris provides a solid introduction that puts these documents into perspective. Whether considering abortive Spanish settlements, English colonial developments, the Lowcountry's differentiated labor system, the various staples cultivated, or the tragedy of war and the shortcomings of Reconstruction, he judiciously fills gaps between the documents. One advantage of his outlook is that he does not treat this story in a vacuum but situates the state and the African Americans who inhabit it within a larger Atlantic world and the national scene. He notes the regime of white supremacy and its collapse, the civil rights movement, the ways in which South Carolina handled desegregation and the reasons behind that policy, the return of African Americans to political influence, and events in the twenty-first century during the Age of Obama. Indeed, his essay is an admirable recounting in capsule form of African Americans in South Carolina's history and is a useful short reference. Students as well as the public will find here a handy tool for their edification.

DANIEL C. LITTLEFIELD

PREFACE AND
EDITORIAL NOTES

African Americans were among the first pioneers in the land that eventually became South Carolina, and for most of the nearly five centuries that followed their arrival, men, women, and children of African descent have been a majority of the population there. Until relatively recently, however, their history—their vital role in the development of the colony, state, and nation—has either been misrepresented or neglected entirely. Fortunately, historians writing during and after the civil rights movement of the mid-twentieth century have devoted considerable attention to the dynamic story of black South Carolinians. Copious and often brilliant scholarship has highlighted African American history and culture in the state from the sixteenth through the twenty-first centuries in local, regional, national, and global contexts.

Still, this flurry of scholarly activity has not produced a comprehensive synthetic history of African Americans and South Carolina. This work is not intended to satisfy that need, although it is the first substantial overview of that story. Nor does it endeavor to evaluate the diverse historiography of the past few decades. Rather, *Yes, Lord, I Know the Road* offers, within the limits of approximately 100,000 words, a synopsis of five centuries of rich history to guide scholars until someone takes on the monumental challenge of producing that long-awaited monograph. In the introduction, details are sacrificed for the sake of concision, and much that truly deserves extended analysis is by necessity wrapped into broad generalizations. However, this book's most valuable section, the eighty edited documents and images that constitute the bulk of the work, are the true substance of the story. They are, as Herbert Aptheker wrote in the introduction to one of his many documentary readers, "the words of participants, of eye-witnesses. These are the words of the very great and the very obscure; these are the words of the mass. This is how they felt; this is what they saw; this is what they wanted."

This book invites readers to work with these component pieces of history and consider how they inform the bigger story. Reading narrative alongside the sources black Carolinians left behind brings life and relevancy to the past. We more fully empathize with the enslaved woman working in the muck of a rice field as the summer sun beats down on her back and mosquitoes swarm

about her head. We appreciate the determination of a maroon, defiant and diligent, setting up his camp deep in a swamp. We hear the cadence of a Gullah
sermon, the percussive echo of clapping, and the counter-clockwise shuffling
of feet. We feel the bright spotlights front and center at a national political convention. Many of these source documents are previously unpublished; many
others have been long out of print. It is my hope that the collection will spark
new conversations, inspire fresh questions, and point new ways for historians
to pursue innovative scholarly work.

The documents are presented in seven chapters, roughly chronologically, beginning with the first slave rebellion in North America in 1526 near the mouth
of the Pee Dee River. Documents then chronicle the first few generations of
black South Carolinians and trace the complex transformation of Africans into
African Americans through the Stono Rebellion of 1739. Following that, the
material highlights the implications of a growing black majority and the passage
of a harsh new slave code, the negotiated terrain between African Americans
and whites within the South Carolina plantation regime, and the development
of a unique African American culture through the late antebellum period.

Freedom in early South Carolina was a luxury few African Americans enjoyed. Nearly 400,000 others who first experienced freedom during and after
the Civil War joined those few in the revolutionary era of Reconstruction and
contributed to the sources presented for that period. The aftermath of Reconstruction in South Carolina and the arrival and solid establishment of the Jim
Crow era in the New South are examined, as well as the service of black soldiers
in World War I and World War II, their eventual return to a continuing hostile state, and the counterpoint between Jim Crow and the budding civil rights
movement in the Palmetto State. As W.E.B. Du Bois put it, South Carolina's
African American veterans "returned from fighting," and, importantly, they "returned fighting." They were not alone.

Next, documentation demonstrates the black community's pushback as it
sowed the seeds of destruction for Jim Crow in South Carolina. Not content to
simply bring down a body of discriminatory state laws, South Carolina African
Americans also joined in the blossoming national civil rights movement and
played a vital role in the revolutionary redefinition of America. The records
show that the racial landscape of South Carolina from the late 1970s on had
little in common with that of just a generation earlier. Racism had not disap-
peared in the Palmetto State, but the foundations of a truly open society were
clearly evident. By 2008, as Barack Obama swept through South Carolina on
the way to the White House, he did not "see a white South Carolina or a black
South Carolina," just a South Carolina composed of individuals who were
learning to deal with one another simply as people, not members of races.[1]

■

The documents in this book have been selected primarily on the basis of considerations of historical significance and typicality. A great effort has also been made to choose documents that illustrate the rich diversity of the African American experience in South Carolina. African American sources have been privileged, although documents produced by others are included when their content speaks to or significantly and directly affected African American life. Some documents are reprinted in their entirety, although most have been extracted and edited for length. In all cases, the basic essence of the content, context, general structure, and author's intent have been preserved. Where it is not obvious from the numbering of sections or chapters, ellipses [...] have been used to indicate omissions. Although the intention has been to present the documents as coherent entries, in the case of some of the longer sources, some detail and at times entire topics have been sacrificed for the sake of space. In every case, citations to the full works are provided. Text in square brackets indicates new editorial information or slight modifications to preserve continuity. Explanatory footnotes are generally limited to providing sufficient information to place the documents within their context or to identify relevant individuals and issues that might not be familiar to readers.

ACKNOWLEDGMENTS

This book had its origins with the first courses I ever taught, in my first job out of graduate school. In planning my classes in U.S., African American, and South Carolina history, I attempted to personalize the syllabi as much as possible for my students. Since most of them were South Carolina natives, I sought to pique their interest by emphasizing the role of their state in whichever larger story I was telling. Indeed, very often I needed to make no extra effort, since the Palmetto State has always figured prominently in America's history. This was especially the case in dealing with the state's African American past. When my search for a good primary source reader proved futile, I went into the archives and library stacks and collected hundreds of documents to complement my lectures and course reading assignments with the voices of South Carolina African Americans from every historical period.

This book, in a much-condensed form, is the result. The process of taking the materials, writing a long introduction, and developing it all into a book to be published by a major university press took much longer than I ever imagined it would. In the process, I accumulated countless debts. My first debt is to my students, without whom this project would have never existed. I am also thankful to the staffs of several libraries and manuscript collections for their help in identify new sources, tracking down obscure publications, and navigating miles of microfilm and countless boxes of documents: the South Caroliniana Library, Division of Rare Books and Special Collections, the Coleman Koresh Law Library, and the Thomas Cooper Library, at the University of South Carolina in Columbia; the South Carolina Historical Society; the South Carolina Department of Archives and History; the Avery Research Center at the College of Charleston; the Beaufort County Library; the Richland County Public Library; and the Heritage Library Foundation of Hilton Head Island. The interlibrary loan departments at the University of South Carolina Aiken and the University of South Carolina Beaufort proved that there was no book they could not track down and get into my hands. I also could not have completed this work without the generous financial support of the Sea Islands Institute and Faculty Development Committee at USCB.

For special reprint permissions, I thank the Alan Paton Center and Struggle Archives; the American Bible Society; and Congressman James Clyburn. I also thank the Crisis Publishing Company, which publishes the magazine of the National Association for the Advancement of Colored People, for allowing me to use material first published in the December 1927, September 1946, and August–September 1963 issues of *The Crisis.* Thanks are also due Nikky Finney, the South Carolina Historical Society, the South Caroliniana Library, Tracy S. Bailey, the University of North Carolina Press, the University of South Carolina Library Political Collections, and the University of South Carolina Press.

Friends, family, and colleagues across the country visited libraries when I could not, suggested new places for me to look, and helped me interpret what I found. Ed Baptsit, Lou Benfonte, Mary Lou Brewton, Emory Campbell, Mari Crabtree, Alexia Helsley, Mac James, Chip Landrum, Dan Littlefield, Maggi Morehouse, Larry Rowland, Steve Wise, and Peter Wood freely offered their help, their time, and enthusiasm for my project. Benjamin Nelson performed masterfully as my Spanish translator. My administrators at USCB—especially Jane Upshaw, Al Panu, Gordon Haist, Lynn McGee, and Babet Villena-Alvarez—were cheerleaders at every step along the way. My great friend and mentor Walter Edgar planted the seed for this book in my mind nearly two decades ago and has been constant and more than generous with his support ever since.

And, as always, Kim and Daegan—the time I've spent on this book is all time I've borrowed from you. Thank you for your generosity, your support, and your love.

Introduction

The first people of African descent to occupy the territory that would eventually become South Carolina were brought as slaves by the Spanish explorer Lucas Vásquez de Ayllón on an expedition that landed near present-day Port Royal in the summer of 1526.[1] From its inception, however, Ayllón's colony seemed doomed to fail, and, following the conquistador's death in October of that year, a group of settlers mounted a coup, jailed his successor, and began to severely mistreat the slaves and the local indigenous population. Each group, in turn, retaliated. After the Natives killed a number of the colonists, the slaves rose up, set fire to the village, and mounted what would be the first slave rebellion in North America. Bloodied, starving, and despondent, the Spanish survivors returned to their base in the Caribbean and abandoned the first European colony in what is now the United States.[2]

The history of men and women of African descent in South Carolina therefore began with a powerful demonstration of agency and with determination to be free. Indeed, the rebels of the Ayllón expedition were the first people of African descent to set foot on the ground that would eventually become the United States, and thus African American history was born on the Carolina coast in blood and fire.[3] The flame of communal self-reliance sparked in the Lowcountry would continue to burn for another five centuries. From the early sixteenth century, African American men and women would be a driving force in South Carolina's and America's history. When Hernando de Soto marched through the territory in 1540, his retinue included several African slaves. One of these Spanish-speaking Africans, named Gomez, fled with a royal Indian prisoner back to the town of Cofitachequi (near present-day Camden). There, they "held communication as husband and wife."[4] More Africans would accompany Spanish and French explorers over the next century, but even though the Spanish Crown granted conquistadores permission to settle parts of the region with fifty Africans, no Europeans were able to sustain a settlement in the area until the English succeeded in doing so in 1670.[5]

The English, though, were more active in the Caribbean in the seventeenth century. In the 1620s, English explorers established the colonies of St. Christopher, Nevis, and Barbados. Once sugarcane was introduced from Brazil in the 1640s, Barbados quickly became the cultural, social, and economic model for the rest of the English West Indies and, later, for South Carolina.[6] Major planters, spurred by an insatiable demand for sugar worldwide that sent the price of land soaring, squeezed out smaller ones, and the Brazilian model of African slavery quickly supplanted white indentured servitude as the laboring engine that lined the pockets of the upper echelons of a highly stratified social structure.[7]

Less than two decades after the introduction of sugar cultivation, African slaves outnumbered white colonists on the island. This rapid introduction of so many Africans made the maintenance of order by the shrinking white minority of vital importance. Accordingly, in 1661 Barbadian officials carefully drafted an act "for the better order and governing of Negroes." This document explicitly laid out the proper roles and legally acceptable behavior of both masters and slaves, and it would be amended from time to time as circumstances demanded. Emigrants who had been squeezed out by owners of large plantations and who were therefore unable to pursue the opportunities for riches in Barbados took both the spirit and the text of its slave code with them to other developing English colonies.[8] Indeed, as the historian Jack P. Greene writes, "South Carolina and the Lower South culture that developed out of those small beginnings was as much the offspring of Barbados as was Jamaica or the other English Caribbean colonies."[9]

John Colleton, a Royalist exile in Barbados, observed the constant outmigration of whites from the island with a keen eye toward his own gain. After the Restoration, in 1660, King Charles II rewarded Colleton and a small group of colleagues for their loyalty to the Crown with a charter, issued in March 1663, for the colony of Carolina, encompassing all the territory between Virginia and Florida.[10] In 1669 these eight Lords Proprietors drafted what they intended to be the governmental framework for the new colony, the Fundamental Constitutions of Carolina. Though it was never adopted by the Carolina Assembly, many of its provisions were in fact implemented in practice, and its language was largely responsible for the rapid settlement of Carolina that followed its drafting and circulation. The document's terms offered policies of relative religious tolerance, liberal terms for citizenship, generous headrights (including an allowance for each slave imported), low property qualifications for office holding and the franchise, and honorific titles for elites, provisions that were attractive to immigrants from all walks of life.[11] In addition, the grant to every freeman of the "absolute power and authority over his negro slaves" suggested that those who sought to replicate the highly successful plantation world of the West Indies would not be disappointed.[12]

In the first two decades of the new colony's existence, more than half the white settlers who arrived in Carolina were from Barbados, and many of these colonists brought along African slaves.[13] Often, these slave owners held a somewhat paternalistic view of the bondsmen of their household, and this relatively close relation between master and slave on the frontier significantly shaped the early development of institutionalized bondage in Carolina. Still, as the number of slaves increased, their presence conjured the same dread of slave revolt in masters' minds as had obtained in the Caribbean, especially after slave unrest and rebellion began to plague the West Indies late in the seventeenth century.[14] In 1703 Carolina officials sought to check the importation of potentially troublesome slaves by placing a higher import duty on Caribbean bondsmen than on those brought directly from Africa.[15]

Still, the African trade ultimately provided most of the enslaved men and women brought to colonial South Carolina. The most likely destination in British North America for slaves taken from Africa was Charles Towne (renamed Charleston after the American Revolution), South Carolina.[16] Carolina merchants made handsome fortunes serving as American factors for the African trade. Successful slave traders understood that white purchasers had a well-formed notion of what they wanted in a slave. Indeed, a slave's country of origin and skill set most often determined his or her desirability and price at auction. White Carolinians demonstrated a well-developed knowledge of African geography and ethnicity in making their slave selections. Early on (and in contrast with masters from other British North American colonies), they believed they had identified certain appearances and tribal markings, skills, personality traits, and other qualities as indicative of the bondsman's place of origin. South Carolinians preferred Gambians (from Senegambia and the Windward Coast) and Gold Coast Coromantees over all others because of their supposed propensity for hard work and their knowledge of rice cultivation, and, though market forces were often stronger than Carolina purchasers' ability to always have their first preference, slaves from these "preferr'd" areas made up nearly half of all African imports.[17] Toward the end of the eighteenth century, South Carolinians demonstrated an even more refined understanding of their slave purchases, changing their slave demands from broad geographic identifiers to more specific ethnic identifications.[18]

Europeans tapped into a long-established slave trade among Africans that had an enormous geographic reach across the continent. Those captives who were not retained by their host society or channeled into the trans-Saharan trade to the north were transferred to barracoons (slave pens) along the west coast for purchase by European traders. Their journeys to the point of embarkation sometimes took as long as four months by foot, and loss of life from capture to barracoon averaged between 10 and 15 percent. Depending on the location, captives of many different ethnicities often found themselves thrown together to await export to an unknown world.[19]

The Middle Passage from Africa to America was a time of unfathomable physical and psychological suffering for those who experienced it—as many as 15 million men, women, and children who crossed the Atlantic only to find more horrors as slaves in the Americas. The intensity of shared suffering on-board slave ships provided diverse survivors with a new way of perceiving themselves, a reorientation of identity in which ethnicity was gradually replaced by race as a criterion for community inclusion. This reevaluation of self was an early and fundamental stage of African American ethnogenesis.[20] Traders imported approximately 365,000 slaves into the North American colonies (later states) from the 1600s to 1807, the last year the trade was legal. Of these, probably 150,000 (approximately 43 percent) entered through South Carolina to feed the insatiable demand for bound laborers.[21]

Despite the economic benefits enjoyed by slaveholders, the burgeoning black population struck a note of fear in the minds of many whites. Officials made several attempts to stem the population imbalance, though none was fully successful.[22] Yet it was not just the sheer numbers of African slaves that alarmed white Carolinians but their "insolent and mischievous" demeanors.[23] Slaves' defiance could take many forms. Isolated acts of day-to-day resistance could include slowing work, feigning illness, breaking tools, or sabotaging production. More serious and direct forms of defiance included running away, committing arson, poisoning, and engaging in outright rebellion.[24] The fact that Carolina's African population was also relatively well armed (hundreds of black men had been authorized in 1704 to serve as militiamen in colonial and Indian conflicts) was also unsettling to the free population.[25]

Continuing reports of slave unrest in the Caribbean and Virginia and an armed rebellion in New York in 1712 raised the level of anxiety in South Carolina. That year, the colony finally enacted a comprehensive slave code, borrowing, in places nearly verbatim, a 1688 Barbadian statute that was a slightly altered version of the island's original 1661 slave code.[26] When the Carolina colony revised the slave code in 1712, officials copied the preamble to the Barbados statute, maintaining that Africans were of such "barbarous, wild, savage natures" that they were ungovernable under laws and customs designed for more "civilized" white citizens, and, as such, they must be restrained from committing the "disorders, rapines, and inhumanity to which they are naturally prone and inclined." The Carolina "Act for the Better Governing and Ordering of Negroes and Slaves" defined slaves as chattel and echoed the Fundamental Constitutions in granting a master the right to discipline them in any way he saw fit. This Act became the prototype for other American colonies as they codified chattel slavery.[27]

Interestingly, South Carolina masters often honored the letter of the law in the breach. Slaves were regularly granted passes to move freely between plantations, travel to the Charles Towne market, even do so armed.[28] However, the continued rise of the black population heightened the sense of unease among the free population. The governor's report to the Proprietors in 1708 alerted them to a startling demographic shift in the past half-decade: though the number of white Carolinians had increased by 7 percent, the black population had grown at more than five times that rate. This had produced a slim, though unmistakable, black majority. By 1720 ever-increasing African imports and a 5 percent natural rate of increase (which far exceeded that of white settlers) had produced a black population that outnumbered whites by two to one. In some districts, such as Goose Creek and St. James Santee, the ratio was closer to four to one.[29]

Many whites feared that black armies in the fields could too easily become armies of rebellion, and the not-unreasonable apprehension of revolt was ever present. Many rumors of conspiracy were undoubtedly the product of white paranoia, but some had a basis in fact, although none of the planned rebellions over the next two decades materialized due to divided leadership and small numbers of participants. In 1739, however, the numbers of runaways had noticeably increased, and some of these reached St. Augustine, where they were greeted with "great honours" by the welcoming Spanish. Coupling these events with news of slave unrest in the Caribbean, Carolinians sensed something more definite afoot. To discourage a feared insurrection, officials in Charles Towne publicly executed two slaves being held on suspicion of conspiracy to rebel and displayed their dead bodies as reminders of the costs of insubordination.[30] In case that message was not properly received, the Commons House passed legislation requiring all white males to carry weapons when they attended church on Sundays, the day when whites were least able to directly supervise their slaves and thus the most likely day for an uprising.[31]

Despite their best attempts to avoid a deadly surprise, South Carolinians were stunned in September 1739 by the onslaught of the Stono Rebellion, the largest slave revolt in British North American history. Twenty Angolan slaves attacked a store at Stono (near Charles Towne), seized weapons, and, leaving a path of destruction in their wake, marched south toward freedom in Spanish Florida. Beating drums along the way, they welcomed other slaves who rushed to join them, and their numbers swelled to approximately a hundred by the second day.

However, in an unlikely coincidence, the rebels encountered Lieutenant Governor William Bull, who was returning to Charles Towne from his Sheldon plantation over the same road. Bull narrowly escaped, and he raced to Charles Towne and rallied the militia to hunt down the rebels. The two groups first collided midway between Beaufort and Charles Towne, and skirmishes over the next week resulted in the killing of approximately sixty rebels and the capture of dozens more. Still, white Carolinians continued on their war footing since two-thirds of the rebels remained at large. Every white male traveled with a firearm, armed guards stood watch at ferry crossings, and officials hired Native American allies to hunt down fugitives. Nearly the entire business of the state ground to a halt while white Carolinians dealt with the rebellion. Within a week, as many as sixty more rebels were found and executed and decapitated, their heads placed on pikes as warnings to future subversives.[32]

Even after the ruthless defeat of the Stono rebels, white Carolinians' fears were not put to rest. Some whites fled the Lowcountry altogether, especially when rumors of yet another rebellion circulated in December. A few months later, a slave named Peter betrayed another plot that involved as many as two hundred slaves who were rising to attack and burn Charles Towne. Again, ghastly public executions meant to awe the black majority did little to reassure the rebels' white captors. Skittish whites suspected slave arsonists in the great fire that burned nearly a third of Charles Towne in the fall of 1740.[33]

The Stono rebels' ultimate goal, of course, was to permanently escape bondage, and many other slaves successfully made good their escapes during this period. As the South Carolina slave population increased in the eighteenth century, the number of runaways grew as well. The historian Daniel Littlefield estimates that approximately one-fifth of 1 percent of all Carolina slaves fled their bonds in the decades immediately following the Stono Rebellion. Though this number represented a small number of fugitives, the open threat that escape posed to the institution itself drew widespread attention. By the 1760s, more than a hundred slaves were escaping their bonds each year, and advertisements offering descriptions of the fugitives and rewards for their capture were common in newspapers.[34]

In the spring of 1740 the Commons House responded to Stono and the rising numbers of runaways with the passage of new legislation. The first was a £100-per-head import duty on African slaves intended to slow the introduction of supposedly "barbarous and savage" saltwater Africans. Those funds, in turn, would be used to encourage white European immigration to counter the still-growing black majority.[35] The most ambitious legislation passed, however, was a new comprehensive slave code, which, on its face, was one of the strictest in the colonies. Meant to forestall another Stono, the Act regulated nearly every aspect of slave life, from slaves' clothing to when and where they could gather. Moreover, the code imposed new duties on white masters. Believing that slaves who were treated well had little reason to revolt violently revolt, the Act of 1740 set minimum standards of care and limited the length of the work day.

However, as the memories of Stono faded, South Carolinians often honored the legislation of 1740 in the breach. At least one historian estimates that even after the passage of the slave code, black Carolinians enjoyed greater freedoms than slaves in any other colony, frequently including even the ability to bear arms. Lax enforcement of slave laws was tolerated in Carolina slave society for two simple and related reasons: enslaved laborers constituted a large majority of the state's population, and, more important, slave labor produced tremendous profits.[36]

The drive for profit among Carolinians was at least as old as the colony itself. The Lords Proprietors had hoped to make a fortune exporting some cash crop to an overseas market, and the Barbadian influence in the first generations guaranteed some degree of African slave labor to produce those riches.[37] After experiments with a handful of other crops, Carolinians eventually developed rice as a viable cash crop, and by the 1720s it had become their most valuable export. Within another decade, South Carolina was producing 20 million pounds of rice per year, and on the eve of the American Revolution South Carolina's annual rice shipments exceeded 66 million pounds. The value of South Carolina's exports accounted for nearly a third of the total exports of the British North American colonies to the mother country, and rice firmly established South Carolina as the wealthiest colony of them all.[38]

The true engine of this growth, of course, was the thousands of slaves that worked the crop, and their labor was not their only contribution. Many Africans arrived in South Carolina with a prior knowledge of rice and rice cultivation. In fact, historians believe that slaves from rice-growing regions of Africa may have known far more about the crop than their masters. Much of the knowledge and technical skill necessary for successful rice crops, including irrigation systems and techniques for cultivation, harvesting, and processing, came from Africans. As white Carolinians developed a keen understanding of the ethnic backgrounds of the slaves presented at market, they began to express a preference for slaves from known rice-producing areas in Africa.[39]

Slaves and their owners were thus well aware that success in rice agriculture depended on the full participation of Africans. Accordingly, South Carolina masters were forced to accommodate themselves to the desires of their slaves to a degree unequaled in any other colony. The most notable negotiation through which slaves labored for the master while extracting an expanded ability to shape the conditions of their own lives was the task system. Under this labor regime, a slave would be assigned and held accountable for a specific task to be completed in a day. The basic task unit was hoeing or otherwise working a quarter of an acre. The same labor regime was practiced successfully for

Lowcountry indigo and Sea Island cotton. There were other tasks that did not directly apply to crop cultivation, such as chopping wood, splitting fence rails, threshing rice, and barrel making, that could also be assigned to enslaved workers in daily quota amounts.[40]

Not only did this labor system facilitate the smooth running of large plantations with minimal white supervision, but also it created a clear incentive for enslaved men and women to be efficient workers. Once the enslaved person completed his or her task, the rest of the day belonged to that person. An energetic bondsman might complete an assigned task around lunchtime or even perform two tasks in a single day, clearing a full day for his or her own use. The resulting free time might be put to use tending a garden plot or a small number of livestock, resources that could be utilized for home consumption but also offered for sale. It was understood by masters and slaves alike that a slave's off time was inviolable.[41] This arrangement was one of the cracks within the plantation system that allowed the enslaved to develop a degree of sociocultural and economic autonomy, thus making them in some ways independent of their masters.

The free time and isolation from whites made possible through the task system, coupled with the large African-born portion of the slave population, also fostered the development of a rich culture unlike that found anywhere else in the colonies. Since slave birthrates remained low for much of the eighteenth century, planters were forced to rely on the African trade to maintain their workforce. This created an increasingly Africanized world in which new arrivals reinforced African folkways, which persisted for much longer in South Carolina than elsewhere. The Gullah slaves of the Sea Islands, for instance, spoke a unique creole language that was a fusion of English and West African languages and grammatical patterns, constructed their dwellings on West African models, maintained African foodways whenever possible, and worshipped in a style with parallels to West and Central African practices.[42]

The Gullahs' retention in their spiritual lives of the African antecedents also survived in part because masters seldom offered their slaves religious instruction or made attempts to convert them to Christianity. Many eighteenth-century owners feared that conversion would entitle their bondsmen to freedom, while others believed that the Bible's message of deliverance might encourage flight or rebellion.[43] Those masters who did encourage their slaves to accept Christianity were also sure to stress biblical injunctions for slaves to obey their masters and encouraged interpretations of scripture that clearly made a distinction between the spiritual equality of men in God's eyes and equality in this world.

However, slaves often interpreted evangelicals' halfhearted message of spiritual equality as a critique of human bondage, even when that message was not intended. In the Revolutionary era, slaves also understood the ideologies upon which the nation's Founders based their struggle for independence as applying equally to themselves. American colonists' assertions that all men possessed a natural right to self-governance reverberated through slave quarters and unwittingly exposed the Patriot cause to new questions regarding the propriety of slavery.

South Carolina's signatories to the Declaration of Independence fully agreed with its principal author, Thomas Jefferson, that the notion of all men being created equal extended only to white men, yet black Carolinians nonetheless saw the conflict with England as an antislavery struggle from the first stirrings of revolt. In 1765, as white Charlestonians opposed the Stamp Act with chants of "Liberty! Liberty and stamp'd paper," local slaves also chanted "Liberty, liberty," to the dismay of their masters.[44] Slaves also capitalized on the growing unrest by escaping from captivity, making good their own desire for freedom and liberty.

Though black Patriots were scarce in South Carolina, white opposition to arming the state's slaves and fear of insurrection discouraged the recruitment of black enlistees. State officials did amend the code of laws in 1778 so that as many as one-third of the South Carolina militia could be slaves, but they would be limited to service as laborers.[45] And although the state General Assembly defeated a proposal by Henry Laurens to arm slaves for combat, black soldiers did fight alongside Francis Marion and in militia units at Cowpens and King's Mountain.[46] Their opponents, however, had few qualms about arming South Carolina slaves. Once the main theater of war shifted south in 1778, the British command determined "to use slaves as weapons against their masters," offering freedom to slaves of Patriot masters and the chance to take up arms with the Redcoats. In the end, however, this policy hurt the British more than it helped, as it aroused white Patriots and encouraged many former Loyalists to abandon their allegiance.

Following the British surrender, officials in London refused to relinquish any refugee slaves who had been explicitly promised their freedom if they fought for the Crown. It fell to a committee of Loyalist civilians and British officers to determine which African Americans qualified. In early November, the committee heard the testimony of thousands of former slaves, all hoping for passage away from North America. British ships were unable to accommodate all refugees, however, and the families of some slave allies of the British were left behind in Charleston to face reenslavement. Some African Americans desperately dove into Charleston harbor and swam toward the boats loading the navy vessels, hoping for a berth. Most were beaten back by British sailors; others clung to the boats until their fingers were sliced off with cutlasses.[47]

The slaves of evacuating Loyalists, however, hoped to stay off the ships leaving Charleston at all costs. Unknown numbers escaped just ahead of the British evacuation, but many more were forced to sail away with the British, still enslaved. Many of these men and women (and also many former slaves originally promised their freedom but unscrupulously claimed as property by British officers) were sold into slavery in Jamaica or other Caribbean colonies. Overall, more than twelve thousand black evacuees sailed from Charleston in late 1782, and more of them were slaves than were freemen.[48]

Abandoned black Loyalists and other African Americans in South Carolina fared poorly after the war, as well. In the Constitutional Convention of 1787, the Founders put no new restrictions on slavery. South Carolina's delegates certainly desired a strong national government, but they were adamant that the new government so formed not have the power to meddle in their "domestic institutions," namely slavery, the foundation of their social and economic world. Owing largely from pressure from South Carolina and Georgia, the constitution adopted by the convention made no explicit mention of "slavery," yet protected the institution in many ways, offering a fugitive slave clause, protection of the African slave trade for twenty years, promises of military assistance in the event of slave rebellion, and the ability to count a portion of a state's enslaved population toward representation in Congress.

With its most vital institution protected in the nation's foundational law, postwar recovery came easily to South Carolina. The Upcountry bounced back from the ravages of the Revolution and began to develop in ways the Lowcountry had a half-century before. Small subsistence farms gave way to the production of staple crops grown with slave labor for world markets. In the Lowcountry, the production of rice continued. Yet, even though South Carolina would produce as much as 75 percent of the nation's rice through the 1850s, rice would soon be eclipsed by a crop that would reshape not just the state and nation but the entire industrializing world: cotton.

As with rice, South Carolinians had been familiar with cotton as early as the late seventeenth century. By the middle of the next century, Carolina farmers were producing small amounts of Sea Island (or long-staple) cotton for export, encouraged by a bounty offered by the Crown for its production. This type of cotton was known for its long fiber, which was easily separated from the seeds by hand and which produced high-demand luxurious fabrics. Though it thrived along the coast, Sea Island cotton could not be easily grown in the state's interior. Thus, geographic limitations seemed to limit the viability of cotton as a high-yielding staple crop.[49]

Planters had long been were aware of another type of cotton that could be easily grown in most southern climates and soil conditions. Short-staple or upland cotton did not have the geographic limitations of Sea Island cotton, but the shortness of its fiber and the resulting difficulty of separating it from the seed made it far too labor-intensive and time consuming to be profitably grown, even using slave laborers. Only after Eli Whitney's invention, in 1793, of the cotton gin, a mechanical separator, did short-staple cotton become an economically viable alternative. Using a gin, a slave could produce fifty pounds of clean cotton lint per day, as opposed to the single pound that a hardworking enslaved man or woman could clean by hand. As entrepreneurs modified designs through the antebellum years, they developed industrial-size cotton gins that could clean four bales, well over a ton, of cotton per day.[50]

Cotton, especially short staple, had a distinct advantage over rice for most South Carolinians in that it did not require significant outlays of capital to start farming. Besides land, seed, a few tools, and access to a gin, little else was required. Even Upcountry yeoman farmers who sought an entry into the market and who could not share in the wealth made possible by rice in the Lowcountry could now produce a staple for cash, possibly afford slaves, and maybe even become planters in their own right. In the first twenty-five years of short-staple cotton production, four thousand Upcountry households joined the ranks of slaveholders for the first time. This number included the free black planter and gin maker William Ellison, who, by the time of the Civil War, owned nine hundred acres (including the plantation of a former governor), a pew in the Episcopal Church of the Holy Cross in Sumter District, and sixty-three slaves, a number that placed him in the top tenth of all American slave owners.[51] On the eve of the Civil War, South Carolina had a higher percentage of citizens who were slaveholders (45.8 percent) than any other state in the South.[52]

Historians estimate that as much as two-thirds of a slave owner's wealth might be held in the form of slaves, with prime field hands in the Lowcountry selling for an average of between $1,200 and $1,500 each in the antebellum decades. A telling indicator of the incredible value of slaves is that a holding of as few as three bondsmen represented a greater capital investment than the average nonslaveholder held in all other forms of property combined. Moreover, slave ownership directly correlated with wealth. The richest districts in the state had the largest black majorities.[53]

However, the rapid turn to cotton cultivation did have a downside, especially for the enslaved African Americans who worked in the cotton fields. Cotton was a soil-intensive crop, and the toll it took on Carolina farmland was severe. In what was called "land butchery" by some, South Carolina cotton farmers often farmed a plot until it became completely leeched of nutrients and was therefore unproductive. Then, rather than fertilize it (which would have taken slaves' labor away from cotton production itself), they abandoned the land and put new plots under cultivation. It was the labor that was scarce and dear, not the land. Indeed, the new, rich land of the Deep South acted as a magnet for many South Carolina planters, who knew that they could reap many times their current profits by moving their holdings out of the state. Between the end of the first cotton boom and the Civil War, nearly 200,000 white South Carolinians emigrated west seeking fertile cotton land.[54]

That same migration included as many or more enslaved African Americans, who had no say in whether or not they relocated.[55] The historian Ira Berlin has named this forced migration the "Second Middle Passage."[56] Forced movement to the Deep South caused the dissolution of one in three slave marriages and separated a fifth of all slave children from their parents.[57] The never-ending threat of sale was devastating to the psyche of the enslaved.[58]

For those who remained, their spirituality continued to be a primary way they dealt with loss and uncertainty, yet the religious life of nineteenth-century South Carolina slaves would be different from that of previous generations. In an attempt to shield themselves from the increasing criticisms of abolitionists, many Carolina masters in the 1830s adopted an outwardly paternalistic relationship to their slaves. This often extended to an interpretation of their Christian duty as *pater familias* that required them to provide religious instruction for their bondsmen. To this end, some slave owners supported the construction of chapels to be used by slaves, obtained or wrote catechisms to instruct them, and even urged the legislature to repeal the 1834 law that criminalized teaching slaves to read so that they could consume these texts and the Bible.[59] By the Civil War, the various denominations in South Carolina had thousands of black members, including a number of majority-black congregations.[60]

The early years of the Second Great Awakening in the South featured a message of egalitarianism, even if only spiritual. Baptist and Methodist denominations were especially appealing to African Americans because these groups sometimes preached equality and advocated limited freedom. However, their halting moves toward a critique of slavery did not survive into the nineteenth century. As slavery continued to grow and to tighten its grip on the state, South Carolina ministers of every stripe accommodated and shifted to preach support for the institution, marshalling scripture and history to their arguments.[61] As the historian Barry Hankins points out, it was not a great leap from the idea that conversion made slaves better to the belief that conversion simply made better slaves. Slaves still read an emancipatory meaning into scripture, but masters interpreted the scriptures as a useful tool for controlling their bondsmen.[62]

Whites did not control access to God's word, however. Many slaves and black lay preachers led religious instruction and conversions of their own through a multidenominational black church that the historian Albert Rabateau calls their "invisible institution." Meeting secretly usually under the cover of night, African Americans freely combined African traditions and the egalitarian spirit of the Bible into a message of salvation particularly suited to their situation. Throughout the antebellum years, this independent religious life remained an important part of black culture and an effective defense against the dehumanizing impact of bondage. Christianity did not become, as many white evangelicals would have had it, a religion that encouraged docility and submission in slaves. Rather, enslaved South Carolinians stressed the egalitarian spirit of the evangelical movement, equality of all men in the eyes of God, and the promise of deliverance, both in heaven and on earth.[63]

Although they lived within the long shadow of slavery, a small but significant free black population existed in South Carolina as well. Most of these people had been born of a free mother, manumitted by their owner, or allowed to save money and purchase their own freedom. The census of 1790 showed 1,801 free people of color in the state, and that number grew to nearly ten thousand by the time of the Civil War.[64] However, there were significant limits to their freedom. After 1792 all free people of color between the ages of fifteen and sixty had to pay an annual tax and register with the local court. When accused of crimes, they were tried before a slave court. After the tumult of the Denmark Vesey insurrection scare in 1822, all free black men also had to have a "respectable" white citizen willing to vouch for their security and to serve as their custodian.[65] Laws and custom severely curtailed the occupations and wages available to black workers, limited their access to educational opportunities, and precluded their enjoyment of the many whites-only institutions in cities. Frighteningly, free blacks were sometimes kidnapped and sold as slaves.[66]

Despite these overwhelming burdens, free Carolinians of color were often still able to carve out a surprising degree of success for themselves and their families. Charleston had one of the South's largest free brown elite classes. A third of the state's free population of color lived in Charleston, and in 1860 they owned property valued at nearly $1.5 million. This amount also included approximately $300,000 worth of property in slaves, as Charleston was also home to 137 of the state's 171 black masters. Though some of these black slave owners hoped to prosper from the labor of their bondsmen, many others acquired slaves as the only way to provide security for their enslaved family members, who, under the state's 1841 law outlawing manumission, could not be legally freed.[67]

As a class, free black South Carolinians represented a contradiction to whites who believed African Americans could not survive without the "beneficent" guidance of slave owners. They realized that their freedom existed essentially at the suffrance of whites. The free brown elite especially often made conspicuous attempts to put as much distance between itself and the enslaved population as possible to maintain its tenuous privilege in society. Members of this elite often identified more with the interests of whites than with those of slaves and seized any opportunity to demonstrate their distinction from the latter. They established their own social, cultural, and charitable organizations, acquired wealth, literacy, and often slaves, and sometimes served on slave patrols, and they were largely successful in creating their own hierarchy of skin color and carving out a distinct niche for themselves between the "degraded" enslaved masses and whites, a model often also seen in Caribbean slave societies.[68]

And when slavery, the institution that sustained their place at least one rung from the bottom levels of Carolina society, was threatened, the elite made its allegiance clear. When South Carolina seceded, eighty-two members of the brown elite sent a message to the governor pledging their unflagging loyalty. They claimed citizenry as their birthright, cited with pride the white blood running through their veins, and offered up their lives and all they held dear to the defense of South Carolina. Even in a state where paranoid legislators debated the merits of selling all free blacks into slavery, these free brown elites continued to profess their loyalty to the white South. For the free nonwhite population, this was the cost of retaining a foothold in white society.[69]

The truth was that the South Carolina master class never fully trusted African Americans, slave or free. Although whites may have viewed free blacks with amused condescension and some masters surely interpreted their slaves' apparent cheerfulness and deference as contentment with their enslavement, others acknowledged a shared humanity in the men and women they enslaved and lived in constant fear of slave rebellion and violence at the hands of their bondsmen. The state's large black population cast a shadow over every white person's imagination.

A string of rebellion plots in Columbia (1805), Camden (1815), and Ashepoo (1816), though discovered and thwarted before they were launched, kept whites on edge. The wave of new legislation in the first two decades of the century aimed at controlling and monitoring the slave population betrayed any illusions white Carolinians may have held regarding "contented bondsmen." Moreover, between 1810 and 1820 the black population increased by nearly a third, and its rate of growth would outpace that of the white population for the rest of the antebellum period.[70] National events also made South Carolina masters even more anxious, especially with the publication of the debates preceding the Missouri Compromise of 1820, many of which were highly critical of slavery.

Denmark Vesey, a Charleston carpenter and an AME lay preacher who had purchased his freedom with lottery winnings, read transcripts of the Missouri debates closely and relished the idea of slavery coming under attack. Though free, Vesey continued to socialize with the city's slave population, and he began plotting a rebellion with many of them in 1820. During more than a year of planning, Vesey and his co-conspirators gathered arms and carefully developed their scheme to raid the Charleston arsenal, kill as many whites as possible, free themselves and other slaves, whom they assumed would flock to their aid, and sail away to the black republic of Haiti.[71]

However, two enslaved recruits betrayed the plot several weeks before the scheduled July 1822 rebellion, and local authorities quickly mobilized to thwart the uprising.[72] Over the next month, Charleston officials arrested 131 free and enslaved African American suspects, 72 of whom were quickly tried, convicted, and sentenced to death. Vesey and five of his lieutenants were hanged in a public execution that drew thousands of spectators. As a lesson to other potential rebels, authorities forbade burials or funeral rites for the conspirators and dismembered many of the corpses. More mass hangings took place in the following weeks, and as the death toll mounted, only the economic considerations of the loss of slave property and labor slowed the pace.[73]

Besides the executions, the white response to the plot was swift and thorough. Vesey's AME church was closed and later demolished by Charleston authorities. In December, the state legislature passed the Seaman's Act, which required that any free black mariners on board a ship entering Charleston Harbor be housed in the city jail until their ship left port. Under penalty of jail and fine, the ship's captain had to pay for the board of his black sailors. Violation of the law could also result in the sailor's being sold into slavery.[74]

Vesey had hoped to strike a serious blow against the stability of the South Carolina slave system, and the events of the next decade, both within the state and elsewhere, did little to settle whites' nerves. Maroon raids, rumors of rebellion plots, and suspicious fires in the Lowcountry kept South Carolinians on edge.[75] Northerners continued to agitate the slavery question. When David Walker, a free black man and a former member of Vesey's church in Charleston, published his militant *Appeal to the Colored Citizens of the World* in Boston in 1829, whites feared abolitionists concealed in their midst. On the basis of his intimate knowledge of South Carolina's slaves, Walker wagered that, if properly armed, they could destroy "every white person on the whole continent of America."[76] In response, South Carolina chartered state-supported military schools in Columbia and Charleston (the institution that would eventually become The Citadel) to train an organic military force to meet such a threat.[77]

Nat Turner came closer to accomplishing that feat in 1831 than any other North American slave rebel had before, and his revolt in Virginia sparked ceaseless rumors in South Carolina of emboldened and inspired slaves planning their own uprisings.[78] Feeling that slavery was truly under siege, white South Carolinians began to question the value of a union containing influences so seemingly bent on bringing down their peculiar institution and resolved to defend it at all costs. It was not just the slaves that whites feared but their allies in the North, who made South Carolina one of their regular targets of abuse. As critics of slavery continued to excoriate South Carolina slave owners, men like John C. Calhoun began to defend the institution as "a positive good" and led the campaign to silence all debate on the issue before Congress.[79]

However, when this "gag rule" was repealed and slavery expansion and slaveholders' rights again became a hot topic of political debate, radicals in 1850 demanded anew that their state secede from the Union. When that movement failed, South Carolinians attempted to intimidate critics of slavery into silence. Men like Senator James H. Hammond warned Northerners not to threaten "King Cotton" lest their own economic interests take a severe hit. Congressman Preston Brooks of Edgefield District took a more direct approach when he beat the abolitionist senator Charles Sumner senseless with a cane on the floor of the Senate.[80]

The election of the Republican Abraham Lincoln to the presidency in 1860 was the final straw for South Carolina. When a man pledged to the nonextension of slavery headed to the White House, the state's congressional delegation resigned, the General Assembly called for a Secession Convention to be held in December. South Carolinians believed their very survival was at stake, for if slavery did not survive this administration, not only would their whole economic world come crashing down but also the race war they were certain would follow would turn their fair state into another Haiti. Accordingly, delegates voted unanimously to dissolve the union between South Carolina and the United States of America. Six other Deep South states quickly followed South Carolina's lead, and once Fort Sumter struck the spark of civil war in April 1861, four other states from the Upper South joined them in the conflict as well as in the newly formed Confederate States of America.[81]

Some of the first Confederate territory to be retaken by Union forces in the Civil War was in and around the Beaufort area. On November 7, 1861 ("Day of the Big Gun Shoot," as it was remembered by the African American population), Union gunboats overpowered Confederate forces at the Battle of Port Royal Sound. Area planters scrambled to gather their belongings and flee the Yankee advance, but they met with resounding refusals on the parts of their nearly ten thousand slaves to abandon their plantations. The former slaves' hesitant greeting of the victorious Union troops marked the birth of Reconstruction in the South. These former slaves were quickly designated "contrabands of war," and, under a new wage-labor system, they went back to work to harvest the ripening cotton crop. The freedpeople organized their own time and demonstrated to doubtful federal officials that they could work efficiently without being under the control and compulsion of slave owners. Missionaries and teachers from the North also played a role in the "Port Royal Experiment," establishing schools that would help former slaves master the skills they would need in freedom. It was, many historians agree, a model of what Reconstruction could have been.[82]

Port Royal marked more than a Union advance, however. It signified the beginnings of South Carolina slave owners' forced recognition that the paternalistic and mutually cherished relationship they thought they had with their slaves was an illusion. As masters and their sons went off to war and left their wives and overseers in charge, the façade continued to crumble. Though few slaves left the plantations if the Union Army was not nearby, they often slowed work or stopped altogether, and feigned deference fell by the wayside.[83] Eventually, many Carolina masters would share the conclusion of a Charleston man who wrote that "the conduct of the Negro in the late crisis of our affairs has convinced me that we were all laboring under a delusion. . . . If they were content, happy and attached to their masters, why did they desert him in the moment of his need and flock to an enemy, whom they did not know?"[84]

Besides the Beaufort area, Union forces quickly made inroads all along the South Carolina coast. In February 1862 the Confederates abandoned the forts that defended Georgetown to concentrate their efforts on holding Charleston. When Union ships took over the port, the events of Port Royal were repeated: as many planters fled inland, slaves remained to seek their freedom. Not even the public execution by one of the remaining slaveholders of six slaves who had tried to reach the safety of the Union fleet could stop the mass exodus.[85] In May, a Charleston slave, Robert Smalls, not only made haste to reach the gunboats offshore but also, with his family and crew with him, commandeered the Confederate steamer the CSS *Planter*, sailed past the unsuspecting guns at Fort Sumter, and presented himself and his prize to the blockading Union fleet.[86]

Although General David Hunter had already begun organizing Sea Island freedmen into military units, the Emancipation Proclamation officially declared that black enlistees would be accepted into the Union Army. Despite racial prejudice, dangerous assignments, early pay inequities, and the risk of re-enslavement or torture if captured by Confederates, black soldiers fought heroically. Perhaps their most notable engagement of the war was the assault in July 1863 on Charleston's Fort Wagner by the Fifty-fourth Massachusetts United States Colored Troops (USCT). Despite heavy losses, black troops there showed extraordinary valor and erased any remaining doubts as to their fitness and reliability as warriors.[87]

The African American population of the Beaufort area marked January 1, 1863, the day the Emancipation Proclamation became effective, with a great celebration. Thousands of former slaves gathered with Northern dignitaries at Fort Saxton, the headquarters of the First South Carolina Colored Volunteers, to hear Beaufort planter-turned-abolitionist William Henry Brisbane read the proclamation aloud for the first time. Although the former slaves in the gathering had already technically been freed as "contraband of war" when they reached Union lines and despite the fact that the proclamation had limited immediate impact on those bondsmen still beyond federal control, with each Union advance thereafter and, more important, with each Carolina bondsman's quest to reach the Union lines, emancipation gradually came to the Palmetto State.[88]

As the war ground toward a conclusion in 1865, Abraham Lincoln seemed poised to offer conciliatory terms to the Confederacy. However, events on the ground in South Carolina were intended to be decidedly less than pacifying. In January, ahead of his arrival in South Carolina and after consulting with black leaders, General William T. Sherman issued Special Field Order 15, which granted confiscated and abandoned lands along the coast to former slaves. On February 1, 1865, Sherman's army crossed the Savannah River into South Carolina and trooped across the state facing little resistance. Heading toward Columbia, they left a path of destruction thirty miles wide and dozens of towns in ruins. From Columbia, Sherman and tens of thousands of contrabands who had attached themselves to his army continued their march toward North Carolina.[89]

The end came quickly. In February, an army of black soldiers including the Third and Fourth South Carolina Regiments marched triumphantly into Charleston, where, to the sounds of soldiers' voices singing "John Brown's Body" and "Battle Cry of Freedom," they were welcomed by masses of former slaves.[90] Federal troops continued to spread across the state in late spring with a policy of publicly announcing emancipation wherever they went. Most black South Carolinians learned that they were no longer slaves from the mouths of Union soldiers, though some planters took the initiative and announced the new order to their former bondsmen. And, on April 14, 1865, the anniversary of the surrender of Fort Sumter, Unionists held a grand celebration there and witnessed the raising of the same flag that had been lowered four years earlier. A crowd of thousands that included Robert Smalls, Robert Vesey (son of Denmark), and the radical abolitionist William Lloyd Garrison joined in the singing of "The Star-Spangled Banner" before the cannons of the Charleston battery roared salutes.[91]

With the Civil War and slavery a thing of the past, black South Carolinians tested the boundaries of their newfound freedom. One of the initial ways they, like former slaves across the South, conceptualized "the feel of freedom" was by moving beyond the borders of their former masters' lands and living largely as they pleased. Those who had been moved out of the path of the Union Army returned to the parts of the state they considered home, as did some others who had been sold to owners in the Deep South years earlier.[92] Thousands of former slaves picked up and moved to Charleston, and what had been a sizable white majority in the city before the war became a black majority of four thousand by 1870.[93] Others traveled great distances seeking long-lost family members.

However, the initial desire "to move about" most often eventually gave way to more practical concerns such as meeting immediate household needs. Since most land in the South was eventually returned to white control, most freedpeople, if they were to work, had to work the land of another as tenants or sharecroppers. Sometimes, the landowners were their former owners. By mid-1866 most former slaves were living either on the plantation where they had toiled as bondsmen or somewhere close by.[94]

Though the former slaves' postwar living arrangements may have seemed similar to those that prevailed before the war, other important things had changed significantly. The biggest differences, of course, were the labor relations between whites and blacks. No longer able to command African Americans' toil as a property right, many former masters were loath to deal with former slaves as free agents who could negotiate labor contracts. Clashes over terms were commonplace. Most former slaves sought fair compensation, labor that could be done alongside family members, and an end to physical punishment and gang-style labor. For their part, whites hoped to ensure a reliable labor supply by limiting former slaves' mobility and suppressing competition. Violent attempts by whites to coerce "their" black workers into signing contracts were sometimes met with threats by blacks to leave the area entirely and offer their services to more amenable employers elsewhere. Only with the oversight of the much maligned (by whites) Freedman's Bureau was a semistable labor system fashioned.[95]

Outside the context of work, most African Americans chose to distance themselves from whites rather than confront them whenever possible. By the mid-1870s, membership in predominantly black churches had climbed sharply, while African American membership in predominantly white denominations declined. The number of black Methodists in the state, for example, shrank by *more than* 99 percent from 1860 to 1876.[96] With the notable exception of Charleston's brothels, called by one historian "the most color-blind places in the state," social interaction between white and black Carolinians was kept to a bare minimum.[97]

One unintended consequence of this self-segregation was an increase in already heightened anxiety among whites. What was often intended by former slaves as means to remove themselves as far from slavery and its memories as possible was viewed with circumspection by whites, who were often left feeling uncomfortable at their inability to supervise or control their black neighbors.[98] Alarmed South Carolina whites moved to reassert as much control over the black population as they could short of outright slavery. As soon as President Andrew Johnson appointed a provisional governor, white Carolinians eagerly embraced the opportunity to right the perceived wrongs of the past few months. Governor Benjamin Perry quickly moved for South Carolina's rapid "restoration" back into to the Union. To that end, he called elections for a constitutional convention in September 1865. The rules that governed who was eligible to elect delegates to the convention were the same as those that had been in place prior to the war: only white landowners or taxpayers age twenty-one or older could vote. Meeting under the same roof in Columbia where the first secession convention had been held in 1860, the convention was dominated by antebellum white elites.[99]

Though delegates reluctantly repealed the state's ordinance of secession, they notably stopped short of following President Johnson's instructions to declare it null and void. Similarly, though recognizing that slavery had not survived the war, delegates did not extend citizenship or voting right to the freedmen. Further, all laws passed prior to the approval of the new constitution were explicitly left in full force, meaning that freedmen remained subject to the harsh sections of the code that had previously applied specifically to "free negroes." These sections imposed restrictions on entering and leaving the state, a ban on carrying arms, and restrictions on assembly and the teaching of reading and writing.[100]

Nonetheless, Johnson approved the constitution. White South Carolinians held elections in October and sent many former high-ranking Confederate heroes to Columbia, the state capital. The first regular session of the legislature that convened in December then proceeded to pass three statutes that became known as the "Black Codes." These restrictive laws, passed in similar form by all states of the former Confederacy, were the General Assembly's attempt to restrict the civil liberties of freedmen. Among other provisions, the laws declared anyone unable to prove he or she was employed guilty of "vagrancy" and allowed such persons to be hired out as convict labor for no pay. All males and unmarried females also had to pay a special tax, nonpayment of which could lead to charges of vagrancy. Interracial marriages were forbidden, as were the practice of certain trades without an expensive license and the ownership of firearms without the permission of the legislature. Mobility was limited. Children of impoverished parents or those whose parents did not properly teach them "habits of industry and honesty" could be forcibly apprenticed. The codes also established a separate court system for African Americans and included a list of crimes and punishments applicable only to freedmen.[101]

Congressional Republicans viewed the Black Codes as nothing more than a poorly veiled attempt to re-create slavery by another name and refused to seat the state's delegation when it arrived in Washington. Congress then proceeded to pass, over Johnson's veto and vehement Southern opposition, a Civil Rights Act that prohibited states from discriminating against citizens on the basis of color. Three months later, it approved and sent to the states for ratification the Fourteenth Amendment to the Constitution, guaranteeing African Americans' citizenship and equal protection under the laws. The state legislature rejected the Fourteenth Amendment by a vote of 95–1 in the House (the equally lop-sided Senate vote was not recorded).[102]

When Radical Republicans gained veto-proof majorities in both houses of Congress in 1866, they forcefully took charge of Reconstruction, dissolving Southern state governments and dividing the region into five military districts subject to martial law. The Carolinas comprised the Second Military District and fell under the command of General Daniel Sickles. As military governor, Sickles would direct the new course by which rebellious states might reenter the Union, which included calling a constitutional convention (delegates to which would be chosen by universal male suffrage), crafting a new constitution that guaranteed black suffrage, and ratifying the Fourteenth Amendment.[103]

Although whites attempted to derail the process by withholding their votes for delegates to the constitutional convention, nearly nine out of ten registered black voters showed up at the polls with "yes" ballots, and plans for the convention went forward. When the delegates convened in Charleston in January, a large majority of them were black, and contemporaries marveled at the possibility that many of the delegates to the Constitutional Convention of 1868 had been the slaves of members of the Secession Convention of 1860.[104] The document eventually crafted by the convention was designed to create a new order in South Carolina in which equal opportunity regardless of race reigned supreme.

When voters went to the polls under the new constitution, Republicans rolled to large majorities across the state, and of the 156 members of the state legislature, 85 were African American.[105] By the end of Reconstruction, 487 black South Carolinians would be elected to state or national posts, including U.S. representative, lieutenant governor, state attorney general, state treasurer, and state supreme court justice. African Americans won greater political power in South Carolina than in any other state of the Union.

To whites, these new circumstances truly seemed like a "world turned upside down," a political nightmare where members of an incompetent and inferior race would lord it with vengeance over their former masters.[106] What finally motivated white South Carolinians to once again flex their political muscle, however, was not social disruption but economic concerns. Besides the charges of incompetency unceasingly directed by whites at black lawmakers and other Republicans, accusations of graft, bribery, and corruption were ubiquitous. In many cases, the charges were accurate.[107] Corruption became the Achilles heel that divided the Republican Party, gave enemies an effective weapon with which to attack Reconstruction, and ultimately undermined programs meant to benefit freedmen.[108]

The white crusade against Republican corruption in South Carolina also gave white officials effective political cover for a shift in tactics that included harassment and intimidation as tools with which to overthrow what they viewed as an illegitimate government. After the federal army was quietly drawn down in the state, with fewer than nine hundred troops remaining in the months following the ratification of the 1868 constitution, responsibility for maintaining law and order became the responsibility primarily of local officials who had just taken office. Violence became endemic in the state, independent dens of the Ku Klux Klan roamed the countryside attempting to reorder society along their chosen lines, and murder and mayhem plagued allies of Reconstruction.[109]

So that they could demonstrate that they were not, in fact, powerless, state Republicans reorganized the state militia to protect black Carolinians and defend elected officials from assassination. Since most native whites refused to serve alongside (and especially *under*) freedmen, the nearly 100,000-strong militia was nearly all black. This show of force initially seemed to check Klan depredations, yet it soon became evident that without federal intervention the nightmare might never end. President U. S. Grant agreed, and in April 1871 he signed the Ku Klux Klan Act into law and took the unprecedented step of suspending habeas corpus in nine upcountry counties that were declared to be in rebellion.[110] However, realizing they had little to fear from an overburdened federal apparatus, Klan members soon resumed their activities.[111] The historian Richard Zuczek rightly notes that "Republicans—at the state and federal levels—dealt in bluff, while conservatives dealt in blood."[112]

At the same time, Republican unity was beginning to crack. A Liberal Republican faction developed to oppose Grant's re-election, convinced that he and his followers were corrupt and that the goals of Reconstruction—the destruction of both slavery and Confederate nationalism—had been met and should not be artificially propped up by federal authority. The fusion of the Liberal Republicans with progressive Democrats was an ominous sign that Radical Reconstruction was quickly losing support in the North. Republican divisions were replicated in South Carolina as well in the run-up to the election of 1872, and state Republicans began to turn on themselves.[113]

Feeling their power, conservatives also began reorganizing themselves politically to put an end to "Negro rule." The South Carolina Democratic Party, long dormant, now exploded into activity in the run-up to the 1876 election and nominated General Wade Hampton III, a Confederate military hero, for governor. Hampton condemned outright violence but did encourage conspicuous demonstrations of force, a policy he called "peaceful coercion."[114] Still, the election season was a bloody one, with riots erupting in Hamburg, Charleston, Cainhoy, and Ellenton, where a white mob captured and executed dozens of African Americans, including state representative Simon Coker. Finally, just three weeks before the election, Grant ordered more than 1,100 troops to South Carolina to oversee the remainder of the election season.[115]

There were few certainties after the elections of November 7, 1876, amid accusations of voter fraud from both Democrats and Republicans and claims by both sides to have won disputed contests. Yet, as South Carolinians attempted to make sense of their state's electoral quandary, they were also squarely in the middle of the disputed Rutherford Hayes-Samuel Tilden presidential election. The state's votes were contested in that election as well, and not until the famous "Compromise of 1877" were the state and federal elections settled. In exchange for the Southerners' guarantee not to filibuster Hayes's election, Northern Republicans promised several concessions: the removal of federal troops from the South, the appointments of several Southern Democrats to federal offices, the channeling of federal funds to the rebuilding of the South, and last, the granting to Southern whites of ultimate control of the "Negro problem."[116]

On April 3, 1877, as expected, Hayes announced that federal troops would be pulled out of South Carolina. With nothing to stand in the way of a violent Democratic coup and after much deliberation, the Republicans quietly left the State House on April 10, and Reconstruction fizzled to a conclusion in South Carolina and the rest of the South. Except for the illegality of slavery and the existence of the relatively toothless Fourteenth and Fifteenth Amendments, much in the early South Carolina spring of 1877 resembled the spring of 1861. White Democrats controlled the government, whites held the reins of the economy, and most African Americans, though no longer bondsmen, fell back into the "mudsill" class. Just as federal troops had surrendered and withdrawn from the state in April 1861, so a similar scene unfolded sixteen years later.[117]

Hampton's Bourbon government was surprisingly tolerant with regard to racial matters, at least as long as African Americans did not attempt to rise above their "place" in society or government.[118] However, even before Hampton left the governorship for the U.S. Senate, South Carolina officials began the process of disfranchising African Americans, who, at 60.7 percent of the population, still made up a larger proportion of the state's population than did blacks in any other state in the nation.[119] In 1877 the General Assembly redrew precinct boundaries and reduced the numbers of polling places, particularly in black-majority counties.[120] Four years later, the state General Assembly passed the "Eight Box Law," essentially a literacy test for voting whereby voters had to be able to read to identify the appropriate ballot boxes. The law also required all voters to reregister to vote by June 1, 1882, or risk being barred from ever again voting in the state. Moreover, local white registration officials were given broad powers to determine a voter's eligibility.[121] Increasingly, black voters were also barred from voting in local Democratic primaries. This essentially limited black participation in the political process in a state with only one viable party. The number of black voters dropped from more than ninety-one thousand in 1876 to fewer than fourteen thousand in 1888, and the number of black legislators shrank from a high of ninety-six in 1872 to just seven in 1890.[122]

Even though most black Carolinians resigned themselves to their new political powerlessness, racial tensions remained high in the final decades of the nineteenth century. Few black Carolinians dared approach the ballot box, but they still remained the targets of white violence. And, although the state's Civil Rights Act technically protected public equality until 1889, whites drew a color line across South Carolina society long before the official appearance of Jim Crow legislation in the state. Churches, schools, and social organizations were almost entirely segregated.[123] Even farming, the occupation of the majority of South Carolina workers, divided along racial lines in the late 1880s. As the South's agricultural sector took a significant hit in that decade, shared suffering could not unite the races. Beleaguered agriculturalists organized segregated self-help organizations: the Southern Farmers' Alliance for whites and the Colored Farmers' Alliance for African Americans.[124]

The rise of Benjamin Tillman, an Edgefield County farmer, into the leadership of the white Alliance did nothing to ease racial tensions among farmers, though few whites sought such an end. Tillman often boasted of his role in overthrowing Reconstruction in South Carolina, as well as his participation in the Hamburg and Ellenton massacres of 1876, and even his message of agricultural reform in the late 1880s smacked of racial demagoguery. He also feared that conservatives might appeal to black voters, thereby snuffing out his budding political movement and reopening a door to social equality through political opportunity.[125]

Tillman ran for governor in 1890 and dominated the race, losing only two counties while winning others with as much as 95 percent of the vote. He was easily reelected in 1892. Before handpicking his replacement and moving on to the U.S. Senate in 1895, Tillman resolved to accomplish one of the most important items on his state agenda: the disfranchisement of African Americans. The Eight Box Law and other legislation had been effective, but some black voters still showed their faces on election days. Nothing short of total exclusion would satisfy Tillman, and he led the push for a state constitutional convention to craft a document that would disfranchise African Americans and fundamentally replace the progressive constitution of 1868.[126]

At the convention, suffrage was a main topic of debate. The handful of black delegates raised their voices in opposition to their disfranchisement, but their entreaties represented a powerless minority. Despite their resistance, the new constitution featured a poll tax, a property qualification, and a literacy test that, though technically satisfying the terms of the Fifteenth Amendment, would de facto disqualify most African Americans from voting. Tacked onto the restrictions was a list of disqualifying criminal convictions, compiled by white delegates as a collection of offenses believed to be those most often committed by African Americans. The document also established segregated schools and banned interracial marriages and, for the first time, statutorily defined who was considered a black person as one who had "one eighth or more negro blood."[127]

The 1895 constitution officially ushered in the Jim Crow era in South Carolina, and, with the support of the *Plessy vs. Ferguson* "separate but equal" ruling from the U.S. Supreme Court the following year, the state quickly completed the process of de jure segregation. Custom accomplished the rest by establishing "appropriate" behaviors for African Americans, with breaches punishable by vigilante mob. The number of lynchings grew in the first years of the twentieth century, and their occurrence was openly endorsed by Tillman as well as, later, by Governor Cole Blease, who in 1911 declared lynching to be "necessary and good" and just the year before had had campaign posters printed that praised him as "A Governor Who Lauds Lynching."[128]

A handful of progressive whites did help fund black-uplift organizations such as the Jenkins Orphanage, in Charleston, and the South Carolina Industrial Home for Negroes, in Columbia, but they seldom questioned the appropriateness of black subordination. In fact, an underlying motivation for white support of black uplift was not so much that it would benefit African Americans but that it would help reduce a drain on society that might negatively affect whites. Most benefits that came to black communities during the Progressive era were the result of African Americans themselves. Black Progressives established independent hospitals and health associations, homes for troubled youth, private schools, and black civic organizations on the local and state levels that promoted uplift and self-improvement.[129]

When the United States entered World War I, in April 1917, African Americans took President Woodrow Wilson at his word that the war would "make the world safe for democracy," including, they hoped, South Carolina. Most welcomed the war that might usher in sweeping changes after generations of oppression, and large numbers of men enthusiastically offered their services to their nation. However, South Carolina officials rejected black volunteers until the federal government specifically ordered that they be accepted. To whites, black military service would not only suggest some uncomfortable level of equality but also lead to potential labor shortages.[130]

Passage of the Selective Service Act of 1917 made the question of black service a moot point. The draft made no racial distinctions, and the total number of black draftees in South Carolina eventually outnumbered the number of white draftees by 7,500, the largest difference of any state. Moreover, no amount of white outrage or fear of racial violence could sway the War Department's decision to train black soldiers at camps in Columbia and Spartanburg. Once their training was complete, black soldiers left South Carolina for Europe with a salary of $30 per month and a determined patriotism that, they hoped, would pay dividends upon their return.[131]

Black South Carolina troops served in segregated units, though most worked in support roles and saw little if any combat. However, when they faced the enemy on the front lines, black South Carolinians performed with valor. Although no black soldier received a medal from the government during the Great War, Corporal Freddy Stowers of Sandy Spring was posthumously awarded the Congressional Medal of Honor in 1991 for conduct "above and beyond the call of duty" in rallying his troops in a battle in September 1918. Stowers, who fought and died serving in an American unit under French command, was the only African American to earn the honor in either world war.[132]

When black soldiers began returning home in 1919, they fully expected their sacrifices to be repaid with tolerance and respect. However, racial tensions, a revived Ku Klux Klan, and a racially motivated riot in Charleston in May suggested they would be sorely disappointed. The comment of Congressman James F. Byrnes of South Carolina confirmed their suspicions. "The war has in no way changed the attitude of the white man toward the social and political equality of the negro," he said in a speech to Congress, "because this is a white man's country, and will always remain a white man's country."[133]

Really at issue was African Americans', especially returning soldiers', new assertiveness and their refusal to toe the racial line. Many whites would have agreed with the Columbia police officer that "some of the overseas men have come back with foolish notions in their head."[134] Allies in Europe, especially the French, did not share America's intractable racism and recognized the bravery of black soldiers and even the richness of their culture. It was clear, though, that African Americans who had just fought one war for democracy abroad would have to begin one immediately for equality back at home. Many of these "New Negroes" returned radicalized, determined to claim their rightful place in American society and to force the nation to live up to its potential.[135]

Whites, on the other hand, were adamant that the social order not be upset. Though one white Columbia organization resolved that year to promote "the just treatment of the negro and the cultivation of harmony between the races," this pledge was based on the understanding that the "state shall be dominated by its white citizens."[136] This outlook dovetailed nicely with many conservative South Carolinians' caginess regarding the new morality of the Roaring Twenties and what seemed to them like an assault on traditional values. In the reborn Ku Klux Klan, these Carolinians had an "unsavory" ally.[137] Employing violence and intimidation as their Reconstruction forebears had done, the KKK opposed all things "non-American," including Catholics, Jews, and, of course, African Americans. The Speaker of the South Carolina House of Representatives hosted a banquet at the Klan headquarters in 1927, and some pundits attributed Byrnes's defeat in the 1927 U.S. Senate race to his public refusal to join a local klavern of the KKK.[138]

Besides the Klan and much of white society, even the environment seemed set against South Carolina African Americans in the 1920s. The boll weevil and severe droughts devastated crops, mortally wounding the state's Sea Island cotton industry. While the rest of America seemed to be riding an uninterrupted wave of prosperity, South Carolina's agricultural sector, the primary employer of the state's black residents, spiraled toward collapse. Farm values fell by half, at least a third of all farms were mortgaged, and 70 percent of farmers could make ends meet only by going further into debt.[139]

Desperate black Carolinians left the state in droves. Though African American families had been leaving the state for years, the disastrous crop yields of the early 1920s amplified this trend to the level of mass exodus. In just the eight-month period that followed the meager harvest of 1922, more than fifty thousand black farmers abandoned the state. The environment was also no respecter of race, and defeated black farmers joined many of their despondent white neighbors in their emigration. During the 1920s, more than half of South Carolina's counties lost population.[140]

Those African Americans who remained juggled economic survival with racial uplift and self-improvement. Local chapters of the National Association for the Advancement of Colored People (NAACP) helped replace white teachers in black schools with black teachers, organized YWCAs and public libraries, and ran voter registration drives.[141] Though older African Americans were often wary of the consequences of questioning the established order, a younger generation of black Carolinians refused to be silenced. Reformers, including Mamie Garvin Fields, Septima Poinsette Clark, Mary Modjeska Monteith Simkins, and Benjamin Mays, were laying the foundation for the civil rights movement that would follow at midcentury.

However, that movement would have to take a back seat to simple survival after the onset of the Great Depression. Those South Carolinians who thought things could not get worse after the dreadful 1920s found themselves sadly mistaken as cotton prices plummeted to their lowest in more than a generation and per capita income in the state dropped to nearly half what it had been the previous decade, from $261 in 1929 to $151 in 1933. African Americans were hit particularly hard. Although the General Assembly voted to amend the state constitution to expand assistance programs, the changes benefited primarily the disabled and white pensioners.[142]

Roosevelt's New Deal offered more help to African Americans than the state could or would provide. By the fall of 1933, one-fourth of all Carolinians were on some form of federal relief, and many more benefited from various New Deal programs.[143] However, racism cast a shadow over South Carolina's recovery. Most government programs maintained segregation, paying black workers less and employing them less often than whites. Some programs, such as the National Recovery Act, led some white employers to simply fire black workers rather than pay them equal wages. Others balked at any policy or appointment that smacked of racial equality. Nonetheless, for the first time since Reconstruction, African Americans received support from the federal government, and the aid kept many of them afloat in South Carolina.[144]

Although Jim Crow survived the worst of the Great Depression, so too did the spark of reform for equal rights in South Carolina. Small victories in the late 1930s and early 1940s offered hope of greater ones to come. In 1940, in the face of Klan reprisals and economic intimidation, the Greenville chapter of the NAACP launched an ambitious voting rights campaign. The next year, a group of black teachers in Charleston asked for wages equal to those of similarly certified white teachers, and after three years of bureaucratic stalling and a high-profile court case the school system relented. Richland County was forced to follow suit after a case brought in that county in 1945.[145] That summer, reformers organized a statewide conference of the NAACP and immediately endorsed the national association's call for an end to segregation and disfranchisement.[146]

For a growing number of African Americans, securing voting rights meant gaining access to the state's Democratic Party. The impact of the New Deal and Roosevelt's popularity with African Americans resulted in a significant shift in black identification away from the Republican Party and toward the national Democratic Party. However, South Carolina Democrats, untrusting and fearful of the potential strength of these black voters, continued in their crusade to exclude them. In 1944 state Democrats incorporated themselves as a private club that would allow only members to vote in party primaries, effectively shutting out African Americans. Because the party so thoroughly dominated state politics, whichever white candidate won the party primary would inevitably win the general election as well.[147]

In response, black activists in the state organized the Progressive Democratic Party and pledged themselves to challenging the validity of the white South Carolina Democrats at the upcoming national party convention.[148] Although they claimed some forty-five thousand members and sent a delegation to Chicago, the national Democratic Party chose to seat only the regular Democrats. However, the PDP persisted in its voter registration drive back home and, determined to operate in all respects as a proper political party, nominated its own candidate for the U.S. Senate that year. Osceloa McKaine thus became the first black Democrat in a southern state to stand for national office in the twentieth century. Though intimidation and fraud marked the 1942 South Carolina elections, black voters responded with even more determination to have their political voices heard.[149]

Black veterans, barred by state election laws from submitting absentee ballots during World War II, were also among the vanguard pressing for changes upon their return home. They had embraced A. Philip Randolph's "Double V" campaign in the fight—double victory over fascism abroad and racism at home—and were unwilling to accept the same oppression they had left behind when they shipped out.[150] However, they soon found out that the second "V" might be harder to accomplish than the first. The severe beating and blinding of returning veteran Isaac Woodward—while still in uniform—at a bus stop in Batesburg in 1946 was proof that the fight for equality in South Carolina was far from over.

White vets and their families also wanted changes in their state, and they elected Strom Thurmond, a decorated war hero, former state senator, and judge, to serve as governor. The Edgefield Democrat presented himself to the electorate as the reform candidate, and once in office he passed through the General Assembly an impressive body of legislation, ranging from the legalization of divorce to the elimination of the state's poll tax. Though this record made him appear quite liberal relative to other Southern politicians, his handling of the Willie Earle lynching case in 1947 solidified his reputation. Earle had been lynched by a Pickens County mob after being arrested and charged with the murder of a white man. What made the crime remarkable was the swift investigation Thurmond ordered and the resulting arrest and trial of twenty-one men for Earle's lynching. In many South Carolinians' minds, though each defendant was acquitted by a jury, the fact that the case was brought at all marked the dawn of a new era.[151]

The Earle case and the Woodward beating prompted President Harry Truman to make civil rights a top priority of his administration, though doing so likely cost him Southern support in his reelection campaign in 1948.[152] Buoyed by the president's support, black South Carolinians also intensified their agitation. Membership in the NAACP statewide swelled from eight hundred in 1939 to fourteen thousand in 1948.[153] Militant black activists in Charleston and Columbia brought multiple salary equalization suits against South Carolina school districts and continued to attack educational inequalities, while more moderate reformers upstate worked with white leaders behind the scenes to secure improved job opportunities, urban renewal, local condemnation of the KKK, and even some acceptance of black voting rights.[154]

The membership rolls of the South Carolina Progressive Democratic Party were growing as well, and in 1947 the group, in coordination with the national NAACP, helped bring an end to the state's all-white Democratic primary. In 1946 George Elmore, a registered voter and secretary of the Richland County PDP, filed a federal class action suit after being denied the right to vote in the primary. Judge J. Waites Waring, an eighth-generation Charlestonian, ruled in favor of the plaintiffs and scolded Carolinians for effectively denying its citizens the right to vote. "It is time," he declared in his opinion, "for South Carolina to rejoin the Union." When the state Democratic Party Executive Committee responded by requiring primary voters to swear an oath to uphold strict seg-regationist policies, Waring declare the requirement null and void. A month later, in August 1948, thirty-five thousand black South Carolinians voted in the Democratic primary.[155]

The old "Solid South" was crumbling, and white South Carolina Democrats felt themselves under siege. Rather than remain within a party that had to actively court black votes to survive, much less the party of a president who was pressing for federal civil rights legislation, many white South Carolina Democrats bolted the party to form the Dixiecrat or States' Rights Democratic Party. With like-minded politicians from other Southern states, they nominated Thurmond for the presidency in 1948 on a platform opposing federal action on civil rights. In November, Dixiecrats polled more than a million votes, tallied thirty-nine electoral votes, and showed the nation the fierce resistance that awaited unwelcome federal action.[156]

Black South Carolinians were not intimidated. In 1948 parents of black schoolchildren in Clarendon County brought suit to obtain school buses for their school district, of which there were none for black students. Though the case was dismissed on a technicality, its spirit was resurrected in 1950 when the NAACP spearheaded a new case, brought by a veteran, Harry Briggs, and dozens of other black parents within the school district. This case struck directly at the constitutionality of school segregation and eventually made it to the United States Supreme Court on appeal. There, the case was heard alongside four similar cases, including *Brown vs. Board of Education of Topeka, Kansas,* and the five cases together went on for another two years.

Hoping to get out ahead of a Supreme Court decision that might strike down "separate but equal," indeed hoping to show through decisive action that such a decision would be unnecessary, Governor Byrnes instructed the state assembly to "provide for the races substantial equality in school facilities."[157] Legislators responded by increasing funding to public education, with nearly two-thirds of the increase going toward black schools and buses. However, the goal of the "equalization" campaign was not the good of black students; *Plessy's* "separate" had to be maintained at any cost, even if that meant attempting to bring its "equal" descriptor more closely in line. Legislators also proactively passed new laws that they hoped might frustrate any possible federal directive to integrate.[158]

The state's massive spending campaign did nothing to sway the Supreme Court. When the Court, in May 1954, handed down its unanimous ruling that "separate educational facilities are inherently unequal," it realized many white South Carolinians' worst nightmare. White officials encouraged "massive resistance" to the desegregation ruling. Black families that signed petitions or that had participated in court cases found themselves subject to physical and economic intimidation. The 1956 session of the state legislature was dubbed the "Segregation Session" for its preoccupation with seeking ways to frustrate integration; it even passed a law that made it illegal for any public employee to be a member of the NAACP.[159] Thurmond, by then a U.S. senator, led the fight against *Brown* in Washington, coauthoring a "Declaration of Southern Principles" or "Southern Manifesto" that attacked the ruling and urging constituents to resist integration by any lawful means.[160] The next year, Thurmond filibustered on the floor of the Senate for more than twenty-four hours in an unsuccessful effort to block civil rights legislation.

African Americans in the state did not just passively endure the abuse, and they forced the cracks in the façade of Jim Crow in South Carolina to open wider. With the courts and the federal government increasingly in their corner, the state's civil rights advocates began focusing their energies on peaceful, direct action protests. Black college students held massive civil rights protests, boycotted classes when their gatherings were broken up by police, staged sit-ins at segregated lunch counters, and defiantly served out jail sentences for violating local segregation laws. Black lawyers rallied to defend jailed Freedom Riders from the Congress of Racial Equality (CORE) in Rock Hill in 1961 just as other activists in the city were staging a boycott of segregated city buses that would eventually put the local line out of business.[161] Activists held other demonstrations over the next several years from the mountains to the Lowcountry, often singing a version of the old Johns Island folk song "We Shall Overcome," a song that would become the anthem of the civil rights movement, as they marched.[162]

The activities of highly visible conservative whites urging massive resistance and interposition, not to mention still-common acts of violence, reflected poorly on the state's image. Business leaders did not want South Carolina to become another Arkansas, a state whose highly publicized fight against integration in the late 1950s led investors to abandon the state.[163] In 1961 a group of prominent Greenville businessmen formed an advisory committee that urged other state leaders to end segregation for their own sakes. The next year, the Greenville Chamber of Commerce appointed a biracial committee to consider the racial changes facing the city.[164] The new generation of metropolitan elites valued economic development over the preservation of the racial status quo.

South Carolinians also did not want the world to view their higher education system in the same light as that of Alabama and Mississippi. In 1962 a riot followed the integration of the University of Mississippi. In January, Governor George Wallace of Alabama promised to uphold "segregation now, segregation tomorrow, segregation forever" and to do all in his power to keep his state's flagship university lily-white.[165] Yet, when faced with the prospect of integration in South Carolina's public universities, Governor Fritz Hollings warned legislators that, no matter what their personal beliefs, they must choose to be "a government of laws rather than a government of men . . . realize the lesson of one hundred years ago, and move on for the good of South Carolina and our United States." Integration, he said, "should be done with dignity. It must be done with law and order."[166] In January, Harvey Gantt was not harassed when he enrolled at Clemson College. This "integration with dignity" was repeated the following September at the University of South Carolina. By May 1965, all of the state's public colleges and universities and nearly half of its private institutions had abandoned their segregationist admissions policies. By 1968 14 percent of black South Carolinian students attended formerly all-white colleges.[167]

Desegregation in the state's public schools was more problematic. The *Brown* ruling had not set a deadline by which schools must desegregate, and a follow-up ruling a year later was not much more specific, essentially sending the issue back to the lower courts with the stipulation that efforts should proceed "with all deliberate speed." In response, South Carolina legislators repealed the state's compulsory school attendance law on the theory that equal protection of the laws would not apply if all students were not required to attend school.[168]

It would take nine years of legal wrangling before two black high school students in Charleston became the first to attend formerly all-white schools. However, the Civil Rights Act of 1964 required school districts to provide desegregation plans or risk losing federal support, and by that fall Columbia's city schools and fourteen other school districts had been integrated. Though this precipitated a massive "white flight" from public schools into quickly organized private ones, desegregation processes picked up speed thereafter. In 1967 the state legislature passed a new compulsory education law, and the next year courts ruled freedom-of-choice plans unconstitutional and decreed that all school districts must eliminate their dual segregated school systems immediately. Despite pressure from two of the state's Republican congressmen to disobey the federal mandate, Governor Robert McNair told South Carolinians that "obedience of the law" required them to "adjust to the circumstances."

When the state's public schools opened in the fall of 1970, all districts operated on a unitary, desegregated system.[169]

In the midst of the desegregation fight, lawmakers nonetheless marked the Civil War centennial by passing a concurrent resolution authorizing the flying of the Confederate battle flag from atop the State House dome.[170] Although the General Assembly ostensibly passed the resolution to commemorate the centennial of the war, opponents accused them of raising a symbol of racism and states'-rights defiance as South Carolina faced increasing threats from federally mandated integration. The flag was not, critics argued, just a memorial to the war's dead but an emblem intended to flaunt African Americans' subordination at a time when whites' grip on control over them was slipping.[171]

Despite the resilience of the Lost Cause, South Carolina handled the stresses of the growing civil rights movement in a peaceful and orderly fashion, not kicking and screaming like so many of its sister states. The historian Walter Edgar argues that throughout the state's history, South Carolinians have most often sought to ensure "the good order and the harmony of the whole community."[172] In their quiet dismantling of Jim Crow in the civil rights era, state leaders certainly support that claim. Governors pledged themselves to peaceful compliance with court orders, newspapers generally encouraged order, business leaders stressed the advantages of peaceful compliance, and religious leaders placed particular emphasis on the Golden Rule. Thus, South Carolinians, described by one Northerner as "emotionally the deepest Deep South state of them all," acquiesced in what the Charleston New and Courier called "a strategic retreat with honor, a refusal to commit suicide" and what conservative state senator Edgar Brown called "a conspiracy for peace."[173]

Of course, the results were not what most white Carolinians would have chosen, and they would have been happy to see the old ways maintained. They remained committed to white supremacy, just less so than to law and order. The die-hard segregationist Marion Gressette reacted to the desegregation of Clemson by admitting, "We have lost this battle but we are engaged in a war. But this war cannot be won by violence or by inflammatory speeches. I have preached peace and good order too long to change my thinking." If major change was to continue, African Americans and their allies would have to keep pressure on conservative lawmakers not inclined to voluntarily retreat from Jim Crow.[174]

In June 1963 the state NAACP published a list of demands for remedies to specific racial problems and targeted eight major cities for demonstrations if the demands were not met. Columbia leaders and businesses were quick to respond, desegregating Main Street businesses and beginning the process of public school desegregation by the end of the year. Several other targeted cities followed suit, and even smaller towns not specifically mentioned by the

NAACP voluntarily began to repeal segregation ordinances. Orangeburg was the most noteworthy holdout, and in 1968 a protest at a segregated bowling alley led to a heavy-handed response by state troopers and National Guardsmen that left three black students dead and dozens of others seriously wounded. The next year, however, a successful three-month strike by black hospital workers in Charleston led an observer to the conclusion that African Americans in South Carolina, previously powerless and voiceless, had clearly demonstrated their "power to disturb . . . institutions and customs which have remained on dead center for SO long that most people have come to take them for granted."[175]

Politically, as well, black Carolinians showed their strength. The Voting Rights Act of 1965 rendered white registrars powerless to stop thousands of black voters from registering to vote: 220,000 did so by 1970 (up from just 58,000 in 1958). A growing majority of African Americans supported the Democratic Party, especially as the state Republican Party steadily crept to the right. In 1968 the number of black delegates to the state Democratic convention was proportional to the number of blacks in the state population, and that convention elected twelve black delegates to the Democratic national convention in Chicago. As a result, South Carolina's delegation would be the only one from the Deep South that did not have its credentials challenged.[176]

In 1970 three African Americans became the first of their race to win seats in the state General Assembly in the twentieth century, and Democratic governor John West appointed two African American advisers to his staff. In four years another ten African Americans were elected to the General Assembly, and they formally established a Black Caucus that year. In 1983 the civil rights leader I. DeQuincey Newman became the first black state senator since the 1880s— and he was elected from a district that was 64 percent white.[177] With only slight growing pains (relative to most other southern states), South Carolina had become something like an open, biracial society. At the turn of the century, African Americans made up 19 percent of the membership of the state General Assembly; this figure, though far below blacks' overall proportion of the population, represented greater progress in a generation than at any time except for the Reconstruction era.[178] Nationally, James Clyburn of Sumter won election in 1992 to represent the Sixth Congressional District (a seat once held by John C. Calhoun), becoming the first black congressman from the state since his distant relative George Washington Murray in 1897. Clyburn was elected House majority whip in 2007, the third most powerful position in the U.S. House of Representatives.[179]

The rising political clout of black citizens was felt in even some of the most unexpected places. Strom Thurmond, who had run for president as a Dixiecrat in 1948 on a segregationist platform and who bolted the Democratic Party for the Republicans when it began to lean to the left, well understood the shifting political math of the times and adjusted accordingly. In 1971 he appointed Thomas Moss, a civil rights activist and son of an Orangeburg sharecropper, to his staff as a senior aide and field representative and tasked him with making inroads with black constituents.[180] This was the first such appointment by a member of Congress from South Carolina, and in every one of Thurmond's subsequent reelection campaigns (through 1996, when he was ninety-four), the number of black voters who supported the former segregationist increased. Though never renouncing his segregationist past, Thurmond voted for a twenty-five year extension of the Voting Rights Act in 1982 and supported the establishment of the federal Martin Luther King Jr. holiday in 1983.[181]

From the 1970s on, political campaigns in South Carolina smacking of overt racism most often went down to defeat, and some candidates for office believed that victory required an outright and explicit rejection of the caste system of the past.[182] However, racial divisions remained quite visible at the ballot box. With the possible exception of the biracial coalition that carried the state for Jimmy Carter in 1976, African Americans increasingly voted the Democratic ticket in state and national elections. Whites continued their growing identification with the GOP, and the success of Ronald Reagan's "Southern Strategy" in the state suggested that appeals to racism, though arguably subconscious, still resonated with conservative Southern whites.[183]

However, a new generation of black and white South Carolina leaders who rose to prominence in the 1980s, 1990s, and early 2000s sought to help their state make a sharp break from the racial shortcomings of its past. In 1984 and 1988 Jesse Jackson ran presidential campaigns that won hundreds of Democratic Party delegates and proved that white Americans would vote for a black candidate if he had the right message.[184] The civil rights veteran Ernest A. Finney had once turned down an invitation to join the U.S. Justice Department because, he said, his struggle was in South Carolina. In 1985 he became the first African American justice of the South Carolina Supreme Court since Reconstruction, and he was elected Chief Justice in 1994. From that post, he continued his crusade to make equal educational opportunity a reality in his state.[185] In 1996 Governor David Beasley, a Republican, risked political suicide by proposing that the Confederate battle flag flying over the State House, a symbol he acknowledged stood for racism and slavery in some citizens' minds, be removed.[186] In 2003 Governor Mark Sanford issued a formal apology for the Orangeburg Massacre of 1968.[187]

It is noteworthy, though, that Sanford had to travel to Augusta, Georgia, to participate in an NAACP-sponsored event in 2006.[188] In 1999 the organization had called for an economic boycott of South Carolina until the Confederate flag was removed from the State House grounds, and the boycott remained in force even though legislators had ordered the flag lowered from the dome to the Confederate memorial in 2000.[189] Soon after, Congressman Clyburn wrote that "as long as the Confederate Battle flag flies in a place of honor and maintains a cloak of currency, lingering effects of our state's segregationist past will continue to infiltrate our daily lives and color our official conduct."[190] Only following the murder of nine members of Charleston's Emanuel AME church in June 2015 by a neoconfederate supporter of the flag was this cloak of currency pulled back enough for realistic discussions about its removal to begin. Under pressure and after weeks of emotional debate, the General Assembly met in special session and voted to remove the divisive banner from the Statehouse grounds. The day after the removal of the flag, the NAACP lifted its boycott.

In South Carolina, the lingering effects of generations of racism persist. The African American unemployment rate in the state was 11.8 percent in the first quarter of 2015, whereas the rate for whites was just 4.6 percent.[191] From 2008 to 2012, per capita income for African Americans was $15,398, just 55 percent of that for whites.[192] Recently the U.S. Census Bureau documented 29.5 percent of South Carolina African Americans as living below the poverty line, more than three times the percentage of whites.[193] Black and white South Carolinians also remained far apart in their assessments of recent race relations in the state. According to one 2000 poll, 37 percent of African Americans in the state thought that race relations remained the most important problem facing the state, an opinion shared by just 15 percent of whites. A total of 58 percent of African Americans believed that the criminal justice system in the state treated nonwhites "more harshly" than whites, whereas only 12 percent of whites believed this to be the case.[194]

But, as the state moved into the twenty-first century, the fact that racism and racial inequalities had not been completely wiped out did not keep white and black South Carolinians from noting with satisfaction just how far their state had come. Indeed, South Carolinians from just one generation earlier might not have recognized the racial atmosphere that pervaded the state. As the historian Walter Edgar pointed out in 1997, "the South Carolina of 1962 is as dead as the South Carolina of 1862."[195] Cleveland Sellers, who was shot in the back during the Orangeburg Massacre of 1968, agreed in 2003 that those dark days had been vanquished but offered a slightly different assessment: "The Palmetto State is still haunted by the ghost of Jim Crow." At the same event where Sellers offered his remarks, Harvey Gantt noted that "South Carolina has come a long way" in the forty years since he integrated Clemson, but he admonished his audience that "race is still too much a factor."[196]

On January 26, 2008, however, a crowd of hundreds of black and white South Carolinians chanted in unison "Race doesn't matter!" Barack Obama had just won the South Carolina Democratic primary, taking 55 percent of the vote in a three-way race. In his victory speech, Obama told the crowd that

"The choice in this election is not about regions or religions or genders. It's not about rich versus poor, young versus old, and it is not about black versus white."[197] "I did not travel around this state and see a white South Carolina or a black South Carolina," he went on. "I saw South Carolina. . . . This election is about the past versus the future."[198] Looking to that future, exit polls showed that 75 percent of South Carolina Democratic voters said that "they were ready to elect a black president."[199]

Yet, according to the legal scholar Kareem Crayton, "You can't get a Barack Obama . . . if you don't have a Harvey Gantt."[200] Born in Jim Crow–era Charleston, Gantt participated in sit-ins to desegregate the city's lunch counters, integrated "Pitchfork" Ben Tillman's college, graduated from Clemson with honors, and entered a public sphere that had been off limits to his parents' generation.[201] He ran twice, unsuccessfully, for the U.S. Senate but keeps a framed memento of his first national campaign, in 1990, hanging in his hallway. A photograph shows a young man proudly wearing a "Gantt for US Senate" T-shirt. It is signed "To Harvey—an early inspiration, Barack Obama."[202]

Gantt acknowledges that "South Carolina has come a long way," and he appreciates that he represents neither the beginning nor the end of African Americans' long journey in the state. Each step forward rested upon a foundation often created through suffering and laid by previous determined generations. His ancestors, like those of First Lady Michelle Obama, lived and died on Sea Island rice plantations. Gantt's friends point out that he "knew his place in the continuum of history." His achievements were not just his own but "part of a journey that started on a slave ship over 400 years ago."[203] That journey would continue into the twenty-first century. "Clearly, from my vantage point," Gantt told a Columbia audience in 2003, "we have much to do."[204]

CHAPTER 1

"The people commonly called Negroes"

BECOMING AFRICAN AMERICANS
IN SOUTH CAROLINA

∎

1.1. The Rebellion of San Miguel de Guadalpe (1526)

Lucas Vasquez de Ayllón received the first contract to settle the region north of Florida for the Spanish, and he and his expedition, which included several African slaves, landed somewhere on the South Carolina coast in the summer of 1526. By the fall, Ayllón was dead and his settlement was coming unraveled. In addition to a mutiny by the Spanish survivors and an attack by Native Americans, a rebellion by the expedition's African slaves, the first in the history of North America, doomed the mission to failure. ::

After [Ayllón's men] were there for a few days, unhappy with the land and with the crazy languages or guides that they had brought, they agreed to go populate the coast further toward the west, and they went to a great river (forty or forty-five leagues from there, more or less) that is called Gualdape:[1] and there along the coast they set up their camp, and they began to build houses, because there were not any, except for some small shacks far away from each other, and all the land was very flat and had many swamps, but the river was very powerful and had many good fish; and the river's entrance was so low, even with its swelling, that boats could not enter. And since they were lacking sustenance and they did not find it on the land, and the cold temperatures were very great, because that land, where they ended up, is thirty-three degrees above sea level and was flat, many people got sick and many died; and the soldier [Ayllón]

Gonzalo Fernandez de Oviedo y Valdéz, *Historia General y Natural de las Indias, Islas y Tierra-Firme del Mar Océano* (1535; reprint, Madrid: Real Academia de la Historia, 1853), 627–32.

later got sick and died. . . . But among the soldiers and people who remained, they did not lack a pair of mutinous, disconcerted men, who put everyone to work: of them, Ginés Doncel was the leader . . . who joined with another man of such bad sense as his, who was called Pedro de Bazán. . . .

Ginés Doncel, after he saw the soldier Ayllón dead, as a man without counsel and who trusted in his ability and intelligence that he could be captain of those who remained, said, under the pretext that they were unhappy with the land, that he would take them away from there, and giving others false pretexts, he took into custody the lieutenant and the magistrates, and put them in great need. . . . At that time the Indians killed some runaway Spaniards. . . . Some good men, not being able to withstand the tyranny and arrogance of the said Ginés Doncel and his faction, got together, and especially two *hidalgos*, named Oliveros and Monesterio, and with others who assembled themselves on their own, agreed to talk to Ginés so that he would release those he had in custody, making him understand that he was doing wrong, and that it was a bad deed. . . . Of this talk and threat, Ginés Doncel kept a perpetual enmity with Oliveros, because he was a proper man, and was rounding up others to not consent to the tyranny of Ginés and to undo it; and Ginés began to deal with Bazán on how they would kill Oliveros and Monesterio. And one night that they were going to put into effect their bad intention, it happened that some black slaves set fire to Ginés's house on their own; and the prisoners were also there, and all took part to put out the burning fire: and so the prisoners left from where they were being detained. At that same time, Bazán went to kill the said Monesterio, who was in his lodging; as Monesterio was a man of good spirits, he left for Bazán and began to abuse him, because Bazán was armed. And also at that time, Oliveros was looking for Ginés Doncel (who had armed himself and was hidden underneath a bed) and he wanted to take him into custody. . . . And [Monesterio and Oliveros] later turned to where the fire was burning, and Ginés was still hidden: and finally he gave himself up to custody, and the authorities and the magistrates were set free, and it was ordered to drag and behead the said Bazán. . . .

With Ginés and others of his confederation in custody, those that remained agreed to come to these islands, and they put that in effect: and they placed the body of the soldier[2] in the flatboat, in order to bring him to this city of Santo Domingo, where he had his house and post, or the Puerto de Plata,[3] for it was half of a strong wit that was well received to bring him from there to this city; but because they had bad navigation, at the end they gave him a great burial in the ocean. . . .

■

1.2. The King Buzzard (1928)

Enslaved men and women were aware of African complicity in the slave trade. The story presented here, recorded by the folklorist E.C.L. Adams in the Congaree in the 1920s, resembles a traditional Igbo tale in which the spirit of a deceased person returns to the world as an animal if he or she has murdered another person in life. Here, the Chief who enslaved his own people is remembered as one who is damned to return as the lowest of all animals and made to wander for eternity, never able to return to the land of his ancestors. ::

A group around a campfire

Tom: I wonder wey Tad.

Cricket: I ain' know. Look like he wants to git out er draggin' dis here seine.[4] He leff here ever since 'fore day. Say he guh see kin he kill a turkey.

Voice: Who wid him?

Cricket: Ain' nobody wid him. He leff here by his self.

Tom: I sho'ain't loves to wander 'round dese here swamps by my lonesome.

Cricket: Tad is a ole swamper. I reckon he know wuh he doin'.

Voice: He ain' token nothin' to eat wid him, an' it atter midnight. I reckon he must er had some kind er trouble.

Cricket: Looks to me like I hear sump'n comin'.

(Tad approaches, his clothes badly torn. He is wet and covered with yellow mud.)

Tom: Tad, wey you been? You sho' looks like you loves to wander 'round dese here swamps by you'self.

Tad: Look at me. Is I look like I been enjoyin' myself?

Tom: You sho' is tored up. A bear must er had you.

Tad: I seen sump'n wuss 'an a bear.

Voice: Wuh it been?

Tad: I been walkin' 'long on de edge er Big Alligator Hole, an'de air been stink; an' I walk on an' I see sump'n riz up in front er me bigger 'an a man. An' he spread he whing out 'an say, "Uuh!" He eye been red an' he de nastiest lookin' thing I ever see. He stink in my nostrils. He so stink, he stink to my eye an' my year. An' I look at him an' see he been eat a dead hog right dere in de night time. I ain' never see buzzard settin' on a carcass in de night 'fore dis. An' he look so vigus, he look like he ain' care ef he stay dere an' fight or no.

E.C.L. Adams, *Nigger to Nigger* (1928), reprinted in E.C.L. Adams, *Tales of the Congaree* (Chapel Hill: University of North Carolina Press, 1987), 120–21. Reprinted courtesy of the University of North Carolina Press.

An' he been so oneasy an' frighten, till I ain' kin do nothin', an' 'fore I knowed it, I jump at him. An' he riz up—makin' dat same dreadful sound—an' start flyin' all 'round me. Look like he tryin' to vomick on me. An' I dodge, an' dere in de moonlight dat ole thing circle 'round—look like he guh tackle me. An' he spew he vomick every which er way, an' I see de leaf an' de grass wuh it fall on dry up. All de air seem like it were pizen.

An' I turned to leff, an' it keep on gittin' nigher an' nigher to me. An' I ain' know wuh would er happen, ef I ain' git in a canebrake wey he ain' kim fly. An' I crawl 'round for God knows how long, an' when I find myself, I been lost. Jesus know I ain' never wan' see no more buzzard like dat.

Cricket: My God!

Voice: Wuh kind er buzzard dat?

Tad: God knows.

Tom: Dat ain' no buzzard. I hear 'bout dat ole thing 'fore dis.

My pa tell me dat 'way back in slavery time—'way back in Af'ica—dere been a nigger, an' he been a big nigger. He been de chief er he tribe, an' when dem white folks was ketchin' niggers for slavery, dat ole nigger nuse to entice 'em into trap. He'd git 'em on boat wey dem white folks could ketch 'em an' chain 'em. White folks nused to gee him money an' all kind er little thing, an' he'd betray 'em. An' one time atter he betray thousands into bondage, an' de white folks say de ain' guh come to dat coast no more—dat was dey last trip—so dey knocked dat nigger down an' put chain on him an' brung him to dis country.

An' when he dead, dere were no place in heaven for him an' he were not desired in hell. An' de Great Master decide dat he were lower den all other mens or beasts, he punishment were to wander for eternal time over de face er de earth. Dat as he had kilt de sperrits of men an' womens as well as dere bodies, he must wander on an' on. Dat his sperrit should always travel in de form of a great buzzard, an' dat carrion must be he food.

An' sometimes he appears to mens, but he doom is settled, an' e ain' would er hurt Tad, kaze one er he punishment is dat he evil beak an' claw shall never tech no livin' thing. An' dey say he are known to all de sperrit world as de King Buzzard, an' dat forever he must travel alone.

∎

1.3. The Fundamental Constitutions of Carolina (1669)

The Fundamental Constitutions of Carolina were adopted by the eight Lords Proprietors in March 1669 to serve as the fundamental laws of the Carolina colony. Drafted with the help of the philosopher John Locke, the Constitutions were intended largely

John Locke, "The Fundamental Constitutions of Carolina," in *The Works of John Locke, in Nine Volumes,* vol. 9 (London: C. Baldwin, 1824), 175–99.

to protect Proprietary interests and establish a feudal government while avoiding the development of anything resembling a democracy. Unpopular with most settlers, the Constitutions were never ratified by the colonial assembly. ::

Our sovereign lord the King having, out of his royal grace and bounty, granted unto us the province of Carolina, with all the royalties, properties, jurisdictions, and privileges of a county palatine[5] . . . with other great privileges; for the better settlement of the government of the said place, and establishing the interest of the lords proprietors with equality and without confusion; and that the government of this province may be made most agreeable to the monarchy under which we live and of which this province is a part; and that we may avoid erecting a numerous democracy, we, the lords and proprietors of the province aforesaid, have agreed to this following form of government, to be perpetually established amongst us, unto which we do oblige ourselves, our heirs and successors, in the most binding ways that can be devised. . . .

Seventy-one. There shall be a parliament, consisting of the proprietors or their deputies, the landgraves, and caziques,[6] and one freeholder out of every precinct, to be chosen by the freeholders of the said precinct, respectively. They shall sit all together in one room, and have every member one vote.

Seventy-two. No man shall be chosen a member of parliament who has less than five hundred acres of freehold within the precinct for which he is chosen; nor shall any have a vote in choosing the said member that hath less than fifty acres of freehold within the said precinct. . . .

Ninety-five. No man shall be permitted to be a freeman of Carolina, or to have any estate or habitation within it, that doth not acknowledge a God, and that God is publicly and solemnly to be worshipped. . . .

One hundred and seven. Since charity obliges us to wish well to the souls of all men, and religion ought to alter nothing in any man's civil estate or right, it shall be lawful for slaves, as well as others, to enter themselves, and be of what church or profession any of them shall think best, and, therefore, be as fully members as any freeman. But yet no slave shall hereby be exempted from that civil dominion his master hath over him, but be in all things in the same state and condition he was in before. . . .

One hundred and ten. Every freeman of Carolina shall have absolute power and authority over his negro slaves, of what opinion or religion soever. . . .

One hundred and twenty. These fundamental constitutions, in number a hundred and twenty, and every part thereof, shall be and remain the sacred and unalterable form and rule of government of Carolina forever. Witness our hands and seals, the first day of March, sixteen hundred and sixty-nine.

■

1.4. Governor Announces Black Majority

Twelve years after passing its first comprehensive slave code, South Carolina officials noted that there had been a significant population shift in the preceding five years. Though the white population had continued to grow, the number of Africans in the province had increased 30 percent faster than the number of white, resulting in a slim black majority. The black-to-white ratio would grow to approximately two to one by 1720 and remain relatively constant until the American Revolution. ::

Carolina 17th Sept., 1708
MAY IT PLEASE YOUR LORDSHIPS,

Wee the governour and council of Her Majesty's province of Carolina having received from their lordships the lords proprietors your lordships letter to them dated Whitehall May 7th, 1707 intimating it to be Her Majesty's pleasure and express commands that from time to time we should transmit to your lordships frequent and full informations of the state and condition of this government.

In obedience therefore to Her Sacred Majesty's command and your lordships instructions we have carefully enquired into the present state and circumstances of this province as it more immediately respects the information your lordships require of us and of which we pray your lordships to accept the following account.

The number of the inhabitants in this province of all sorts are computed to be nine thousand five hundred and eighty souls of which there are thirteen [hundred] and sixty freemen, nine hundred free women, sixty white servant men, sixty white servant women, seventeen hundred white free children, eighteen hundred Negro men slaves, eleven hundred Negro women slaves, five hundred Indian men slaves, six hundred Indian women slaves, twelve hundred Negro children slaves, and three hundred Indian children slaves. . . .

The whole number of the militia of this province is nine hundred and fifty fit to bear arms viz. two regiments of foot both making up sixteen companys fifty men one with another in a company to which must be added a like number of Negro men slaves the capt. of each company by an act of assembly being obliged to enlist traine up and bring into the field for each white one able slave armed with gunn or lance for each man in his company and the governors troop of guards . . . to take care of the women and children in time of allarum and invasion. . . .

Facsimile in *Records in the British Public Records Office Relating to South Carolina, 1701–10*, vol. 5 (Atlanta: Foote and Davies, 1947), 203–10.

The comoditys exported from this province to England are rice, pitch, tarr, buck and doe skins in the haire and Indian drest; also some few furs as beaver, otter, wild cat, raccons, buffaloe and bear skins, some ox and cow hides, a little silk, white oak pipe staves sometimes some other sorts. We are sufficiently provided with pine fit for masts and yeards[7] of severall sizes both pine and cyprus which may be afforded very reasonable and supplied at all times in the year, there being no frost or snow considerable enough to hinder bringing them down the rivers. . . .

Wee are also often furnished with Negroes from the American islands chiefly from Barbadoes and Jamaica from whence also comes a considerable quantity of English manufactures and some prize goods (viz.) clarett [and] brandy, taken from the French and Spaniards. . . .

The trade of this province is certainly increased of late years, there being a greater comsumption yearly of most commodities imported, and the inhabitants by a yearly addition of slaves are made the more capable of improving the produce of the colony. Notwithstanding, tis our opinion the value of our import is greater (if we include Negroes and the commodities that are consumed here) then our export by which means it comes to pass that wee are very near drained of all our silver and gold coins. Nor is there any remedy to prevent this but by a number of honest laborious persons to come amongst us that would consume but little, by which means the produce of the country being increased might in time make our exportation equalize if not exceed our importation. . . .

We are, my lords,
Your lordships most obedient humble servants,
N. Johnson, Thos. Broughton, Robert Gibbs, Geo. Smith, Richard Beresford

■

1.5. Governor Urges Curtailing of the African Slave Trade (1711)

Robert Gibbes (1644–1715)—sheriff, assemblyman, Proprietary Deputy, chief justice, and interim governor of Carolina province from 1710 to 1712—presented his annual report on the affairs of the colony to the Assembly in May 1711. After offering a glowing description of the general happiness and prosperity of Carolina, he solemnly urges lawmakers to consider curtailing the importation of African slaves into the colony. ::

. . . And, Gentlemen, I desire you will consider the great quantities of negroes that are dayly brought into this government, and the small number of whites

"A South Carolinian," *A Refutation of the Calumnies Circulated against the Southern and Western States, Respecting the Institution and Existence of Slavery among Them* (Charleston, S.C.: A. E. Miller, 1822), 28–29.

that comes amongst us, and how many are lately dead and gon off. How insolent and mischeivous the negroes are become, and to consider the Negro Act[8] already made, doth not reach up to some of the crimes they have lately been guilty off; therefore it might be convenient by some additional clause of said Negro Act to appoint either by gibbets,[9] or some such like way, that, after executed, they may remain more exemplary, than any punishment hitherto hath been inflicted on them; and also that masters of negroes may be obliged to provide and allow their negroes sufficient dyet and cloathing, and that their worke and correction may be with moderation, that they may be comfortable, which may the better encourage them to live peaceably and honestly with their masters."

The next month, Gibbes made stronger suggestions to the Assembly.

"We further recommend unto you the repairs of the fortifications about Charleston, and the amending of the Negro Act, who are of late grown to that height of impudence, that there is scarce a day passes without some robbery or insolence, committed by them in one part or other of this province. . . ."

■

1.6. An Act for the Better Ordering and Governing of Negroes and Slaves (1712)

To keep the rising black population in check, South Carolina first passed a comprehensive slave code in 1696. That law was based almost entirely on the Barbados slave code of 1688. The 1712 Slave Code excerpted here was an expanded version of the original. To its predecessor was added a preamble, a near-verbatim copy of the preamble to the Barbadian code that offered African savagery as the rationale for adopting a separate code of laws for slaves, who were unfit to be governed by laws intended for whites. Though it offers great insight into the mind of the slave-owning class, the Act also provides a fascinating picture of slave life by describing in detail the conditions and behaviors it hoped to correct. ::

WHEREAS, the plantations and estates of this Province cannot be well and sufficiently managed and brought into use, without the labor and service of negroes and other slaves; and forasmuch as the said negroes and other slaves brought unto the people of this Province for that purpose, are of barbarous, wild, savage natures, and such as renders them wholly unqualified to be governed by the laws, customs, and practices of this Province; but that it is absolutely necessary, that such other constitutions, laws and orders, should in this Province be made and enacted, for the good regulating and ordering of them, as may restrain the

The Statues at Large of South Carolina; Edited, under Authority of the Legislature, vol. 7 (Columbia, S.C.: A. S. Johnson, 1840), 352–65.

disorders, rapines and inhumanity, to which they are naturally prone and inclined; and may also tend to the safety and security of the people of this Province and their estates; to which purpose,

I. *Be it therefore enacted,* by his Excellency, William, Lord Craven, Palatine, and the rest of the true and absolute Lords and Proprietors of this Province, by and with the advice and consent of the rest of the members of the General Assembly, now met at Charlestown, for the South-west part of this Province, and by the authority of the same, That all negroes, mulatoes, mustizoes or Indians, which at any time heretofore have been sold, or now are held or taken to be, or hereafter shall be bought and sold for slaves, are hereby declared slaves; and they, and their children, are hereby made and declared slaves, to all intents and purposes; excepting all such negroes, mulatoes, mustizoes or Indians, which heretofore have been, or hereafter shall be, for some particular merit, made and declared free, either by the Governor and council of this Province, pursuant to any Act or law of this Province, or by their respective owners or masters; and also, excepting all such negroes, mulatoes, mustizoes or Indians, as can prove they ought not to be sold for slaves. And in case any negro, mulatoe, mustizoe or Indian, doth lay claim to his or her freedom, upon all or any of the said accounts, the same shall be finally heard and determined by the Governor and council of this Province.

II. And for the better ordering and governing of negroes and all other slaves in this Province, *Be it enacted* by the authority aforesaid, That no master, mistress, overseer, or other person whatsoever, that hath the care and charge of any negro or slave, shall give their negroes and other slaves leave, on Sundays, hollidays, or any other time, to go out of their plantations, except such negro or other slave as usually wait upon them at home or abroad, or wearing a livery; and every other negro or slave that shall be taken hereafter out of his master's plantation, without a ticket, or leave in writing, from his master or mistress, or some other person by his or her appointment, or some white person in the company of such slave, to give an account of his business, shall be whipped; and every person who shall not (when in his power,) apprehend every negro or other slave which he shall see out of his master's plantation, without leave as aforesaid, and after apprehended, shall neglect to punish him by moderate whipping, shall forfeit twenty shillings, the one half to the poor, to be paid to the church wardens of the Parish where such forfeiture shall become due, and the other half to him that will inform for the same, within one week after such neglect; and that no slave may make further or other use of any one ticket than was intended by him that granted the same, every ticket shall particularly mention the name of every slave employed in the particular business, and to what place they are sent, and what time they return; and if any person shall presume to give any negro or slave a ticket in the name of his master or mistress, without his or her consent, such person so doing shall forfeit the sum of twenty shillings; one half to the poor, to be disposed of as aforesaid, the other half to the person injured, that will complain against the person offending, within one week after the offence committed. And for the better security of all such persons that shall endeavor to take any runaway, or shall examine any slave for his ticket, passing to and from his master's plantation, it is hereby declared lawful for any white person to beat, maim or assault, and if such negro or slave cannot otherwise be taken, to kill him, who shall refuse to shew his ticket, or, by running away or resistance, shall endeavor to avoid being apprehended or taken.

III. *And be it further enacted* by the authority aforesaid, That every master, mistress or overseer of a family in this Province, shall cause all his negro houses to be searched diligently and effectually, once every fourteen days, for fugitive and runaway slaves, guns, swords, clubs, and any other mischievous weapons, and finding any, to take them away, and cause them to be secured; as also, for clothes, good's, and any other things and commodities that are not given them by their master, mistress, commander or overseer, and honestly come by; and in whose custody they find any thing of that kind, and suspect or know to be stolen goods, the same they shall seize and take into their custody, and a full and ample description of the particulars thereof, in writing, within ten days after the discovery thereof, either to the provost marshall, or to the clerk of the parish for the time being, who is hereby required to receive the same, and to enter upon it the day of its receipt, and the particulars to file and keep to himself; and the clerk shall set upon the posts of the church door, and the provost marshall upon the usual public places, or places of notice, a short brief, that such lost goods are found; whereby, any person that hath lost his goods may the better come to the knowledge where they are; and the owner going to the marshall or clerk, and proving, by marks or otherwise, that the goods lost belong to him, and paying twelve pence for the entry and declaration of the same, if the marshall or clerk be convinced that any part of the goods certified by him to be found, appertains to the party inquiring, he is to direct the said party inquiring to the place and party where the goods be, who is hereby required to make restitution of what is in being to the true owner; and every master, mistress or overseer, as also the provost marshall or clerk, neglecting his duty in any the particulars aforesaid, for every neglect shall forfeit twenty shillings.

IV. And for the more effectual detecting and punishing such persons that trade with any slave for stolen goods, *Be it further enacted* by the authority aforesaid, That where any person shall be suspected to trade as aforesaid, any justice of the peace shall have power to take from him suspected, sufficient recognizance, not to trade with any slave contrary to the laws of this Province; and if it shall afterwards appear to any of the justices of the peace, that such person hath, or hath had, or shipped off, any goods, suspected to be unlawfully come by, it shall be lawful for such justice of the peace to oblige the person to appear at the next general sessions, who shall there be obliged to make reasonable proof, of whom he bought, or how he came by, the said goods, and unless he do it, his recognizance shall be forfeited.

V. *And be it further enacted* by the authority aforesaid, That no negro or slave shall carry out of the limits of his master's plantation any sort of gun or fire arms, without his master, or some other white person by his order, is present with him, or without a certificate from his master, mistress or overseer, for the same; and if any negro or slave shall be so apprehended or taken, without the limits aforesaid, with any gun or fire arms as aforesaid, such arms shall be forfeited to him or them that shall apprehend or take the same; unless the person who is the owner of the arms so taken, shall in three months time redeem the arms so taken, by paying to the person that took the same, the sum of twenty shillings.

VI. *And be it further enacted* by the authority aforesaid, That every master or head of any family, shall keep all his guns and other arms, when out of use, in the most private and least frequented room in the house, upon the penalty of being convicted of neglect therein, to forfeit three pounds.

VII. And *whereas*, great numbers of slaves which do not dwell in Charlestown, on Sundays and holidays resort thither, to drink, quarrel, fight, curse and swear, and profane the Sabbath, and using and carrying of clubs and other mischievous weapons, resorting in great companies together, which may give them an opportunity of executing any wicked designs and purposes, to the damage and prejudice of the inhabitants of this Province; for the prevention whereof, *Be it enacted* by the authority aforesaid, That all and every the constables of Charlestown, separately on every Sunday, and the holidays at Christmas, Easter and Whitsonside,[10] together with so many men as each constable shall think necessary to accompany him, which he is hereby empowered for that end to press, under the penalty of twenty shillings to the person that shall disobey him, shall, together with such persons, go through all or any the streets, and also, round about Charlestown, and as much further on the neck as they shall be informed or have reason to suspect any meeting or concourse of any such negroes or slaves to be at that time, and to enter into any house, at Charlestown, or elsewhere, to search for such slaves, and as many of them as they can apprehend, shall cause to be publicly whipped in Charlestown, and then to be delivered to the marshall; . . . and the marshall shall in all respects keep and dispose of such slave as if the same was delivered to him as a runaway, under the same penalties and forfeiture as hereafter in that case is provided; and every constable of Charlestown which shall neglect or refuse to make search as aforesaid, for every such neglect shall forfeit the sum of twenty shillings.

VIII. *And be it further enacted* by the authority aforesaid, That no owner or head of any family shall give a ticket to any slave to go to Charlestown, or from plantation to plantation, on Sunday, excepting it be for and about such particular business as cannot reasonably be delayed to another time, under the forfeiture of ten shillings; and in every ticket in that case given, shall be mentioned the particular business that slave is sent about, or that slave shall be dealt with as if he had no ticket.

IX. *And be it further enacted* by the authority aforesaid, That upon complaint made to any justice of the peace, of any heinous or grievous crime, committed by any slave or slaves, as murder, burglary, robbery, burning of houses, or any lesser crimes, as killing or stealing any meat or other cattle, maiming one the other, stealing of fowls, provisions, or such like trespasses or injuries, the said justice shall issue out his warrant for apprehending the offender or offenders, and for all persons to come before him that can give evidence; and if upon examination, it probably appeareth, that the apprehended person is guilty, he shall commit him or them to prison, or immediately proceed to tryal of the said slave or slaves . . . and diligently weighing and examining all evidences, proofs and testimonies, (and in case of murder only, if on violent presumption and circumstances,) they shall find such negro or other slave or slaves guilty thereof, they shall give sentence of death, if the crime by law deserve the same, and forthwith by their warrant cause immediate execution to be done, by the common or any other executioner, in such manner as they shall think fit, the kind of death to be inflicted to be left to their judgment and discretion; and if the crime committed shall not deserve death, they shall then condemn and adjudge the criminal or criminals to any other punishment, but not extending to limb or disabling him, without a particular law directing such punishment, and shall forthwith order execution to be done accordingly.

X. And in regard great mischiefs daily happen by petty larcenies committed by negroes and slaves of this Province, *Be it further enacted* by the authority aforesaid, That if any negro or other slave shall hereafter steal or destroy any goods, chattels, or provisions whatsoever, of any other person than his master or mistress, being under the value of twelve pence, every negro or other slave so offending, and being brought before some justice of the peace of this Province, upon complaint of the party injured, and shall be adjudged guilty by confession, proof, or probable circumstances, such negro or slave so offending, excepting children, whose punishment is left wholly to the discretion of the said justice, shall be adjudged by such justice to be publicly and severely whipped, not exceeding forty lashes; and if such negro or other slave punished as aforesaid, be afterwards, by two justices of the peace, found guilty of the like crimes, he or they, for such his or their second offence, shall either have one of his ears cut off, or be branded in the forehead with a hot iron, that the mark thereof may remain; and if after such punishment, such negro or slave for his third offence, shall have his nose slit; and if such negro or other slave, after the third time as aforesaid, be accused of petty larceny, or of any of the offences before mentioned, such negro or other slave shall be tried in such manner as those accused of murder, burglary, &c. are before by this Act provided for to be tried, and in case they shall be found guilty a fourth time, of any the offences before mentioned, then such negro or other slave shall be adjudged to suffer death, or other punishment, as the said justices shall think fitting; and any judgment given for the first offence, shall be a sufficient conviction for the first offence; and any after judgment after the first judgment, shall be a sufficient conviction to bring the offender within the penalty of the second offence, and so for inflicting the rest of the punishments; and in case the said justices and freeholders, and any or either of them, shall neglect or refuse to perform the duties by this Act required of them, they shall severally, for such their defaults, forfeit the sum of twenty-five pounds.

. . .

XII. *And it is further enacted* by the authority aforesaid, That if any negroes or other slaves shall make mutiny or insurrection, or rise in rebellion against the authority and government of this Province, or shall make preparation of arms, powder, bullets or offensive weapons, in order to carry on such mutiny or insurrection, or shall hold any counsel or conspiracy for raising such mutiny, insurrection or rebellion, the offenders shall be tried by two justices of the peace and three freeholders, associated together as before expressed in case of murder, burglary, &c., who are hereby empowered and required to try the said slaves so offending, and inflict death, or any other punishment, upon the offenders, and forthwith by their warrant cause execution to be done, by the common or any other executioner, in such manner as they shall think fitting; and if any person shall make away or conceal any negro or negroes, or other slave or slaves, suspected to be guilty of the beforementioned crimes, and not upon demand bring forth the suspected offender or offenders, such person shall forfeit for every negro or slave so concealed or made away, the sum of fifty pounds; *Provided, nevertheless,* that when and as often as any of the beforementioned crimes shall be committed by more than one negro, that shall deserve death, that then and in all such cases, if the Governor and council of this Province shall think fitting, and accordingly shall order, that only one or more of the said criminals should suffer death as exemplary, and the rest to be returned to the owners, that then, tho owners of the negroes so offending, shall bear proportionably the loss of the said negro or negroes so put to death, as shall be allotted them by the said justices and freeholders; and if any person shall refuse his part so allotted him, that then, and in all such cases, the said justices and freeholders are hereby required to issue out their warrant of distress upon the goods and chattels of the person so refusing, and shall cause the same to be sold by public outcry, to satisfy the said money so allotted him to pay, and to return the overplus, if any be, to the owner; *Provided, nevertheless,* that the part allotted for any person to pay for his part or proportion of the negro or negroes so put to death, shall not exceed one sixth part of his negro or negroes so excused and pardoned; and in case that shall not be sufficient to satisfy for the negro or negroes that shall be put to death, that the remaining sum shall be paid out of the public treasury of this Province.

XIII. *And be it further enacted* by the authority aforesaid, That the confession of any slave accused, or the testimony of any other slave, that the justices and free-holders shall have reason to believe to speak truth, shall be held for good and convincing evidence in all petty larcenies or trespasses, not exceeding forty shillings; but no negro or other slave shall suffer loss of life or limb, but such as shall be convicted, either by their own free and voluntary confession, or by the oath of christian evidence, or, at least, by the plain and positive evidence of two negroes or slaves, so circumstantiated as that there shall not be sufficient reason to doubt the truth thereof, and examination being always made, if the negroes or slaves that give evidence, do not bear any malice to the other slave accused; excepting in the case of murder, in which case, the evidence of one slave, attended with such circumstances as that the justices and freeholders shall have no just reason to suspect the truth thereof, of which they are hereby made judges, or upon violent presumption of the accused person's guilt, the said justices and freeholders may declare the accused person guilty, and may give sentence of death upon him accordingly, and award execution, as before directed by this Act.

. . .

XV. *And be it further enacted* by the authority aforesaid, That in case any negro or slave shall run from his master or mistress, with intent to go off from this Province, in order to deprive his master or mistress of his service, such negro or slave, being declared guilty of the same by two justices and three freeholders, as aforesaid, shall suffer the pains of death; and in case any negro or slave shall be guilty of enticing or persuading any other negro or slave to run from their master's or mistress's service, in order to go off from this Province, and being convicted of the same, before two justices and three freeholders, he shall be severely whipped, not exceeding forty lashes, and shall also be branded in the forehead with a hot iron, that the mark thereof may remain. But if any negro or other slave shall so tempt and practice with any negro or negroes, or other slave or slaves, and him or them so tempted, actually convey away, or send off from this Province, or be taken in the very act of taking or carrying him or them away, in order to carry him or them off and from this Province, such negro or slave, so tempting and persuading the other negro or slave, as aforesaid, being found guilty of the fact, by two justices and three freeholders, as before directed in this Act, shall suffer the pains of death; and the negro or negroes, or other slave or slaves, so consenting to the persuasion and inticement of the other negro, and shall so go off from this Province, or be taken in the very act of running from his or their master or mistress, in order to go off from this Province, and being adjudged guilty of the same, by two justices and three freeholders, as aforesaid, they, the said two justices and three freeholders, shall give sentence of death, or other punishment, as they shall think fitting, against the criminal or criminals, and by their warrant cause execution to be done accordingly.

XVI. Now, forasmuch as the loss of the negroes and other slaves that shall suffer death, or be killed, by this Act, would prove too heavy for the owners of them to bear, and that the owners of negroes and slaves may not be discouraged to detect and discover the offences of their negroes and slaves, and that the loss may be borne by the public, whose safety, by such punishments, is hereby provided for and intended, *Be it therefore enacted* by the authority aforesaid, That in all cases whatsoever, where any negro or other slave, by the appointment and provision of this Act, shall suffer death, then all such justices and freeholders who adjudged such negro or other slave to suffer death, immediately after return thereof given, shall inquire, by the best means they are able, of the full and true value of such negro or slave, and make certificate thereof to the public receiver for the time being, therein requiring him to pay out of the public treasury the full value of the said negro or slave, to the owner thereof. . . .

XVII. *And be it further enacted* by the authority aforesaid, That if any negro or slave whatsoever, shall offer any violence to any christian or white person, by striking, or the like, such negro or other slave, for his or her first offence, by information given, upon oath, to the next justice, shall be severely whipped, or caused to be whipped, by the constable, who is hereby required to do the same, under the penalty of forty shillings, by order of any justice of the peace; for the second offence of that nature, by order of the justice of the peace, he shall be severely whipped, and his nose slit, or be burned in some part of his face with a hot iron, that the mark thereof may remain; and for the third offence, be left to two justices and three freeholders, to inflict death, or any other punishment, according to their discretion; and any judgment given after the first judgment, shall be sufficient conviction to bring the offenders within the penalty for the second offence, and after the second, within the penalty of the third offence. And in case any negro or slave shall so assault and beat any white person, by which the said white person is maimed and disabled, in such case, the slave shall be punished as in the third offence, for offering violence to any white person, by striking, or the like, is appointed; *Provided always,* that such striking, conflict or maiming, be not by command of, or in the lawful defence of, their master, mistress, or owner of their families, or of their goods.

. . .

XIX. *And be it further enacted* by the authority aforesaid, That every slave of above sixteen years of age, that shall run away from his master, mistress or overseer, and shall so continue for the space of twenty days at one time, shall, by his master, mistress, overseer or head of the family's procurement, for the first offence, be publicly and severely whipped, not exceeding forty lashes; and in case the master, mistress, overseer, or head of the family, shall neglect to inflict such punishment of whipping, upon any negro or slave that shall so run away, for the space of ten days, upon complaint made thereof, within one month, by any person whatsoever, to any justice of the peace, the said justice of the peace shall, by his warrant directed to the constable, order the said negro or slave to be publicly and severely whipped, the charges of such whipping, not exceeding twenty shillings, to be borne by the person neglecting to have such runaway negro whipped, as before directed by this Act. And in case such negro or slave shall run away a second time, and shall so continue for the space of twenty days, he or she, so offending, shall be branded with the letter R, on the right cheek. And in case the master, mistress, overseer, or head of the family, shall neglect to inflict the punishment upon such slave running away the second time, the person so neglecting shall forfeit the sum of ten pounds, and upon any complaint made by any person, within one month, to any justice of the peace, of the neglect of so punishing any slave for running away the second time, such justice shall order the constable to inflict the same punishment upon such slave, or cause the same to be done, the charges thereof, not exceeding thirty shillings, to be borne by the person neglecting to have the punishment inflicted. And in case such negro or slave shall run away the third time, and shall so continue for the space of thirty days, he or she, so offending, for the third offence, shall be severely whipped, not exceeding forty lashes, and shall have one of his ears cut off; and in case the master, mistress, overseer or head of the family, shall neglect to inflict the punishment upon such slave running away the third time, the person so neglecting shall forfeit the sum of twenty pounds, and upon any complaint made by any person, within two months, to any justice of the peace, of the neglect of the so punishing any slave for running away the third time, the said justice shall order the constable to inflict the same punishment upon such slave, or cause the same to be done, the charges thereof, not exceeding forty shillings, to be borne by the person neglecting to have the punishment inflicted. And in case such male negro or slave shall run away the fourth time, and shall so continue for the space of thirty days, he, so offending, for the fourth offence, by order or procurement of the master, mistress, overseer or head of the family, shall be gelt;[11] and in case the negro or slave that shall be gelt, shall die, by reason of his gelding, and without any neglect of the person that shall order the same, the owner of the negro or slave so dying, shall be paid for him, out of the public treasury. And if a female slave shall run away the fourth time, then she shall, by order of her master, mistress or overseer, be severely whipped, and be branded on the left cheek with the letter R, and her left ear cut off. And if the owner, if in this Province, or in case of his absence, if his agent, factor or attorney, that hath the charge of the negro or slave, by this Act required to be gelt, whipped, branded and the ear cut off, for the fourth time of running away, shall neglect to have the same done and executed, accordingly as the same is ordered by this Act, for the space of twenty days after such slave is in his or their custody, that then such owner shall loose [sic] his property to the said slave, to him or them that will sue for the same, by information, at any time within six months, in the court of common pleas in this Province. And every person who shall so recover a slave by information, for the reasons aforesaid, shall, within twenty days after such recovery, inflict such punishment upon such slave as his former owner or head of a family ought to have done, and for neglect of which he lost his property to the said slave, or for neglect thereof shall forfeit fifty pounds; and in case any negro slave so recovered by information, and gelt, shall die, in such case, the slave so dying shall not be paid for out of the public treasury. And in case any negro or slave shall run away the fifth time, and shall so continue by the space of thirty days at one time, such slave shall be tried before two justices of the peace and three freeholders, as before directed by this Act in case of murder, and being by them declared guilty of the offence, it shall be lawful for them to order the cord of one of the slave's legs to be cut off above the heel, or else to pronounce sentence of death upon the slave, at the discretion of the said justices; and any judgment given after the first offence, shall be sufficient conviction to bring the offenders within the penalty for the second offence; and after the second, within the penalty of the third; and so for the inflicting the rest of the punishments.

. . .

XXIV. *And be it further enacted* by the authority aforesaid, That every captain or commander of a company within this Province, shall be, and is hereby, impowered, on notice to him given of the haunt, residence or hiding place of any runaway slaves, to raise a convenient party of men, not exceeding twenty, with special order from the general, or lieutenant general, and with them to pursue, apprehend and take the said runaway slaves, either alive or dead; any captain or commander who shall neglect his or their duty therein, shall forfeit the sum of thirty pounds; and for every negro or other slave that they shall take, having been run away above six months from his master, they shall receive forty shillings; and for every negro or other slave that they shall take alive, having been run away above twelve months, four pounds, from the masters or owners of the said negro or other slave; and if killed, they shall receive forty shillings from the public. . . .

XXVI. *And be it further enacted* by the authority aforesaid, That every Indian or slave which shall take up any runaway slave, as aforesaid, and the same shall deliver to the owner or master of the slave, if known, or if not known, then to the marshal, he shall have twenty shillings given him by the owner or master of the said slave, or by the marshal. That in case any negro or other slave shall harbour, conceal, entertain and give victuals to any runaway slave, knowing him or her to be such, that upon complaint made thereof to any justice of the peace, such negro or slave, by order of the justice, shall be severely whipped, not exceeding forty lashes.

XXVIII. And *whereas,* several owners of slaves used to suffer their said slaves to do what and go whither they will, and work where they please, upon condition that their said slaves do bring their aforesaid masters so much money as between the said master and slave is agreed upon, for every day the said slave shall be so permitted to imploy himself, which practice hath been observed to occasion such slaves to spend their time aforesaid, in looking for opportunities to steal, in order to raise money to pay their masters, as well as to maintain themselves, and other slaves, their companions, in drunkenness and other evil courses; for the prevention whereof, *Be it enacted* by the authority aforesaid, That no owner or master or mistress of any family, after the ratification of this Act, shall suffer or permit any slave to do what, go whither, or work where, they please, upon condition aforesaid, under the penalty of the forfeiture of five shillings for every day he, she or they shall suffer any slave to do as aforesaid; *Provided nevertheless,* that nothing in this Act shall be construed or intended to hinder any person from letting their negroes or slaves to hire, by the year, or for any lesser time, or by the day, so as such negro or slave is under the care and direction of his master, or some other person by his order intrusted with the slave, and that the master is to receive the whole of what the slave shall earn.

XXIX. *And be it further enacted* by the authority aforesaid, That no person whatsoever, after the ratification of this Act, shall settle or manage any plantation, cow-pen or stock, that shall he six miles distant from his usual place of abode, and wherein six negroes or slaves shall be imployed, without one or more white persons living and residing upon the same plantation, upon the penalty or forfeiture of forty shillings for each month so offending.

XXX. *And be it further enacted* by the authority aforesaid, That if any negro or other slave, under punishment by his master, or his order, for running away, or any other crimes or misdemeanors towards his said master, unfortunately shall suffer in life or member, which seldom happens, no person whatsoever shall be liable to any penalty therefor. But if any person shall, of wantonness, or only of bloody-mindedness, or cruel intention, violently kill a negro or other slave of his own, he shall pay into the public treasury fifty pounds, current money; but if he shall so kill the slave of another man, he shall pay to the owner of the negro or slave, the full value, and into the public treasury, twenty-five pounds, but not be liable to any other punishment or forfeiture for the same. But if the person so offending be a servant, he or she shall receive, on his or her bare back, nine and thirty lashes, by order of any two justices of the peace before whom the matter shall be proved, and shall also suffer three months imprisonment, without bail or mainprize;[12] which said time of three months that he is imprisoned, he shall serve with his master or mistress, after the expiration of his time, and shall be further liable to serve the owner or owners of such slave so killed, the full term of four years, by order of the said justices of the peace. But if any person shall kill any other person's negro or slave by accident, he shall not be liable to any other penalty but the owner's action at law; but if any person shall find any negro or other slave stealing, the said slave making resistance and refusing to submit himself, it shall and may be lawful for such person to kill the said negro or slave, and he shall not be liable to any damage or action for the same; any law, custom or usage to the contrary notwithstanding.

. . .

XXXIII. To the intent this Act and every clause and branch thereof, may receive full execution, and no person plead ignorance therein, Be if *enacted* by the authority aforesaid, That this Act be read and published by the clerk of the common pleas, at the next court of common pleas after the ratification of this Act, as also by the clerk of the crown, or clerk of assize, at the next general sessions, and also at the head of every company, by order of each respective captain or commander of his company, at his first muster after the ratification of this Act, on penalty of five pounds for each default, to be recovered and disposed of as aforesaid.

XXXIV. Since charity, and the christian religion, which we profess, obliges us to wish well to the souls of all men, and that religion may not be made a pretence to alter any man's property and right, and that no person may neglect to baptize their negroes or slaves, or suffer them to be baptized, for fear that thereby they should be manumitted and set free, *Be it therefore enacted by* the authority aforesaid, that it shall be, and is hereby declared, lawful for any negro or Indian slave, or any other slave or slaves whatsoever, to receive and profess the christian faith, and be thereinto baptized; but that notwithstanding such slave or slaves shall receive and profess the christian religion, and be baptized, he or they shall not thereby be manumitted or set free, or his or their owner, master or mistress lose his or their civil right, property and authority over such slave or slaves, but that the slave or slaves, with respect to his servitude, shall remain and continue in the same state and condition that he or they was in before the making of this Act.

■

1.7. The Stono Insurrection Described by a Descendant of the Leader (c. 1937)

George Cato's account of the Stono Rebellion was given to a Federal Writers Project interviewer in the 1930s, and it offers a rare nonwhite perspective on the event. Although WPA narratives and oral traditions passed down through several generations must be viewed with some degree of circumspection, much of Cato's account is corroborated by other sources. ::

George Cato, a Negro laborer, residing at the rear of 1010 Lady Street, Columbia, S.C., says he is a great-great-grandson of the late Cato slave who commanded the Stono Insurrection in 1739, in which 21 white people and 44 Negroes were slain. George, now 50 years old, states that this Negro uprising has been a tradition in his family for 198 years.

When asked for the particulars, he smiled, invited the caller to be seated, and related the following story:

George P. Rawick, ed., *The American Slave: A Composite Autobiography: Supplement*, series 1, vol. 11: *North Carolina and South Carolina Narratives* (Westport, Conn..: Greenwood, 1977), 98–100.

Yes sah! I sho' does come from dat old stock who had de misfortune to be slaves but who decide to be men, at one and de same time, and I's right proud of it. De first Cato slave we knows 'bout, was plum willin' to lay down his life for de right, as he see it. Dat is pow'ful fine for de Catoes who has come after him. My graddaddy and my daddy tell me plenty 'bout it, while we was livin' in Orangeburg County, not far from where de fightin' took place in de long ago.

My graddaddy was a son of de son of de Stono slave commander. He say his daddy often take him over de route of de rebel slave march, dat time when dere was sho' big trouble all 'bout dat neighborhood. As it come down to me, I thinks de first Cato take a darin' chance on losin' his life, not so much for his own benefit as it was to help others. He was not lak some slaves, much 'bused by deir masters. My kinfolks not 'bused. Dat why, I reckons, de captain of de slaves was picked by them. Cato was teached how to read and write by his rich master.

How it all start? Dat what I ask but nobody ever tell me how 100 slaves between de Combahee and Edisto rivers come to meet in de woods not far from de Stono River on September 9, 1739. And how they elect a leader, my kinsman, Cato, and late dat day march to Stono town, break in a warehouse, kill two white men in charge, and take all de guns and ammunition they wants. But they do it, wid dis start, they turn south and march on.

They work fast, coverin' 15 miles, passin' many fine plantations, and in every single case, stop, and break in de house and kill men, women, and children. Then they take what they want, 'cludin' arms, clothes, liquor and food. Near de Combahee swamp. Lieutenant Governor Bull, drivin' from Beaufort to Charleston, see them and he smell a rat. Befo' he was seen by de army he detour into de big woods and stay 'til de slave rebels pass.

Governor Bull and some planters, between de Combahee and Edisto, ride fast and spread de alarm and it wasn't long 'til de militiamen was on de trail in pursuit of de slave army. When found, many of de slaves was singin' and dancin' and Cap. Cato and some of de other leaders was cussin' at them sumpin awful. From dat day to dis, no Cato has tasted whiskey, 'less he go 'gainst his daddy's warnin'. Dis war last less than two days but it sho' was pow'ful hot while it last.

I reckons it was hot, 'cause in less than two days, 21 white men, women, and chillum, and 44 Negroes, was slain. My granddaddy say dat in de woods and at Stono, where de war start, dere was more than 100 Negroes in line. When de militia come in sight of them at Combahee swamp, de drinkin' dancin' Negroes scatter in de brush and only 44 stand deir ground.

Commander Cato speak for de crowd. He say: "We don't lak slavery. We start to jine de Spanish in Florida. We surrender but we not whipped yet and we is 'not converted.'" De other 43 say "Amen." They was taken, unarmed, and hanged by de militia. Long befo' dis uprisin', de Cato slave wrote passes for slaves and do all he can to send them to freedom. He die but he die for doin' de right, as he see it.

CHAPTER 2

"De bless fa true, dem wa da wok haad"

THE DEVELOPMENT OF
SOUTH CAROLINA'S SLAVE SOCIETY

■

2.1. An Act for the Better Ordering and Governing of Negroes
and Other Slaves in This Province (1740)

In 1740, following the Stono Rebellion and another two abortive slave uprisings, South Carolina lawmakers enacted one of the most stringent and comprehensive slave codes ever written in the colonies. For the first time, South Carolinians codified a precise definition of slavery, that of bondsmen as chattel. Unlike earlier slave codes, the Code written by the legislature abandoned any legal appeal to custom (as had been the case with earlier codes based upon the Barbadian example) and placed the institution upon the explicit legal foundations already developed in other British North American slave societies. However, the Code was not enacted simply to rein in recalcitrant slaves. Rather, significant and careful attention was also given to the actions and practices of masters and other whites in positions of authority over en-slaved men and women. Lawmakers sought to balance a continuing commitment of questionable sincerity to the kind treatment of slaves with the disciplined required necessary to keep bondsmen in good order. There would be no more slave rebellions in the colonial period. ::

WHEREAS, in his Majesty's plantations in America, slavery has been introduced and allowed, and the people commonly called Negroes, Indians, mulattoes and mustizoes, have been deemed absolute slaves, and the subjects of property in the hands of the particular persons, the extent of whose power over such slaves ought to be settled and limited by positive laws, so that the slave may

The Statutes at Large of South Carolina, vol. 7, ed. David McCord (Columbia, S.C.: A. S. Johnson, 1840).

be kept in due subjection and obedience, and the owners and other persons having the care and government of slaves may be restrained from exercising too great rigour and cruelty over them, and that the public peace and order of this Province may be preserved: We pray your most sacred Majesty that it may be enacted,

I ... That all Negroes and Indians, (free Indians in amity with this government,[1] and degrees, mulattoes, and mustizoes, who are now free, excepted,) mulattoes or mustizoes who now are, or shall hereafter be, in this Province, and all their issue and offspring, born or to be born, shall be, and they are hereby declared to be, and remain forever hereafter, absolute slaves, and shall follow the condition of the mother, and shall be deemed, held, taken, reputed and adjudged in law, to be chattels personal, in the hands of their owners and possessors. ...

III ... And for the better keeping slaves in due order and subjection, *Be it further enacted* ... That no person whatsoever shall permit or suffer any slave under his or their care or management, and who lives or is employed in Charlestown,[2] or any other town in this Province, to go out of the limits of the said town, or any such slave who lives in the country, to go out of the plantation to which such slave belongs, or in which plantation such slave is usually employed, without a letter superscribed and directed, or a ticket ... and every slave who shall be found [without a pass] shall be punished with whipping on the bare back, not exceeding twenty lashes. ...

V. *And it shall be further enacted* ... That if any slave who shall be out of the house or plantation where such slave shall live, or shall be usually employed, or without some whiter person in company with such slave, shall refuse to submit or undergo the examination of any white person, it shall be lawful for any such white person to pursue, apprehend, and moderately correct such slave; and if any such slave shall assault and strike such white person, such slave may be lawfully killed. ...

VII. *And be it further enacted* ... That it shall and may be lawful for every justice assigned to keep the peace in this Province ... to disperse any assembly or meeting of slaves which may disturb the peace or endanger the safety of his Majesty's subjects, and to search all suspected places for arms, ammunition or stolen goods, and to apprehend and secure all such slaves as they shall suspect to be guilty of any crimes or offences whatsoever. ...

XVI. And *whereas,* some crimes and offences of an enormous nature and of the most pernicious consequence, may be committed by slaves, as well as other persons, which being peculiar to the condition and situation of this Province, could not fall within the provision of the laws of England; *Be it therefore enacted* . . . [That] if any slave, free Negro, mulattoe, Indian or mustizoe, shall willfully and maliciously set fire to, burn or destroy any sack of rice, corn or other grain, of the product, growth or manufacture of this Province, or shall willfully and maliciously set fire to, burn or destroy any tar kiln, barrels of pitch, tar turpentine or rosin, or any other the goods or commodities of the growth, produce or manufacture of this Province, or shall feloniously steal, take or carry away any slave, being the property of another, with intent to carry such slave out of this Province, or shall willfully or maliciously poison or administer any poison to any person, free man, woman, servant or slave, every such slave, free Negro, mulattoe, Indian, (except as before excepted,) and mustizoe, shall suffer death as a felon.

XVII. *And be it further enacted* . . . That any slave who shall be guilty of homicide of any sort, upon any white person, except by misadventure, or in defense of his master or other person under whose care and government such slave shall be, shall, upon conviction thereof as aforesaid, suffer death; and every slave who shall raise or attempt to raise an insurrection in this Province, shall endeavor to delude or entice any slave to run away and leave this Province, every such slave and slaves, and his and their accomplices, aiders and abettors, shall, upon conviction . . . be executed for example, to deter others from offending in the like kind.

XXII. *And be it further enacted* . . . That if any person in this Province shall, on the Lord's day, commonly called Sunday, employ any slave in any work or labour, (works of absolute necessity and the necessary occasions of the family one excepted,) every person in such case offending, shall forfeit the sum of five pounds, current money, for every slave they shall so work or labour.

XXIII. *And be it further enacted* . . . That it shall not be lawful for any slave, unless in the presence of some white person, to carry or make use of fire arms, or any offensive weapons whatsoever, unless such Negro or slave shall have a ticket or license, in writing, from his master, mistress or overseer, to hunt and kill game, cattle, or mischievous birds, or beasts of prey . . . *provided also,* that no Negro or other slave shall have liberty to carry any gun, cutlass, pistol or other weapon, abroad from home, at any time between Saturday evening after sunset, and Monday morning before sun-rise, notwithstanding a license or ticket for so doing. . . .[3]

XXIV. *And be it further enacted* . . . That if any slave shall presume to strike any white person, such slave, upon trial and conviction before the justice or justices and freeholders . . . shall, for the first and second offence, suffer such punishment as the said justice and freeholders . . . shall in their discretion, think fit, not extending to life or limb; and for the third offence, shall suffer death. But in case any such slave shall grievously wound, maim or bruise any white person, though it by only the first offence, such slave shall suffer death. *Provided always,* that such striking, wounding, maiming or bruising, not be done by the command, and in the defense of, the person or property of the owner or other person having the care and government of such slave, in which case the slave shall be wholly excused, and the owner or other person having the care and government of such slave shall be answerable, as far as by law he ought.

XXII. *And be it further enacted* . . . That if any keeper of a tavern or punch house, or retailer of strong liquors, shall give, sell utter or deliver to any slave, any beer, ale, cider, wine, rum, brandy, or other spirituous liquors, or strong liquor whatsoever, without the license or consent of the owner . . . shall forfeit the sum of five pounds, current money, for the first offence, and for the second offence, ten pounds; and shall be bound in recognizance in the sum of one hundred pounds, current money . . . not to offend in the like kind, and to be of good behaviour, for one year; and for want of such sufficient sureties, to be committed to prison without bail. . . .

XXXIII. And *whereas,* several owners of slaves do suffer their slaves to go and work where they please, upon conditions of paying to their owners certain sums of money agreed upon between the owner and the slave; which practice has occasioned such slaves to pilfer and steal, to raise money for their owners, as well as to maintain themselves in drunkenness and evil courses . . . *Be it enacted* . . . That no owner, master or mistress of any slave, after the passing of this Act, shall permit or suffer any of his, her or their slaves to go and work out of their respective houses of families, without a ticket in writing. . . .

XXXVI. And for that as it is absolutely necessary to the safety of this Province, that all due care be taken to restrain the wanderings and meetings of Negroes and other slaves, at all times, and more especially on Saturday nights, Sundays, and other holidays, and their using and carrying wooden swords, and other mischievous and dangerous weapons, or using or keeping of drums, horns, or other loud instruments,[4] which may call together or give sign or notice to one another of their wicked designs and purposes; and that all masters, overseers and others may be enjoined, diligently and carefully to prevent the same, *Be it enacted* . . . That it shall be lawful for all masters, overseers and other persons whosoever, to apprehend and take up any Negro or other slave that shall be found ... to disarm, take up and whip: And whatsoever master, owner or overseer shall permit or suffer his or their Negro or other slave or slaves, at any time hereafter, to beat drums, blow horns, or use any other loud instruments or whosoever shall suffer and countenance any public meeting or feastings of strange Negroes or slaves in their plantations, shall forfeit ten pounds, current money, for every such offence, upon conviction or proof. . . .

XXXVII. And *whereas,* cruelty is not only highly unbecoming those who profess themselves Christians, but is odious in the eyes of all men who have any sense of virtue of humanity; therefore, to restrain and prevent barbarity being exercised towards slaves, *Be it enacted* . . . That if any person of persons whosoever, shall willfully murder his own slave, or the slave of any other person, every such person, shall, upon conviction thereof, forfeit and pay the sum of seven hundred pounds, current money, and shall be rendered, and is hereby declared altogether and forever incapable of holding, exercising, enjoying or receiving the profits of any office, place or employment, civil or military, within this Province. . . . And if any person shall, on sudden heat or passion, or by undue correction, kill his own slave, or the slave of any other person, he shall forfeit the sum of three hundred and fifty pounds, current money. And in case any person or persons shall willfully cut out the tongue, put out the eye, castrate, or cruelly scald, burn, or deprive any slave of any limb or member, or shall inflict any other cruel punishment, other than by whipping or beating with a horsewhip, cow-skin, switch or small stick, or by putting irons on, or confining or imprisoning such slave, every such person shall, for every such offence, forfeit the sum of one hundred pounds. . . .

XXXVIII. *And be it further enacted* . . . That in case any person in this Province, who shall be owner, or shall have the care, government or charge of any slave or slaves, shall deny, neglect or refuse to allow such slave or slaves, under his or her charge, sufficient cloathing, covering or food, it shall and may be lawful for any person or persons, on behalf of such slave or slaves, to make complaint to the next neighboring justice, in the parish where such slave or slaves live or are usually employed. . . .

XLIV. And *whereas,* many owners of slaves, and others who have the care, management and overseeing of slaves, so confine them so closely to hard labor, that they have not sufficient time for natural rest; *Be it therefore enacted* . . . That if any owner of slaves ... shall work or put to labor any such slave or slaves, more than fifteen hours in for [*sic*] and twenty hours, from the twenty-fifth day of March to the twenty-fifth day of September, or more than fourteen hours in for and twenty hours, from the twenty-fifth day of September to the twenty-fifth day of March, every such person shall forfeit any sum not exceeding twenty pounds, nor under five pounds, current money, for every time he, she or they shall offend herein. . . .

XLV. And *whereas,* the having of slaves taught to write, or suffering them to be employed in writing, may be attended with great inconveniences; *Be it therefore enacted* . . . That all and every person and persons whatsoever, who shall hereinafter teach or cause any slave or slaves to be taught, to write, or shall use or employ any slave as a scribe in any manner of writing whatsoever, hereafter taught to write, every such person and persons, shall, for every such offense, forfeit the sum of one hundred pounds. . . .

XLVII. And *whereas,* many disobedient and evil minded Negroes and other slaves, being the property of his Majesty's subjects of this Province, have lately deserted the service of their owners, and have fled to St. Augustine and other places in Florida, in hopes of being there received and protected; and *whereas,* many other slaves have attempted to follow the same evil and pernicious example, which, (unless timely prevented,) may tend to the very great loss and prejudice of the inhabitants of this Province; *Be it therefore enacted* . . . That from and after the passing of this act, any white person or persons, free Indian or Indians, who shall, on the south side of Savannah river, take and secure, and shall from thence bring to the work house in Charlestown, any Negroes or other slaves, which within the space of six months have deserted, or who shall hereafter desert, from the services of their owners or employers, every such white person or persons, free Indian or Indians, on evidence of the said slaves being taken as aforesaid . . . shall be paid . . . for each grown man slave brought alive, the sum of fifty pounds; for every grown woman or boy slave above the age of twelve years brought alive, the sum of twenty five pounds; for every Negro child under the age of twelve years, brought alive, the sum of five pounds; for every scalp of a grown Negro slave with the two ears, twenty pounds; and for every Negro grown slave, found on the south side of St. John's river, and brought alive as aforesaid, the sum of one hundred pounds; and for every scalp of a grown Negro slave with the two ears, taken on the south side of St. John's river, the sum of fifty pounds.

LVI. And *whereas,* several Negroes did lately rise in rebellion, and did commit many barbarous murders at Stono and other parts adjacent thereto; and *whereas,* in suppressing the said rebels, several of them were killed and others taken alive and executed; and as the exigence and danger the inhabitants at that time were in and exposed to, would not admit of the formality of a legal trial of such rebellious Negroes, but for their own security the said inhabitants were obliged to put such Negroes to immediate death; to prevent, therefore, any person or persons being questioned for any matter or thing done in the suppression or execution of the said rebellious Negroes, as also any litigious suit, action or prosecution that may be brought, sued or prosecuted or commenced against such person or persons for or concerning the same; *Be it enacted ... That all and every act ... committed and executed, in and about the suppressing and putting all and every the said Negro and Negroes to death, is and are hereby declared lawful, to all intents and purposes whatsoever, as fully and amply as if such rebellious Negroes had undergone a formal trial and condemnation, notwithstanding any want of form or omission what-ever in the trial of such Negroes; and any law, usage or custom to the contrary thereof in any wise notwithstanding ...*

■

2.2, 2.3. Two Poetic Views of Miscegenation (1732)

These poems on miscegenation appeared in the South Carolina Gazette *in March 1732 and speak to the intense societal anxieties provoked by interracial sex (both consensual and forced).* ::

Anonymous, "The Cameleon Lover"

If what the Curious have observ'd be true,
That the Cameleon will assume the Hue
Of all the Objects that approach its Touch;
No Wonder then, that the Amours of such
Whose Taste betrays them to a close Embrace
With the dark Beauties of the Sable Race,
(Stain'd with the Tincture of the Sooty Sin,)
Imbibe the Blackness of their Charmer's Skin.

***

Sable, "The Cameleon's Defence"

All Men have Follies, which they blindly trace
Thro' the dark Turnings of a dubious Maze:
But happy those, who, by a prudent Care,
Retreat betimes, from the fallacious Snare.
The eldest Sons of Wisdom were not free,

From the same Failure you condemn in Me.
If as the Wisest of the Wise have err'd,
I go astray and am condemn'd unheard,
My Faults you too severely reprehend,
More like a rigid Censor than a Friend.
Love is the Monarch Passion of the Mind,
Knows no Superior, but no Laws confin'd;
But triumphs still, impatient of Controul,
O'er all the proud Endowments of the Soul.

■

2.4, 2.5. Henry Laurens Discusses Ethnic Preference of Slave Purchases (1755, 1756)

Merchant and rice planter Henry Laurens was a partner in Austin and Laurens, the largest slave-trading house in North America. From 1748 to 1762 Laurens's firm brokered the sale of more than ten thousand slaves. It was Laurens's business to know what types of slaves his purchasers most desired. In the following letters, he describes the preferences of South Carolina planters and his ideal slave cargo. ::

To Smith & Cliffton

17th July 1755
Gentlemen,
. . . We now have before us your kind favour of the 23d May handed by Capt. Jeffries of the *Pearl* . . . he deliver'd us a pretty Cargo of Slaves for the numbers of them 243 . . . which we ran off upon an average at £33.17 / Sterling some of the Men so high as £290, many at £280, and but few under £270, none for a longer credit than for the month of January.

. . . If you will be half concern'd with us in a hundred Slaves proviso you can purchase that number of very healthy People, Two thirds at least Men from 18 to 25 Years old, the other young Women from 14 to 18 the cost not to exceed Twenty five Pounds Sterling per head. . . . There must not be a Callabar amongst them. Gold Coast or Gambia's are the best, next to them the Windward Coast are prefer'd to Angola's. . . . Pray observe that our People like tall Slaves best for our business & strong withal. Such as are small, meagre, or otherwise ordinary wont sell better here than with you. . . .

Henry Laurens papers, South Carolina Historical Society, Letter book, 1755–57, 37/2, Microfilm Roll 45/131.

To Richard Oswald & Co.

17th May 1756

Gentlemen,

The foregoing is a third recital of our last to your good selves. We have now before us your esteem'd favour of the 5th of March advising of your intentions that your Ship the *St. Andrew*, Capt Hood, should proceed from Gambia to this place & that we may expect her the latter end of June. Should she reach us the next Ship & with such a Cargo as were ship'd by your Friends in the *St. Paul* two Years ago we might hope that as things now appear to render you pretty good Sale. . . . The Slaves from the River Gambia are preferr'd to all others with us save from the Gold Coast & as we trust your Ships will leave the Coast much before the Traders which are obliged to go up the River 'tis highly probable she will be ahead of all from that Quarter. Indeed we do not imagine there will be many come from that River to this place the present Summer as we wrote early to our Friends at Bristol, Liverpoole, & Lancaster not to have a thought of sending Slaves to our Market until the differences should be adjusted between Great Brittain & France. This we have reason to believe will divert the Voyage of half a dozen Vessells that were intended this way. . . .

We must acknowledge the great obligation you have laid us under in ordering your Ship to us without Security & shall make it our Endeavour to return the

Ran away from the subscriber, On Sunday, the 27th of July last, a NEW NEGRO, about 19 years of age, about five feet five or six inches high, with his country marks on his face and body. He can speak little or no English, has been in the country about ten months, and is named JIM. Had on when he went away, a blue jacket, with small yellow buttons, with a kind of brown cloth for a cuff on one sleeve; a pair of home-made cotton trowsers, with three large yellow buttons on the waistband, and a hat pretty much worn. A reward of Five Dollars will be paid to any person that will bring him home. The law will be strictly enforced against any person found harboring or clandestinely working him.

Thomas Doyle,
Lenud's ferry, St. James', Santee.

August 16.   eod 9

Slave runaway advertisement. *Charleston City Gazette and Daily Advertiser,* September 4, 1806.

Slave sale advertisement.
South Carolina Gazette, April 26, 1760.

favour by an exertion of the utmost ability we are Masters of to give you all possible content, being very truly—

■

2.6. The Dangers of Slavery (1763)

Many South Carolinians benefited tremendously from the products of slave labor, not to mention the rising value of the colony's slaves themselves. However, as this observer noted, the growing black majority, while admitted to be necessary for the continued vigorous growth of the colony, represented a potential danger to white colonists that could not be ignored. ::

The inhabitants are either white or black; the white are between thirty and forty thousand; all the males, from sixteen years of age to sixty, are mustered, and carry arms in the militia regiments, and form together a body of about seven thousand: Their complexion is little different from the inhabitants of Britain, and they are generally of a good stature and well-made, with lively and

George Milligan Johnston, *Short Description of the Province of South Carolina: With an Account of the Air, Weather, and Diseases at Charlestowne, Written in the Year 1763* (London: King's Arms, 1770), 65–67.

agreeable countenances; sensible, spirited, and open-hearted, and exceed most people in acts of benevolence, hospitality, and charity. The men and women who have a right to the class of gentry (who are more numerous here than in any other colony in North America) dress with elegance and neatness....

The Negro slaves are about seventy thousand; they, with a few exceptions, do all the labour or hard work in the country, and are a considerable part of the riches of the province; they are supposed worth, upon an average, about forty pounds sterling each; And the annual labour of the working slaves, who may be about forty thousand, is valued at ten pounds sterling each. They are in this climate necessary, but very dangerous domestics, their number so much exceeding the whites; a natural dislike and antipathy, that subsists between them and our Indian neighbours, is a very lucky circumstance, and for this reason: In our quarrels with the Indians however proper and necessary it may be to give them correction, it can never be our interest to extirpate them, or to force them from their lands; their ground would be soon taken up by runaway Negroes from our settlements, whose numbers would daily increase, and quickly become more formidable enemies than Indians can ever be, as they speak our language, and would never be at a loss for intelligence.

■

2.7. Henry Laurens Urges Emancipation (1776)

Henry Laurens was a slave trader and owner of more than two hundred slaves. However, he grew to question the moral legitimacy of human bondage. In this letter to his son, Laurens contemplates the ramifications of freeing his bondsmen. However, the elder Laurens's radical notions faded before the end of the war. He did not free his slaves and, as an American diplomat in 1783, insisted that slaves who had escaped from patriot masters during the war be returned by the British. ::

. . . My negroes there all to a Man are strongly attached to me, so are all of mine in this Country; hitherto not one of them has attempted to desert, on the contrary those who are most exposed hold themselves always ready to fly from the Enemy in case of a sudden descent—many hundreds of that Colour have been stolen and decoyed by the Servants of King George the Third—Captains of British Ships of War and Noble Lords have busied themselves in such inglorious pilferage to the disgrace of their Master and disgrace of their Cause.— These Negroes were first enslaved by the English—Acts of Parliament have

A South Carolina Protest against Slavery: Being a Letter from Henry Laurens, Second President of the Continental Congress, to His Son, Col. John Laurens; Dated Charleston, S.C., August 14, 1776 (New York: G. P. Putnam, 1861), 3–21.

established the Slave Trade in favour of the home residing English and almost totally prohibited the Americans from reaping any share of it—Men of War, forts, Castles, Governors, Companies and Committees are employed and authorized by the English Parliament to protect regulate and extend the Slave Trade. Negroes are brought by Englishmen and sold as slaves to Americans— Bristol, Liverpool, Manchester, Birmingham, &ca. &ca. live upon the Slave Trade. The British Parliament now employ their Men of War to steal those Negroes from the Americans to whom they sold them, pretending to set the poor wretches free, but basely trepan and sell them into tenfold worse Slavery in the West Indies, where probably they will become the property of Englishmen again and of those who sit in Parliament; what meanness! what complicated wickedness appears in this scene! O England, how changed! how fallen!

You know, my dear Son,[5] I abhor Slavery. I was born in a Country where Slavery had been established by British Kings and Parliaments as well as by the laws of that Country Ages before my existence, I found the Christian Religion and Slavery growing under the same authority and cultivation.—I nevertheless disliked it—in former days there was no combatting the prejudices of Men supported by Interest, the day I hope is approaching when from principles of gratitude as well as justice every Man will strive to be foremost in shewing his readiness to comply with the Golden Rule; not less than £20000 stg. would all my Negroes produce if sold at public Auction tomorrow. I am not the man who enslaved them, they are indebted to English Men for that favour, nevertheless I am devising means for manumitting many of them and for cutting off the entail of Slavery—great powers oppose me; the Laws and Customs of my Country, my own and the avarice of my countrymen—What will my Children say if I deprive them of so much Estate? These are difficulties but not insuperable. I will do as much as I can in my time and leave the rest to a better hand. I am not one of those who arrogate the peculiar care of Providence in each fortunate event, nor one of those who dare trust in Providence for defence and security of their own Liberty while they enslave and wish to continue in Slavery, thousands who are as well intitled to freedom as themselves. I perceive the work before me is great. I shall appear to many as a promoter, not only of strange but of dangerous doctrines, it will therefore be necessary to proceed with caution, you are apparently deeply interested in this affair, but as I have no doubt of your concurrence and approbation I most sincerely wish for your advice and assistance and hope to receive both in good time.

■

2.8. An Act for the Regulation of the Militia of This State (1778)

Although South Carolina lawmakers refused to allow their slaves to serve in the Continental Army in exchange for their freedom, they did provide for their service in the state militia. Slaves would not be armed and were to perform only manual labor; notably, all compensation for their services would accrue to their owners. Service would not earn freedom for the slaves. ::

WHEREAS, the establishment of a well regulated militia in a free State, will greatly conduce to its happiness and prosperity, and is absolutely essential to the preservation of its freedom; and *whereas,* it is necessary that the laws hitherto enacted for the regulation of the militia of this State, be amended and reduced into one body, for the satisfaction and better information of individuals, and for the interest of the community. . . .

XXX. *And be it . . . enacted* by the authority aforesaid, That every person in this State who hath any property, power or command over any male slave or slaves in this State . . . shall, on the first day of January in every year, return to the captain or commanding officer of the company of the district wherein such person . . . shall reside, a faithful and true list of all male slaves, from the age of sixteen to sixty years, residing in such district, and whereof such person is owner, or hath command and controul as aforesaid; in which list, the names of such slaves shall be specified, on oath, by the person returning the same, to the captain of the district wherein he or she resides, who shall return the same to the commanding officer of the regiment to which such captain belongs; which commanding officer of such regiment shall cause the same, within two months thereafter, to be laid before the President or Governor and Commander-in-chief, as the case may be, and privy council for the time being.

XXXI. *And be it . . . enacted* by the authority aforesaid, That the President or Governor and Commander-in-chief, as the case may be, and to be privy council of the State aforesaid for the time being, are hereby authorized and required, when they shall think it necessary, to order the captains of the militia of this State to enlist in their respective companies a number of such slaves so returned to them as aforesaid, not exceeding one third of such companies, and such as the said captains shall approve of as faithful and fit for service, to be employed as hatchet men or pioneers in such companies, and doing the fatigue

The Statutes at Large of South Carolina, ed. David J. McCord (Columbia, S.C.: A. S. Johnson, 1841), 666–80.

duties thereof; the owners of every such slave so enlisted shall be allowed, out of the treasury of this State, the sum of ten shillings for every day such slave shall be employed or retained in such service. And in case any such slave shall be killed, maimed or wounded in such service, the owner or owners thereof shall be allowed and paid out of the public treasury of this State such a sum of money as shall, by two indifferent freeholders, on oath . . . be deemed equivalent to the loss sustained by such owner of the said slave so killed, maimed or wounded as aforesaid; which valuation shall be made under the hand and seal of the person or persons making the same, and shall be lodged in the public treasury on payment thereof.

XXXII. *And be it . . . enacted* by the authority aforesaid, That every person having any property, command or power over any male slave . . . who shall refuse or neglect to make out and give in such list, in manner as and at the times directed by this Act, shall, for every such offence, forfeit and pay the sum of twenty pounds, current money; and every such person who shall neglect or refuse to send and order any such slave, in time of alarm, to join the company in which such slave shall be enlisted as pioneer or hatchet man as aforesaid, after notice of such enlistment, shall, for every such offence, forfeit and pay the sum of fifty pounds current money; which fines shall be recovered by the majority of the officers of such company in which such slave is enlisted, from the owner or person having command of such slave, in manner as other fines are recoverable by this Act, and shall be paid into the public treasury for the use of this State.

■

2.9. Continental Congress Proposes Arming Slaves (1779)

African Americans had fought in many of the previous colonial wars, and some black soldiers had fought in the early battles of Lexington, Concord, and Bunker Hill. Nonetheless, fearing insurrection, General George Washington and many southerners in the Continental Congress opposed the enlistment of blacks into the ranks of the Continental Army. However, by 1778 manpower shortages and a British offensive into Georgia and South Carolina led to proposals to free and arm three thousand slaves from those states. Despite Congress's unanimous approval, the South Carolina legislature rejected the scheme. ::

Congress resumed the consideration of the report of the committee on the circumstances of the southern states, and the ways and means for their safety and defence: wherein the committee report:

Journals of the Continental Congress, vol. 13 (Washington, D.C.: U.S. Government Printing Office, 1909), 385–88.

"The Old Plantation," by John Rose of Beaufort (c. 1785–95). Courtesy of the
Abby Aldrich Rockefeller Folk Art Museum, Williamsburg, Virginia.

That the circumstances of the army will not admit of the detaching of any
force for the defence of South Carolina and Georgia.

That the continental battalions of those two States are not adequate to their
defence.

That the three battalions of North Carolina continental troops now on the
southern service are composed of draughts from the militia for nine months
only, which term with respect to a great part of them will expire before the end
of the campaign.

That all the other force now employed for the defence of the said States
consists of militia, who from the remoteness of their habitations and the difficulties attending their service ought not to be relied on for continued exertions
and a protracted war.

That the State of South Carolina as represented by the delegates of the said
State and by Mr. Huger,[6] who has come hither at the request of the governor
of the said State, on purpose to explain the particular circumstances thereof, is
unable to make any effectual efforts with militia, by reason of the great proportion of citizens necessary to remain at home to prevent insurrections among
the negroes, and to prevent the desertion of them to the enemy.

That the state of the country and the great numbers of those people among
them expose the inhabitants to great danger from the endeavours of the enemy
to excite them, either to revolt or to desert. That it is suggested by the delegates
of the said State, and by Mr. Huger, that a force might be raised in the said State

from among the negroes which would not only be formidable to the enemy from their numbers and the discipline of which they would very readily admit, but would also lessen the danger from revolts and desertions by detaching the most vigorous and enterprizing from among the negroes. That as this measure may involve inconveniences peculiarly affecting the states of South Carolina and Georgia, the committee are of opinion that the same should be submitted to the governing powers of the said states, and if the said powers shall judge it expedient to raise such a force, that the United States ought to defray the expence thereof; Whereupon, . . .

Resolved, That it be recommended to the states of South Carolina and Georgia, if they shall think the same expedient, to take measures immediately for raising three thousand able bodied negroes.

That the said negroes be formed into separate corps as battalions, according to the arrangements adopted for the main army, to be commanded by white commissioned and non commissioned officers. . . .

Resolved, That congress will make provision for paying the proprietors of such negroes as shall be inlisted for the service of the United States during the war, a full compensation for the property at a rate not exceeding one thousand dollars for each active able bodied negro man of standard size, not exceeding thirty five years of age, who shall be so inlisted and pass muster.

That no pay or bounty be allowed to the said negroes, but that they be cloathed and subsisted at the expence of the United States.

That every negro who shall well and faithfully serve as a soldier to the end of the present war, and shall then return his arms, be emancipated and receive the sum of fifty dollars.

■

2.10. Years of the Haitian Revolution in Charleston (1797)

During the Haitian Revolution (1791–1804), South Carolina slaveholders feared that news of the war might encourage their bondsmen to also rise up in rebellion. The arrival of Haitian refugees in Charleston increased this anxiety that the black revolution might spread to the most Caribbean of the United States. ::

Extract from a letter from Charleston, dated November 21th:

On Saturday last a plot was discovered, which may have saved some lives and some property. Seventeen French negroes intended to set fire to the town in different places, kill the whites, and probably take possession of the pow[d]er magazine and the arms; but luckily one of them turned states evidence. Five have been apprehended, two hung, and the others have escaped into the country.

Pennsylvania Gazette, December 13, 1797.

From the *Charleston State Gazette* of the 22d ultimo:

On Tuesday, the 14th inst. the Intendant received certain information of a *Conspiracy of several French negroes to fire the city,* and to act here as they had formerly done at S. Domingo—as the discovery did not implicate more than ten or fifteen persons, and as the information first given was not so complete as to charge all the ringleaders, the Intendant delayed taking any measures for their apprehension until the plan should be more matured, and their guilt more closely ascertained; but the plot having been communicated to persons, on whose secrecy the city magistrates could not depend, they found themselves obliged on Saturday last to apprehend a number of negroes, and among others the following, charged (together with another not yet taken) as the ringleaders, viz.—Figaro, the property of Mr. Robinett; Jean Louis, the property of Mr. Langstaff; Figaro the younger, the property of Mr. Delaire; and Capelle....

On examination they all at first positively denied their knowledge or concern in the plot; but the younger Figaro, after some time, made a partial confession, and was admitted as evidence on the part of the state. The others were on Monday brought to trial, in the City Hall, before as respectable a court and jury as we ever remember to have been convened. A number of witnesses were examined, and fully proved the guilt of the prisoners; and the court, on mature consideration, unanimously condemned Figaro, Sen. and Jean Louis, to be hung, and Capelle and Figaro the younger to be transported. The rest who were apprehended are under confinement, for further examination.

After the condemnation of Jean Louis, he turned to the two Figaros and said, "I do not blame the whites, though I suffer, they have done right, but it is you who have brought me to this trouble."

Figaro and Jean Louis were yesterday executed in pursuance of their sentence.

■

2.11. The Gullah Beatitudes (2005)

Because of the high concentration of Africans in the Lowcountry in the early eighteenth century and their relative isolation from whites, the enslaved population there was able to retain a great deal of its rich West and Central African heritage. This Gullah culture included parts of several different African languages, which, when combined with English, developed into a distinct creole dialect still spoken by many Sea Islanders. Though much of Gullah culture has been transmitted orally, not

De Nyew Testament: The New Testament in Gullah Sea Island Creole with Marginal Text of the King James Version, © 2005 American Bible Society (New York: American Bible Society, 2005), 12–13. Used by permission.

written, in 2005 the American Bible Society published De Nyew Testament, *a phonetic translation of the New Testament into Gullah. The passage reprinted here presents the Beatitudes from the book of Matthew alongside the King James version.* ::

Matthew 5:1–12

Jedus Teach Bout Dem wa Bless fa True	King James Version
¹ Wen Jedus see all de crowd dem, e gone pontop one high hill. E sed-down dey, an e ciple dem come geda roun um.	¹ And seeing the multitudes, he went up into a mountain: and when he was set, his disciples came unto him:
² Den Jedus staat fa laan um. E say,	² And he opened his mouth, and taught them, saying,
³ "Dey bless fa true, dem people wa ain hab no hope een deysef, cause God da rule oba um.	³ Blessed are the poor in spirit: for theirs is the kingdom of heaven.
⁴ Dey bless fa true, dem wa saaful now, cause God gwine courage um.	⁴ Blessed are they that mourn: for they shall be comforted.
⁵ Dey bless fa true, dem wa ain tink dey mo den wa dey da, cause all de whole wol gwine blongst ta um.	⁵ Blessed are the meek: for they shall inherit the earth.
⁶ Dey bless fa true, dem wa hongry an tosty fa wa right, cause dey gwine git sattify.	⁶ Blessed are they which do hunger and thirst after righteousness: for they shall be filled.
⁷ Dey bless fa true, dem wa hab mussy pon oda people, cause God gwine hab mussy pon dem.	⁷ Blessed are the merciful: for they shall obtain mercy.
⁸ Dey bless fa true, dem dat only wahn fa jes saab de Lawd, cause dey gwine see God.	⁸ Blessed are the pure in heart: for they shall see God.
⁹ Dey bless fa true, dem wa da wok haad fa hep people lib peaceable wid one noda, cause God gwine call um e chullun.	⁹ Blessed are the peacemakers: for they shall be called the children of God.
¹⁰ Dey bless fa true, dem wa oda people mek suffa cause dey da waak scraight wid God, cause God da rule oba um.	¹⁰ Blessed are they which are persecuted for righteousness' sake: for theirs is the kingdom of heaven.
¹¹ "Ya bless fa true wen people hole ya cheap an mek ya suffa an wen dey say all kind ob bad ting bout ya wa ain true, cause ya da folla me.	¹¹ Blessed are ye, when men shall revile you, and persecute you, and shall say all manner of evil against you falsely, for my sake.
¹² Mus be glad fa true, cause ya gwine git a whole heapa good ting dat God	¹² Rejoice, and be exceeding glad: for great is your reward in heaven: for so

da keep fa ya een heaben. Ya mus
memba dat de people wa mek ya suffa
dem ting yah, dey ole people done de
same ting ta de prophet dem wa lib
way back dey.

persecuted they the prophets which
were before you.

■

2.12. Slave Literacy Law (1834)

South Carolina was the first colony to pass legislation limiting slave literacy, which it did in 1740. Despite some objections on religious grounds and a failed attempt by radicals to pass similar legislation in 1833, the state legislature passed the nation's most comprehensive antiliteracy law in 1834. ::

Be it enacted by the honorable, the Senate and House of Representatives, now met and sitting in General Assembly, and by the authority of the same, If any person shall hereafter teach any slave to read or write, or cause, or procure any slave to read or write; such person, if a free white person, upon conviction thereof, shall, for each and every offense against this act, be fined not exceeding one hundred dollars, and imprisoned not more than six months; or if a free person of color, shall be whipped not exceeding fifty lashes, and fined not exceeding fifty dollars, at the discretion of the court of magistrates, and freeholders before which such person of color is tried; and if a slave, to be whipped at the discretion of the court, not exceeding fifty lashes: the informer to be entitled to one-half of the fine, and to be a competent witness; and if any free person of color or slave, shall keep any school or other place of instruction, for teaching any slave or free person of color to read or write, such free person of color or slave, shall be liable to the same fine, imprisonment and corporal punishment as are by this section, imposed and inflicted upon free persons of color and slaves, for teaching slaves to read or write.

■

2.13. Old Man Hildebrand (1928)

Among the people most hated by the enslaved were overseers who abused their power and mistreated slaves. In this early-twentieth- century folk song, black South Carolinians remembered one such man who relished inflicting pain upon slaves. ::

Acts and Joint Resolutions of the General Assembly of the State of South Carolina, Passed in December, 1834 (Columbia, S.C.: E. F. Branthwaite, 1834), 13.

E.C.L. Adams papers, MSS of "Nigger to Nigger," 9887, pp. D76–D77. Courtesy of the South Caroliniana Library, University of South Carolina, Columbia.

Ole man Hildebran' was a bad ole man,
He live in slavery time.
He heart been iron an' he head been stone,
An' he pleasure been a Nigger's groan.
He eye been yallow, an' he soul been dead,
An' he live in slavery time.
Ole man Hildebran'! Ole man Hildebran'! Ole man Hildebran'!

A rawhide whip he hold in de hand,
For he love a chain an' he love a whip;
An' he been a bad ole man,
An' he live in slavery time.
Ole man Hildebran'! Ole man Hildebran'! Ole man Hildebran'!

He nose been split an' he face been cut,
An' he neck been short;
Wid teet' like a hog, an' a mind like a dog,
He smile been a frown, an' voice a growl.
He been a bad ole man,
An' he live in slavery time.
Ole man Hildebran'! Ole man Hildebran'! Ole man Hildebran'!

An' he ooman was a nigger wench
Wid ways crokked as de trail of a black snake;
An' she'd grin at we trouble an' laugh at we pain,
An' she live in slavery time.
Ole man Hildebran'! Ole man Hildebran'! Ole man Hildebran'!

Ole man Hildebran' was a bad ole man,
He live in slavery time.
He's equal wid de niggers now;
De worrums crawls through de holes in he head.
He was a bad ole man,
An' he live in slavery time.
Ole man Hildebran'! Ole man Hildebran'! Ole man Hildebran'!

■

2.14. The "Positive Good" of Slavery (1837)

*In this speech, John C. Calhoun (1782–1850), the most influential antebellum pol-
itician from South Carolina, responds to the reception of abolitionist petitions by
the US Senate. Unlike earlier generations of southern politicians who often apolo-
gized for slavery while urging its maintenance out of necessity, Calhoun countered
mounting antislavery criticism by arguing that slavery was in fact "a good—a positive good" that was "indispensable to the peace and happiness of both" whites and
blacks. Calhoun's viewpoint would dominate proslavery discourse through the Civil
War and influence the postwar ideology of the Lost Cause. ::*

The peculiar institution of the South—that, on the maintenance of which the
very existence of the slaveholding States depends, is pronounced to be sinful
and odious, in the sight of God and man; and this with a systematic design
of rendering us hateful in the eyes of the world—with a view to a general crusade against us and our institutions. This, too, in the legislative halls of the
Union; created by these confederated States, for the better protection of their
peace, their safety, and their respective institution;—and yet, we, the representatives of twelve of these sovereign States against whom this deadly war is
waged, are expected to sit here in silence, hearing ourselves and our constituents day after day denounced, without uttering a word; for if we but open our
lips, the charge of agitation is resounded on all sides, and we are held up as
seeking to aggravate the evil which we resist. Every reflecting mind must see in
all this a state of things deeply and dangerously diseased.

I do not belong to the school which holds that aggression is to be met by
concession. Mine is the opposite creed, which teaches that encroachments
must be met at the beginning, and that those who act on the opposite principle are prepared to become slaves. In this case, in particular, I hold concession
or compromise to be fatal. If we concede an inch, concession would follow
concession—compromise would follow compromise, until our ranks would
be so broken that effectual resistance would be impossible. We must meet the
enemy on the frontier, with a fixed determination of maintaining our position
at every hazard. . . .

They who imagine that the spirit now abroad in the North, will die away of
itself without a shock or convulsion, have formed a very inadequate conception

John C. Calhoun, "Speech on the Reception of Abolition Petitions, Delivered in the Senate, February 6th, 1837," in Richard R. Cralle, ed., *Speeches of John C. Calhoun, Delivered in
the House of Representatives and in the Senate of the United States* (New York: D. Appleton,
1853), 625–33.

of its real character; it will continue to rise and spread, unless prompt and efficient measures to stay its progress be adopted. Already it has taken possession of the pulpit, of the schools, and, to a considerable extent, of the press; those great instruments by which the mind of the rising generation will be formed.

However sound the great body of the non-slaveholding States are at present, in the course of a few years they will be succeeded by those who will have been taught to hate the people and institutions of nearly one-half of this Union, with a hatred more deadly than one hostile nation ever entertained towards another. It is easy to see the end. By the necessary course of events, if left to themselves, we must become, finally, two people. It is impossible under the deadly hatred which must spring up between the two great sections, if the present causes are permitted to operate unchecked, that we should continue under the same political system. The conflicting elements would burst the Union asunder, powerful as are the links which hold it together. Abolition and the Union cannot co-exist. . . .

But let me not be understood as admitting, even by implication, that the existing relations between the two races in the slaveholding States is an evil:—far otherwise; I hold it to be a good,as it has thus far proved itself to be to both, and will continue to probe so if not disturbed by the fell spirit of abolition. I appeal to facts. Never before has the black race of Central Africa, from the dawn of history to the present day, attained a condition so civilized and so improved, not only physically, but morally and intellectually. It came among us in a low, degraded, and savage condition, and in the course of a few generations it has grown up under the fostering care of our institutions, reviled as they have been, to its present comparatively civilized condition. This, with the rapid increase of numbers, is conclusive proof of the general happiness of the race, in spite of all the exaggerated tales to the contrary.

In the mean time, the white or European race has not degenerated. It has kept pace with its brethren in other sections of the Union where slavery does not exist. It is odious to make comparison; but I appeal to all sides whether the South is not equal in virtue, intelligence, patriotism, courage, disinterestedness, and all the high qualities which adorn our nature. I ask whether we have not contributed our full share of talents and political wisdom in forming and sustaining this political fabric; and whether we have not constantly inclined most strongly to the side of liberty, and been the first to see and first to resist the encroachments of power. In one thing only are we inferior—the arts of gain; we acknowledge that we are less wealthy than the Northern section of this Union, but I trace this mainly to the fiscal action of this Government, which has extracted much from, and spent little among us. Had it been the reverse,—if the exaction had been from the other section, and the expenditure with us, this point of superiority would not be against us now, as it was not at the formation of this Government.

But I take higher ground. I hold that in the present state of civilization, where two races of different origin, and distinguished by color, and other physical differences, as well as intellectual, are brought together, the relation now existing in the slaveholding States between the two, is, instead of an evil, a good—a positive good. I feel myself called upon to speak freely upon the subject where the honor and interests of those I represent are involved. I hold then, that there never has yet existed a wealthy and civilized society in which one portion of the community did not, in point of fact, live on the labor of the other. Broad and general as is this assertion, it is fully borne out by history. . . .

I may say with truth, that in few countries so much is left to the share of the laborer, and so little exacted from him; or where there is more kind attention paid to him in sickness or infirmities of age. Compare his condition with the tenants of the poor houses in the more civilized portions of Europe—look at the sick, and the old and infirm slave, on one hand, in the midst of his family and friends, under the kind superintending care of his master and mistress, and compare it with the forlorn and wretched condition of the pauper in the poor house. But I will not dwell on this aspect of the question; I turn to the political; and here I fearlessly assert that the existing relation between the two races in the South, against which these blind fanatics are waging war, forms the most solid and durable foundation on which to rear free and stable political institutions. It is useless to disguise the fact. There is and always has been in an advanced stage of wealth and civilization, a conflict between labor and capital. The condition of society in the South exempts us from the disorders and dangers resulting from this conflict; and which explains why it is that the political condition of the slaveholding States has been so much more stable and quiet than that of the North. The advantages of the former, in this respect, will become more and more manifest if left undisturbed by interference from without, as the country advances in wealth and numbers. We have, in fact, but just entered that condition of society where the strength and durability of our political institutions are to be tested; and I venture nothing in predicting that the experience of the next generation will fully test how vastly more favorable our condition of society is to that of other sections for free and stable institutions, provided we are not disturbed by the interference of others, or shall have sufficient intelligence and spirit to resist promptly and successfully such interference. It rests with ourselves to meet and repel them. I look not for aid to this Government, or to the other States; not but there are kind feelings towards us on the part of the great body of the nonslaveholding States; but as kind as their feelings may be, we may rest assured that no political party in those States will risk their ascendency for our safety. If we do not defend ourselves none will defend us; if we yield we will be more and more pressed as we recede; and if we submit we will be trampled under foot. . . .

■

2.15. The Mudsill Theory (1858)

James Henry Hammond (1807–1864) was a South Carolina politician and planter. His "mudsill theory" of social organization was embraced by elite proslavery ideologues for its justification of slavery and labor exploitation and gave other whites, even those who were not slave owners, a powerful motivation for maintaining the status quo. ::

Speech to the U.S. Senate, March 4, 1858

. . . In all social systems there must be a class to do the menial duties, to perform the drudgery of life. That is, a class requiring but a low order of intellect and but little skill. Its requisites are vigor, docility, fidelity. Such a class you must have, or you would not have that other class which leads progress, civilization, and refinement. It constitutes the very mud-sill of society and of political government; and you might as well attempt to build a house in the air, as to build either the one or the other, except on this mud-sill. Fortunately for the South, she found a race adapted to that purpose to her hand. A race inferior to her own, but eminently qualified in temper, in vigor, in docility, in capacity to stand the climate, to answer all her purposes. We use them for our purpose, and call them slaves. We found them slaves by the common "consent of mankind," which, according to Cicero, *"lex naturae est."*[7] The highest proof of what is Nature's law. We are old-fashioned at the South yet; slave is a word discarded now by "ears polite;" I will not characterize that class at the North by that term; but you have it; it is there; it is everywhere; it is eternal.

The Senator from New York[8] said yesterday that the whole world had abolished slavery. Aye, the name, but not the thing; all the powers of the earth cannot abolish that. God only can do it when he repeals the fiat, "the poor ye always have with you;"[9] for the man who lives by daily labor, and scarcely lives at that, and who has to put out his labor in the market, and take the best he can get for it; in short, your whole hireling class of manual laborers and "operatives," as you call them, are essentially slaves. The difference between us is, that our slaves are hired for life and well compensated; there is no starvation, no begging, no want of employment among our people, and not too much employment either. Yours are hired by the day, not cared for, and scantily compensated, which may be proved in the most painful manner, at any hour in any street in any of your

James Henry Hammon, *Selections from the Letters and Speeches of the Hon. James H. Hammond of South Carolina* (New York: J. F. Trow, 1866), 318–20.

large towns. Why, you meet more beggars in one day, in any single street of the city of New York, than you would meet in a lifetime in the whole South. We do not think that whites should be slaves either by law or necessity. Our slaves are black, of another and inferior race. The status in which we have placed them is an elevation. They are elevated from the condition in which God first created them, by being made our slaves. None of that race on the whole face of the globe can be compared with the slaves of the South. They are happy, content, unaspiring, and utterly incapable, from intellectual weakness, ever to give us any trouble by their aspirations. Yours are white, of your own race; you are brothers of one blood. They are your equals in natural endowment of intellect, and they feel galled by their degradation. Our slaves do not vote. We give them no political power. Yours do vote, and, being the majority, they are the depositories of all your political power. If they knew the tremendous secret, that the ballot-box is stronger than "an army with banners,"[10] and could combine, where would you be? Your society would be reconstructed, your government overthrown, your property divided, not as they have mistakenly attempted to initiate such proceedings by meeting in parks, with arms in their hands, but by the quiet process of the ballot-box. You have been making war upon us to our very hearthstones. How would you like for us to send lecturers and agitators North, to teach these people this, to aid in combining, and to lead them?

CHAPTER 3

"A jubilee of freedom"

LIBERTY AND EMANCIPATION IN SOUTH CAROLINA

■

3.1. Boston King Recalls His Joining the British Army (1798)

Boston King was born a slave around 1760. His early years were marked by unbear-able abuses, and following the British occupation of Charles Town in May 1780 King made his escape to the British lines, hoping to gain his freedom by fighting for the Crown. After the war, King was evacuated by the British and settled in Nova Scotia. He later served as a missionary and schoolteacher in the free black colony of Free-town, Sierra Leone, where he died in 1802. ::

I was born in the Province of South Carolina, 28 miles from Charles-Town. . . . My master being apprehensive that Charles-Town was in danger on account of the war, removed into the country, about 38 miles off. Here we built a large house . . . during which time the English took Charles-Town.[1] Having obtained leave one day to see my parents, who lived about 12 miles off, and it being late before I could go, I was obliged to borrow one of Mr. Waters's[2] horses; but a servant of my masters, took the horse from me to go [on] a little journey, and stayed two or three days longer than he ought. This involved me in the greatest perplexity, and I expected the severest punishment, because the gentleman to whom the horse belonged was a very bad man, and knew not how to shew mercy. To escape his cruelty, I determined to go to Charles-Town, and throw myself into the hands of the English. They received me readily, and I began to feel the happiness of liberty, of which I knew nothing before, altho' I was much grieved at first, to be obliged to leave my friends, and reside among strangers. In this situation I was seized with the smallpox, and suffered great hardships; for

"Memoirs of the Life of Boston King, a Black Preacher. Written by Himself, during his Residence at Kingswood School," *The Methodist Magazine* 21 (March 1798): 105–10 and 21 (April 1798): 157–61.

all the Blacks affected with that disease, were ordered to be carried a mile from the camp, lest the solders should be infected, and disabled from marching.[3] This was a grievous circumstance to me and many others. We lay sometimes a whole day without any thing to eat or drink; but Providence sent a man, who belonged to the York volunteers whom I was acquainted with, to my relief. He brought me such things as I stood in need of; and by the blessing of the Lord I began to recover.

By this time, the English left the place; but as I was unable to march with the army, I expected to be taken by the enemy. However, when they came, and understood that we were ill of the small-pox, they precipitately left us for fear of infection. Two days after, the wagons were sent to convey us to the English Army, and we were put into a little cottage, (being 25 in number) about a quarter of a mile from the Hospital.

Being recovered, I marched with the army to Chamblem.[4] When we came to the headquarters, our regiment was 35 miles off. I stayed at the head-quarters three weeks, during which time our regiment had an engagement with the Americans, and the man who relieved me when I was ill of the small pox, was wounded in battle, and brought to the hospital. As soon as I heard of his misfortune, I went to see him, and tarried with him in the hospital six weeks, till he recovered; rejoicing that it was in my power to return him the kindness he had shewed it was in my power. From thence I went to a place about 35 miles off, where we stayed two months: at the expiration of which, an express came to the Colonel to decamp in fifteen minutes. When these orders arrived I was at a distance from the camp, catching some fish for the captain that I waited upon; upon returning to the camp, to my great astonishment, I found all the English were gone, and had left only a few militia. I felt my mind greatly alarmed, but Captain Lewes,[5] who commanded the militia, said, "You need not be uneasy, for you will see your regiment before 7 o'clock tonight." This satisfied me for the present, and in two hours we set off. As we were on the march, the Captain asked, "How will you like me to be your master?" I answered, that I was Captain Grey's servant. "Yes," said he, "but I expect they are all taken prisoners before now; and I have been long enough in the English service, and am determined to leave them." These words roused my indignation and I said some sharp things to him. But he calmly replied, "If you do not behave well, I will put you in irons, and give you a dozen stripes every morning." I now perceived that my case was desperate, and that I had nothing to trust to, but to wait the first opportunity for making my escape. The next morning, I was sent with a little boy over the river to an island to fetch the Captain some horses. . . . Upon our return to the Captain with the horses we were sent for, he immediately set off by himself. I stayed till about 10 o'clock, and then resolved to go to the English army. . . . Being arrived at the head-quarters, I informed my Captain that Mr.

Lewes had deserted. I also told him of the horses which Lewes had conveyed to the Island. Three weeks after, our light horse[6] went to the island and burnt his house; they likewise brought back forty of the horses, but he escaped. I tarried with Captain Grey about a year, and then left him, and came to Nelson's-ferry.[7] Here I entered into the service of the commanding officer of that place. But our situation was very precarious, and we expected to be made prisoners every day; for the American had 1600 men, not far off; whereas our whole number amounted only to 250: But there were 1200 English about 30 miles off; only we knew not how to inform them of our danger, as the Americans were in possession of the country. Our commander at length determined to send me with a letter, promising me great rewards, if I was successful in the business. I refused going on horse-back, and set off on foot about 3 o'clock in the afternoon; I expected every moment to fall in with the enemy, whom I well knew would shew me no mercy. I went on without interruption, till I got within six miles of my journey's end, and then was alarmed with a great noise a little before me. But I stopped out of the road, and fell flat upon my face till they were gone by. I then arose, and praised the Name of the Lord for his great mercy, and again pursued my journey, till I came to Mums-corner tavern. I knocked at the door, but they blew out the candle. I knocked again and entreated the master to open the door. At last he came with a frightful countenance, and said, "I thought it was the Americans; for they were here about an hour ago, and I thought they were returned again." I asked "How may were there?" he answered, "about one hundred." I desired him to saddle his horse for me, which he did, and went with me himself. When we had gone about two miles, we were stopped by the picket-guard, till the Captain came out with 30 men: As soon as he knew that I had brought an express from Nelson's-ferry, he received me with great kindness, and expressed his approbation of my courage and conduct in this dangerous business. Next morning, Colonel Small gave me three shillings, and many fine promises, which were all that I ever received for this service from him. . . .

Soon after I went to Charles-Town, and entered on board a man of war . . . and then sailed for New York, where I went on shore. . . . A year after I was taken very ill, but the Lord raised me up again in about five weeks. I then went out in a pilot boat. We were at sea eight days, and had only provisions for five, so that we were in danger of starving. On the 9thday we were taken by an American whale-boat. . . . My mind was sorely distressed at the thought of being again reduced to slavery, and separated from my wife and family; and at the same time it was exceeding difficult to escape from my bondage, because the river at Amboy[8] was above a mile over, and likewise another to cross at Staten Island. I called to remembrance the great deliverances the Lord had wrought for me, and besought him to save me this once, and I would serve him all the days of my life. . . .

I used to go to the ferry, and observed, that when it was low water, the people waded across the river; tho' at the same time I saw there were guards posted at the place to prevent the escape of prisoners and slaves. As I was at prayer on Sunday evening, I thought the Lord heard me, and would mercifully deliver me. Therefore putting my confidence in him, about one o'clock in the morning I went down to the river side, and found the guards were either asleep or in the tavern. . . . When I had got a little distance from the shore, I fell down upon my knees, and thanked God for this deliverance. . . . When I came to the river, opposite Staten-Island, I found a boat; and altho' it was very near a whale-boat, yet I ventured into it, and cutting the rope, got safe over. The commanding officer, when informed of my case, gave me a passport, and proceeded to New-York.

When I arrived at New York, my friends rejoiced to see me once more restored to liberty, and joined me in praising the Lord for his mercy and goodness. . . . About which time (in 1783), the horrors and devastation of war happily terminated, and peace was restored between America and Great Britain, which issued universal joy among all parties, except us, who had escaped from slavery, and taken refuge in the English army; for a report prevailed at New-York, that all slaves, in number 2,000, were to be delivered up to their masters, although some of them had been three or four years among the English. This dreadful rumour filled us all with inexpressible anguish and terror, especially when we saw our masters coming from Virginia, North-Carolina, and other parts, and seizing upon their slaves in the streets of New-York, or even dragging them out of their beds. Many of the slaves had very cruel masters, so that the thoughts of returning home with them embittered life to us. For some days, we lost our appetite for food, and sleep departed from our eyes. The English had compassion upon us in the day of distress, and issued out a Proclamation, importing, That all slaves should be free, who had taken refuge in the British lines, and claimed the function and privileges of the Proclamations respecting the security and protection of Negroes.[9] In consequence of this, each of us received a certificate from the commanding officer at New-York, which dispelled all our fears, and filled us with joy and gratitude. Soon after, ships were fitted out, and furnished with every necessary for conveying us to Nova Scotia. We arrived at Burch Town[10] in the month of August, where we all safely landed. . . .

■

3.2. David George Founds the Silver Bluff Church (1793)

The Silver Bluff Baptist Church, founded between 1773 and 1775, was the first separate black church in America and mother church to several other widely scattered Baptist missions in the United States, Canada, the Caribbean, and Africa. Many of the church's founders, including the slave David George, author of the passage reprinted here, abandoned South Carolina in 1778, during the American Revolution, and evacuated to Nova Scotia with the British in 1782. Others remained in the area and, though still enslaved after the war, reconstituted their church in Augusta in the late 1780s. ::

I lived a bad life, and had no serious thoughts about my soul; but after my wife was delivered of our first child, a man of my own colour, named Cyrus, who came from Charlestown, South Carolina, to Silver Bluff, told me one day in the woods, That if I lived so, I should never see the face of God in glory (Whether he himself was a converted man or not, I do not know). This was the first thing that disturbed me, and gave me much concern. I thought then that I must be saved by prayer. I used to say the Lord's prayer, that it might make me better, but I feared that I grew worse; and I continued worse and worse, as long as I thought I would do some thing to make me better; till at last there seemed as if there was no possibility of relief, and that I must go to hell. I saw myself a mass of sin. . . .

Soon after I heard brother George Liele preach, who, as you both know, is at Kingston in Jamaica.[11] I knew him ever since he was a boy. I am older than he; I am about fifty. His sermon was suitable, on *Come unto me all ye that labour, and are heavy laden, and I will give you rest.*[12] When it was ended, I went to him and told him I was so; That I was weary and heavy laden, and that the grace of God had given me rest. Indeed his whole discourse seemed for me. Afterwards brother Palmer,[13] who was pastor at some distance from Silver Bluff, came and preached to a large congregation at a mill of Mr. Gaulfin's;[14] he was a very powerful preacher; and as he was returning home Lord's-day evening, I went with him two or three miles, and told him how it was with me. About this time more of my fellow-creatures began to seek the Lord. Afterwards Brother Palmer came again and wished us to beg Master to let him preach to us; and he had leave, and came frequently There were eight of us now who had found the great blessing and mercy from the Lord, and my wife was one of them, and brother Jesse Gaulfin . . . was another. Brother Palmer appointed a Saturday evening to hear what the Lord had done for us, and the next day he baptized us in the Mill-stream. . . .

Brother Palmer formed us into a church, and gave us the Lord's supper at Silver Bluff. Then I began to exhort in the church, and learned to sing hymns. . . . So I was appointed to the office of an Elder and received instruction from Brother Palmer how to conduct myself. I proceeded in this way till the American war was coming on, when the Ministers were not allowed to come amongst us lest they should furnish us with too much knowledge. The Black people all around attended with us, and as Brother Palmer must not come, I had the whole management, and used to preach among them myself. . . .

I continued preaching at Silver Bluff, till the church, constituted with eight, increased to thirty or more, and till the British came to the city [of] Savannah and took it.[15] My Master was an Antiloyalist; and being afraid, he now retired from home and left the Slaves behind. My wife and I, and the two children we then had, and fifty or more of my Master's people, went to Ebenezer,[16] about twenty miles from Savannah, where the King's forces were. . . .

■

3.3. The Conversion of John Marrant (1815)

John Marrant (1755–1791) was born to a free African American family in New York City. After his father's death, he moved south with his mother, eventually settling in Charleston in 1766. There, he learned to read and write and became a much-sought-after musician. At age thirteen, he was converted by George Whitefield in a revival, but his family did not approve of his newfound faith. He soon left home and became a missionary to the Cherokee. After being impressed into the British navy in the Revolutionary War, Marrant encountered Whitefield again, renewed his walk with God, and was ordained in 1785. ::

One evening I was sent for in a very particular manner to go and play for some gentlemen, which I agreed to do, and was on my way to fulfil my promise; and passing by a large meeting-house, I saw many lights in it, and crowds of people going in. I inquired what it meant, and was answered by my companion, that a crazy man was hallooing there; this raised my curiosity to go in, that I might hear what he was hallooing about: He persuaded me not to go in, but in vain. He then said, "if you will do one thing, I will go in with you." I asked him what that was? He replied, "blow the French horn among them." I liked the proposal well enough, but expressed my fears of being beaten for disturbing them; but upon his promising to stand by and defend me, I agreed. So we went, and with much difficulty got within the doors. I was pushing the people to make room,

John Marrant, *A Narrative of the Life of John Marrant* (Leeds: Davies, 1815), 7–9.

to get the horn off my shoulder to blow it, just as Mr. Whitfield[17] was naming
his text, and looking round, and, as I thought, directly upon me, and pointing
with his finger, he uttered these words "Prepare To Meet Thy God, O Israel."[18]
The Lord accompanied the word with such power, that I was struck to the
ground, and lay both speechless and senseless for twenty-four minutes: when
I was come a little to, I found two men attending me, and a woman throwing
water in my face, and holding a smelling bottle to my nose; and when something more recovered, every word I heard from the minister was like a parcel
of swords thrust into me; and what added to my distress, I thought I saw the
devil on every side of me. I was constrained by the bitterness of my spirit to
halloo out in the midst of the congregation, which disturbing them, they took
me away: but finding I could neither walk nor stand, they carried me as far as
the vestry, and there I remained till the service was over. When the people were
dismissed Mr. Whitfield came into the vestry, and being told of my condition
he came immediately, and the first word he said was, "Jesus Christ Has Got
Thee At Last." He asked where I lived, intending to come and see me the next
day; but recollecting he was to leave the town the next morning, he said he
could not come himself, but would send another minister; he desired them
to get me home, and then taking his leave of me, I saw him no more. When I
reached my sister's house, being carried by two men, she was very uneasy to
see me in so distressed a condition. She got me to bed, and sent for a doctor,
who came immediately, and after looking at me, he went home, and sent me a
bottle of mixture, and desired her to give me a spoonful every two hours; but I
could not take any thing the doctor sent nor indeed keep in bed; this distressed
my sister very much, and she cried out. "The lad will surely die!" She sent for
two other doctors, but no medicine they prescribed could I take. No, no; it
may be asked,—a wounded spirit who can cure? as well as who can bear? In
this distress of soul I continued for three days without any food, only a little
water now and then. On the fourth day, the minister Mr. Whitfield had desired
to visit me came to see me, and being directed up stairs, when he entered the
room, I thought he made my distress much worse. He wanted to take hold of
my hand, but I durst not give it to him. He insisted upon taking hold of it, and
I then got away from him on the other side of the bed; but being very weak I
fell down, and before I could recover he came to me, and took me by the hand
and lifted me up, and after a few words, desired to go to prayer. So he fell upon
his knees, and pulled me down also; after he had spent some time in prayer he
rose up, and asked me how I did? I answered much worse; he then said, "come
we will have the old thing over again;" and so we kneeled down a second time,
and after he had prayed earnestly we got up, and he said again, "how do you do
now?" I replied worse and worse, and asked him if he intended to kill me? "No,
no, said he, you are worth a thousand dead men, let us try the old thing over

again;" and so falling upon our knees, he continued in prayer a considerable time; near the close of his prayer, the Lord was pleased to set my soul at liberty, and being filled with joy, I began to praise the Lord immediately; my sorrows were turned into peace, and joy, and love. The minister said, "How is it now?" I answered, all is well, all happy. He then took his leave of me; but called every day for several days afterwards, and the last time he said, "Hold fast that thou hast already obtained, till Jesus Christ come." I now read the Scriptures very much. My master[19] sent often to know how I did, and at last came himself, and finding me well, asked me if I would not come to work again? I answered no. He asked me the reason, but receiving no answer, he went away.

■

3.4. Testimony of the Vesey Plot (1822)

News of the thwarted Denmark Vesey insurrection in 1822 terrified white South Carolinians. Though some historians have suggested that the plot never actually existed and that the trial and attendant hysteria were part of a well-orchestrated plan to whip white Carolinians into a panic for political reasons, the words of those free and enslaved men and women caught up in the unrest nonetheless offer a fascinating glimpse into the hopes and fears of African Americans in the age of revolution. ::

A negro man[20] testified as follows:

I know Peter, he belongs to Mr. James Poyas; in May last, Peter and myself met in Legare street, at the corner of Lambol street, where the following conversation took place—he asked me the news—I replied, none that I know of—he said, by George! we can't live so. I replied, how will we do? He said, we can do very well, if you can find any one to assist us—will you join? I asked him, how do you mean? He said, why! to break the yoke. I replied, I don't know. He asked me, suppose you were to hear, that the whites were going to kill you, would you defend yourself? I replied, I'd try to escape. He asked, have you lately seen *Denmark Vesey,* and has he spoken to you particularly. I said no. Well then, said he, that's all now; but call at the shop to-morrow after knocking off work, and I will tell you more! We then parted. I met him the next day, according to appointment, when he said to me, we intend to see, if we can't do something for ourselves, we can't live so. I asked him, where he would get men? He said, we'll find them fast enough, we have got enough, we expect men from country and town. But how, said I, will you manage it. Why, we will give them notice, said he, and they will march down and camp round the city. But what, said I, will they do for arms. He answered, they will find arms enough, they all bring down

An Account of the Late Intended Insurrection among a Portion of the Blacks of the City of Charleston, South Carolina (Boston: Joseph W. Ingraham, 1822), 33–36.

their hoes, axes, &c. I said, that won't do to fight with here. He said, stop! let us get candidates from town with arms, and we will then take the guardhouse and arsenal in town, the arsenal on the neck and the upper guardhouse, and supply the country people with arms. How, said I, will you approach those arsenals, &c. for they are guarded? Yes, said he, I know that, but what are these guards, one man here, and one man there, we let a man pass before us. Well, said I, but how will the black people from the country, and those from the islands, know when you are to begin, or how will you get the town people together. Why, said he, we will have prayer meetings at night, and there notify them when to start, and when the clock strikes twelve, *all must move.* But, said I, the whites in the back country, Virginia, &c. when they hear the news, will turn to, and kill you all, and besides, you may be betrayed. Well, said he, what of that, if one gets hanged, we will rise at that minute. We then left his shop, and walked towards Broad street, when he said, I want you to take notice of all the shops and stores in town with arms in them, take down *their numbers, and give them to me.* I said, I will see to it, and then we parted.

About the first of June, I saw in the publick papers a statement that the white people were going to build missionary houses for the blacks, which I carried and showed to Peter, and said, see the good they are going to do for us; when he said, what of that? Have you not heard, that on the 4th of July, the whites are going to create a false alarm of fire, and every *black* that comes out will be *killed,* in order *to thin them?* Do you think they would be so barbarous? (said I) Yes! (said he) I do!—I fear *they have a knowledge of an army from San Domingo,* and they would be *right to do it; to prevent us joining that army, if it should march towards this land!* I was then very much alarmed. We then parted, and I saw no more of him till the guards were very strict, (about a fortnight ago.) At that time I saw Peter and Ned Bennett standing and talking together, at the corner of Lambol and Legare streets. They crossed over and met me by Mrs. Myles's, and Ned Bennett said to me, did you hear what those boys were taken up for the other day? I replied, no! but some say it was for stealing. Ned asked me if I was sure I had never said any thing to the whites about what Peter Poyas had spoken to me about? I replied, no! Says Peter, You never did? No! I answered. Says Ned, to me, how do you stand?

At which I struck the tree box with my knuckles and said, as firm as this box—I'll never say one word against you. Ned then smiled and nodded his head, and said, that will do! when we all separated. Last Tuesday or Wednesday week, Peter said to me, you see, my lad, how the white people have got to windward of us? You won't, said I, be able to do any thing. O, yes! (he said) we will! By George, we are obliged to! He said, all down this way ought to meet and have a collection to purchase powder. What, said I, is the use of powder—the whites can fire three times to our once. He said, but *'twill be such a dead time of* the night, they won't know what is the matter, and our horse companies will go about the streets and prevent the whites from assembling. I asked him—where will you get horses? Why, said he, there are many butcher boys with horses; and there are the livery stables, where we have several candidates; and the waiting men, belonging to the white people of the horse companies, will be told to take away their master's horses. He asked me if my master was not a horseman? I said, yes! Has he not got arms in his house? I answered, yes! Can't they be got at? I said, yes! Then, (said he) it is good to have them. I asked what was the plan? Why, said he, after we have taken the arsenals and guardhouses, then we will set the town on fire in different places, and as the whites come out we will slay them. If we were to set fire to the town first the man in the steeple would give the alarm too soon. I am the captain, said he, to take the lower guardhouse and arsenal. But, I replied, when you are coming up, the centinel will give the alarm. He said, he would advance a little distance ahead, and if he could only get a *grip at his throat he was a gone man,* for his sword was very sharp; he had sharpened it, and had made it so sharp, it had cut his finger, which he showed me. As to the arsenal on the neck, he said, that it was gone as sure as fate, *Ned Bennett would manage that with the people from the country, and the people between Hibbens' ferry and Santee would land and take the upper guardhouse.* I then said, then this thing seems true. My man, said he, God has a hand in it, *we have been meeting for four years, and are not yet betrayed.* I told him, I was afraid, after all, of the white people from the back country, and Virginia, &c. He said that the blacks would collect so numerous from the country, we need not fear the whites from the other parts, for when we have once got the city we can keep them all out. He asked, if I had told my boys. I said no. Then said he, you should do it, for Ned Bennett has his people pretty well ranged. But, said he, take care and don't mention it to those waiting men who receive *presents of old coats, &c. from their masters, or they'll betray us.* I will speak to them. We then parted, and I have not since conversed with him. He said the rising was to take place last Sunday night, (16th June). That *any of the coloured people who said a word about this matter would be killed by the others. The little man, who can't be killed, shot, or taken,* is named Jack, a Gullah negro. Peter said there was a French company in town of three hundred men fully armed—that he was to see Monday Gell, about expediting the rising. I know that Mingo went often to Mr. Paul's to see Edwin, but don't know if he spoke with William. Peter said he had a sword, and I ought to get one. He said he had got a letter from the country; I think from St. Thomas's, from a negro man who belonged to the captain of a militia company, who said he could easily get the key of the house where the company's arms were put after muster, and take them all out, and help in that way. This business originates altogether with the *African congregation,* in which Peter is a leader. When Bennett's Ned asked about those taken up, he alluded particularly to Mr. Paul's William, and asked me if I said any thing to him about it.

■

3.5. Our Wretchedness in Consequence of the Preachers of the Religion of Jesus Christ (1829)

David Walker (1785–1830) was born free in Cape Fear, North Carolina, and moved to Charleston as a young adult. There, he attended the same A.M.E. church as Denmark Vesey, and he may have had some involvement in the 1822 insurrection plot. In the wake of Vesey's trial, Walker moved to Boston, where he published Walker's Appeal to the Colored Citizens of the World *(1829), a scathing critique of American slavery. In addition to calling for slaves to revolt against their masters, Walker's radical pamphlet condemned the South's scriptural defense of slavery and, with examples from his time spent in South Carolina, called out slaveholding Christians for their hypocrisy.* ::

Religion, my brethren, is a substance of deep consideration among all nations of the earth. The Pagans have a kind, as well as the Mahometans, the Jews and the Christians. But pure and undefiled religion, such as was preached by Jesus Christ and his apostles, is hard to be found in all the earth. God, through his instrument, Moses, handed a dispensation of his Divine will, to the children of Israel after they had left Egypt for the land of Canaan or of Promise, who through hypocrisy, oppression and unbelief, departed from the faith.—He then, by his apostles, handed a dispensation of his, together with the will of Jesus Christ, to the Europeans in Europe, who, in open violation of which, have made *merchandise* of us, and it does appear as though they take this very dispensation to aid them in their *infernal* depredations upon us. Indeed, the way in which religion was and is conducted by the Europeans and their descendants, one might believe it was a plan fabricated by themselves and the *devils* to oppress us. But hark! My master has taught me better than to believe it— he has taught me that his gospel as it was preached by himself and his apostles remains the same, notwithstanding Europe has tried to mingle blood and oppression with it. . . .

The Pagans, Jews and Mahometans try to make proselytes to their religions, and whatever human beings adopt their religions they extend to them their protection. But Christian Americans, not only hinder their fellow creatures, the Africans, but thousands of them *will absolutely beat a coloured person nearly to death, if they catch him on his knees, supplicating the throne of grace.* This

David Walker, *Walker's Appeal, in Four Articles; Together with a Preamble to the Colored Citizens of the World* (Boston: David Walker, 1830), 39–49.

barbarous cruelty was by all the heathen nations of antiquity, and is by the Pagans, Jews and Mahometans of the present day, left entirely to Christian Americans to inflict on the Africans and their descendants, that their cup which is nearly full may be completed. . . . Yet the American minister send out missionaries to convert the heathen, while they keep us and our children sunk at their feet in the most abject ignorance and wretchedness that ever a people was afflicted with since the world began. Will the Lord suffer this people to proceed much longer? . . .

Have not the Americans the Bible in their hands? Do they believe it? Surely they do not. See how they treat us in open violation of the Bible!! They no doubt will be greatly offended with me, but if God does not awaken them, it will be, because they are superior to other men, as they have represented themselves to be. Our divine Lord and Master said, "all things whatsoever ye would that men should do unto you, do ye even so unto them." . . . I have known pretended preachers of the gospel of my Master, who not only held us as their natural inheritance, but treated us with as much rigor as any Infidel or Deist in the world—just as though they were intent only on taking our blood and groans to glorify the Lord Jesus Christ. The wicked and ungodly, seeing their preachers treat us with so much cruelty, they say: our preachers, who must be right, if any body are, treat them like brutes, and why cannot we?—They think it is no harm to keep them in slavery and put the whip to them, and why cannot we do the same!—They being preachers of the gospel of Jesus Christ, if it were any harm, they would surely preach against their oppression and do their utmost to erase it from the country; not only in one or two cities, but one continual cry would be raised in all parts of this confederacy, and would cease only with the complete overthrow of the system of slavery, in every part of the country. But how far the American preachers are from preaching against slavery and oppression, which have carried their country to the brink of a precipice; to save them from plunging down the side of which, will hardly be affected, will appear in the sequel of this paragraph, which I shall narrate just as it transpired. I remember a Camp Meeting in South Carolina, for which I embarked in a Steam Boat at Charleston, and having been five or six hours on the water, we at last arrived at the place of hearing, where was a very great concourse of people, who were no doubt, collected together to hear the word of God, (that some had collected barely as spectators to the scene, I will not here pretend to doubt, however, that is left to themselves and their God.) Myself and boat companions, having been there a little while, we were all called up to hear; I among the rest went up and took my seat—being seated, I fixed myself in a complete position to hear the word of my Saviour and to receive such as I thought was authenticated by the Holy Scriptures; but to my no ordinary astonishment, our Reverend gentleman got up and told us (coloured people) that slaves must be obedient to their masters—must do their duty to their masters or be whipped—the whip was made for the backs of fools. . . .

What the American preachers can think of us, I aver this day before my God, I have never been able to define. They have newspapers and monthly periodicals, which they receive in continual succession, but on the pages of which, you will scarcely ever find a paragraph respecting slavery, which is ten thousand times more injurious to this country than all the other evils put together; and which will be the final overthrow of its government, unless something is very speedily done; for their cup is nearly full.—Perhaps they will laugh at or make light of this; but I tell you Americans! that unless you speedily alter your course, *you* and your *Country are gone!!!!!!* For God Almighty will tear up the very face of the earth!!! Will not that very remarkable passage of Scripture be fulfilled on Christian Americans? Hear it Americans!! "He that is unjust, let him be unjust still:—and he which is filthy, let him be filthy still: and he that is righteous, let him be righteous still: and he that is holy, let him be holy still."[21] I hope that the Americans may hear, but I am afraid that they have done us so much injury, and are so firm in the belief that our Creator made us to be an inheritance to them for ever, that their hearts will be hardened, so that their destruction may be sure. This language, perhaps is too harsh for the American's delicate ears. But Oh Americans! Americans!! I warn you in the name of the Lord, (whether you will hear, or forbear,) to repent and reform, or you are ruined!!! Do you think that our blood is hidden from the Lord, because you can hide it from the rest of the world, by sending out missionaries, and by your charitable deeds to the Greeks, Irish, &c.? Will he not publish your secret crimes on the house top. . . . There are not a more wretched, ignorant, miserable, and abject set of beings in all the world, than the blacks in the Southern and Western sections of this country, under tyrants and devils. The preachers of America cannot see them, but they can send out missionaries to convert the heathens, notwithstanding. Americans! unless you speedily alter your course of proceeding, if God Almighty does not stop you, I say it in his name, that you may go on and do as you please for ever, both in time and eternity—never fear any evil at all!!!!!!!! . . .

How can the preachers and people of America believe the Bible? Does it teach them any distinction on account of a man's colour? Hearken, Americans! to the injunctions of our Lord and Master, to his humble followers.

"And Jesus came and spake unto them, saying, all power is given unto me in Heaven and in earth.

"Go ye, therefore, and teach all nations, baptizing them in the name of the Father, and of the Son, and of the Holy Ghost.

"Teaching them to observe all things whatsoever I have commanded you; and lo, I am with you always, even unto the end of the world. Amen."[22]

I declare, that the very face of these injunctions appear to be of God and not of man. They do not show the slightest degree of distinction. "Go ye therefore," (says my divine Master) "and teach all nations," (or in other words, all people) "baptizing them in the name of the Father, and of the Son, and of the Holy Ghost." Do you understand the above, Americans? We are a people, notwithstanding many of you doubt it. You have the Bible in your hands, with this very injunction.—Have you been to Africa, teaching the inhabitants thereof the words of the Lord Jesus? "Baptizing them in the name of the Father, and of the Son, and of the Holy Ghost." Have you not, on the contrary, entered among us, and learnt us the art of throat-cutting, by setting us to fight, one against another, to take each other as prisoners of war, and sell to you for small bits of calicoes, old swords, knives, &c. to make slaves for you and your children? This being done, have you not brought us among you, in chains and hand-cuffs, like brutes, and treated us with all the cruelties and rigour your ingenuity could invent, consistent with the laws of your country, which (for the blacks) are tyrannical enough? Can the American preachers appeal unto God, the Maker and Searcher of hearts, and tell him, with the Bible in their hands, that they make no distinction on account of men's colour? Can they say, O God! thou knowest all things—thou knowest that we make no distinction between thy creatures, to whom we have to preach thy Word? Let them answer the Lord; and if they cannot do it in the affirmative, have they not departed from the Lord Jesus Christ, their master? But some may say, that they never had, or were in possession of a religion, which made no distinction, and of course they could not have departed from it. I ask you then, in the name of the Lord, of what kind can your religion be? Can it be that which was preached by our Lord Jesus Christ from Heaven? I believe you cannot be so wicked as to tell him that his Gospel was that of *distinction*. What can the American preachers and people take God to be? Do they believe his words? If they do, do they believe that he will be mocked? Or do they believe, because they are whites and we blacks, that God will have respect to them? Did not God make us all as it seemed best to himself? What right, then, has one of us, to despise another, and to treat him cruel, on account of his colour, which none, but the God who made it can alter? Can there be a greater absurdity in nature, and particularly in a free republican country? But the Americans, having introduced slavery among them, their hearts have become almost seared, as with an hot iron, and God has nearly given them up to believe a lie in preference to the truth!!! And I am awfully afraid that pride, prejudice, avarice and blood, will, before long prove the final ruin of this happy republic, or land of *liberty!!!!* Can any thing be a greater mockery of religion than the way in which it is conducted by the Americans? It appears as though they are bent only on daring God Almighty to do his best— they chain and handcuff us and our children and drive us around the country like brutes, and go into the house of the God of justice to return him thanks for having aided them in their infernal cruelties inflicted upon us. Will the Lord suffer this people to go on much longer, taking his holy name in vain? Will he not stop them, PREACHERS and all? O Americans! Americans!! I call God—I call angels—I call men, to witness, that your DESTRUCTION *is at hand,* and will be speedily consummated unless you REPENT.

■

3.6. Rules and Regulations of the Brown Fellowship Society (1790)

The Brown Fellowship Society was the premier mutual aid society of Charleston's free African Americans. The organization was founded in 1790 to provide its members with burial plots in its private cemetery, as well as education, medical care, social services, and support for members' widows and children. However, with a steep membership fee and a strict color requirement, it was clear that the group's motto, "charity and benevolence," applied only to the "brown elite," a privileged group of mixed-race Charlestonians who sought to distance themselves from enslaved African Americans and courted favor with white society. The organization continued to function through at least 1916. ::

Whereas we, Free brown men, natives of the City of Charleston, in the State of South Carolina, having taken into consideration the unhappy situation of our fellow creatures, and the distresses of our widows and orphans, for the want of a fund to relieve them in the hour of their distresses, sickness and death; and holding it an essential duty to mankind to contribute all they can towards relieving the wants and miseries, and promoting the welfare and happiness of one another, and observing the method of many other well-disposed persons of the State, by entering into particular Societies for this purpose, to be effectual, we therefore, whose names are underwritten, to comply with this great duty, have freely and cheerfully entered into a society in Charleston, and State aforesaid, commencing the first of November 1790 and have voted, agreed and subscribed to the following rules for ordering and conducting the same. . . .

"Charity and Benevolence."

2 Corinthians ix, 7.

"Every man according as he proposeth in his heart, so let him give, not grudgingly, or of necessity, for God loveth a cheerful giver."

Rule I. This Society shall be known and distinguished by the name of the *Brown Fellowship Society,* and shall consist of any number of persons, not

Rules and Regulations of the Brown Fellowship Society, Established at Charleston, S.C. 1st November, 1790 (Charleston, S.C.: J. B. Nixon, Printer, 1844).

exceeding fifty, nor less than five. No person shall be admitted a member thereof under the age of twenty-one years.

Rule II. The members of this Society shall meet of the first Thursday of every month. . . . Every member within five miles of Charleston who does not attend at the different monthly or extra meetings of the body, when summoned, shall be fined. . . .

Rule XII. In case sickness afflicts any member . . . he shall be entitled to, and allowed a weekly sum of not less than $1.50 . . . and if he dies . . . the President, or presiding officer, who shall order a meeting immediately, and consult on the management of the funeral; and in case the circumstances of such deceased member be low and indigent, that a decent funeral cannot be afforded out of their own estate of effects, the President or presiding officer shall . . . regulate things in as frugal a manner as possible, for the funeral, which charges shall be paid out of the Society's funds, in such manner as before stipulated. Every member in Charleston shall attend the funeral, with a black cape around the left arm, by invitation from the Secretary; and on neglect (if able) to attend, he shall be fined. . . .

Rule XIII. Deceased members who have regularly paid up their contributions to the time of their death, and leaving children, being free heirs in law, in low and indigent circumstances, so that they cannot, out of their estate, be accommodated with learning . . . the Society shall, at their expense, teach or cause to be taught, all children, reading, writing, and arithmetic, and also be supported with every necessary of life until arrived at the age of fourteen years, after which they shall be bound out to some good trade, the male to serve until twenty-one years, after which, should he or they wish to become members of this institution, on application made, and being elected he shall be admitted for one quarter the amount of admission money that may be at the time of his or their application. The female shall be bound to some trade until eighteen years of age. Further provided: in case such deceased members leaving widows, such widows being unfortunately in the like circumstances as above stated . . . she shall be entitled to and allowed a yearly sum of sixty dollars, payable quarterly, during her widowhood. . . .

Rule XV. In conjunction with the institution and motto of charity and benevolence, be it resolved and agreed, that on report of any poor colored orphan or adult , being free, whose case requires needful assistance, on application being made to the Society, the same shall be taken into immediate consideration, and if a majority grants relief, the President shall appoint a committee for the purpose of further consideration on the case and manner of relief, which by them are to be recommended and laid before the Society at their next meeting. The number of indigent shall not exceed five on the bounty at any one period.

Rule XVIII. Resolved that a decent, peaceable, orderly behavior be observed by the members, at the meetings. . . . All debates on controverted points of divinity or matters of nation, shall be excluded from the conversation in this Society. . . .

■

3.7. Charles Ball Describes His Escape from Slavery through South Carolina (1837)

Charles Ball (1780–?) was a Maryland-born slave who in 1805 was sold away from his family to a South Carolina cotton planter. Ball attempted to escape from slavery several times and ultimately succeeded in reaching Philadelphia. This account of his escape through South Carolina appeared in his first autobiography. ::

I was now once more in South Carolina, where I knew it was necessary for me to be even more watchful than I had been in Georgia. I do not know where I crossed the Savannah river, but think it must have been only a few miles above the town of Augusta.

. . . I never moved until long after night, and was cautious never to permit daylight to find me on the road; but I observed that the north-star was always on my left hand. My object was to reach the neighbourhood of Columbia, and get upon the road which I had travelled and seen years before in coming to the south; but the road I was now on must have been the great Charleston road,[23] leading down the country, and not across the courses of the rivers. So many people travelled this road, as well by night as by day, that my progress was very slow; and in some of the nights I did not travel more than eight miles. At the end of a week, after leaving the forks, I found myself in a flat, sandy, poor country; and as I had not met with any river on this road, I now concluded that I was on the way to the sea-board instead of Columbia. In my perplexity, I resolved to try to get information concerning the country I was in, by placing myself in some obscure place in the side of the road, and listening to the conversation of travellers as they passed me. . . . On the third night, about ten o'clock, several wagons drawn by mules passed me, and I heard one of the drivers call to another and tell him that it was sixty miles to Charleston; and that they should be able to reach the river to-morrow. I could not at first imagine what river this could be; but another of the wagoners enquired how far it was to the Edisto, to which it was replied by some one, that it was near thirty miles. I now perceived that I had mistaken my course; and was as completely lost as a wild goose in cloudy weather. . . .

Charles Ball, *Slavery in the United States: A Narrative of the Life and Adventures of Charles Ball* (New York: John S. Taylor, 1837), 416–40.

At length I determined to quit this road altogether, travel by the north-star for two or three weeks, and after that to trust to Providence to guide me to some road that might lead me back to Maryland. . . . I soon found myself in a country almost entirely clear of timber, and abounding in fields of cotton and corn.

. . . I came unexpectedly to a broad river, which I now saw running between me and the town. I took it for granted that there must be a ferry at this place, and on examining the shore, found several small boats fastened only with ropes to a large scow. One of these boats I seized, and was quickly on the opposite shore of the river. I entered the village and proceeded to its centre, without seeing so much as a rat in motion. Finding, myself in an open space I stopped to examine the streets, and upon looking at the houses around me, I at once recognized the jail of Columbia, and the tavern in which I had lodged on the night after I was sold.

. . . It was now in my power to avail myself of the knowledge I had formerly acquired, of the customs of South Carolina. The patrol are very rigid in the execution of the authority, with which they are invested; but I never had much difficulty with these officers, anywhere. From dark until ten or eleven o'clock at night, the patrol are watchful, and always traversing the country in quest of negroes, but towards midnight these gentlemen grow cold, or sleepy, or weary, and generally betake themselves to some house, where they can procure a comfortable fire.

I now established, as a rule of my future conduct, to remain in my hiding place until after ten o'clock, according to my computation of time; and this night I did not come to the road, until I supposed it to be within an hour of midnight, and it was well for me that I practised so much caution, for when within two or three hundred yards of the road, I heard people conversing. After standing some minutes in the woods, and listening to the voices at the road, the people separated, and a party took each end of the road, and galloped away upon their horses. These people were certainly a band of patrollers, who were watching this road, and had just separated to return home for the night. After the horsemen were quite out of hearing, I came to the road, and walked as fast as I could for hours.

. . . As nearly as possible, I confined my travelling within the hours of midnight and three o'clock in the morning. Parties of patrollers were heard by me almost every morning, before day. These people sometimes moved directly along the roads, but more frequently lay in wait near the side of the road, ready to pounce upon any runaway slave that might chance to pass; but I knew by former experience that they never lay out all night, except in times of apprehended danger; and the country appearing at this time to be quiet, I felt but little apprehension of falling in with these policemen, within my travelling hours.

. . . Since leaving Columbia, I had followed as nearly as the course of the roads permitted, the index of the north-star; which, I supposed, would lead me on the most direct route to Maryland; but I now became convinced, that this star was leading me away from the line by which I had approached the cotton country.

. . . I saw, at the distance of half a mile from me, a man moving slowly about in the forest, and apparently watching, like myself, to see if any one was in view. Looking at this man attentively, I saw that he was a black, and that he did not move more than a few rods from the same spot where I first saw him. Curiosity impelled me to know more of the condition of my neighbour; and descending quite to the foot of the hill, I perceived that he had a covert of boughs of trees, under which I saw him pass, and after some time return again from his retreat. Examining the appearance of things carefully, I became satisfied that the stranger was, like myself, a negro slave, and I determined, without more ceremony, to go and speak to him, for I felt no fear of being betrayed by one as badly off in the world as myself.

When this man first saw me, at the distance of a hundred yards from him, he manifested great agitation, and at once seemed disposed to run from me; but when I called to him, and told him not to be afraid, he became more assured, and waited for me to come close to him. I found him to be a dark mulatto, small and slender in person, and lame in one leg. He had been well bred, and possessed good manners and fine address. I told him I was travelling, and presumed this was not his dwelling place. Upon which he informed me that he was a native of Kent county, in the state of Delaware . . . and had run away three weeks before the time I saw him, with the intention of returning to Delaware. . . . He invited me to go into his camp, as he termed it, where he had an old skillet, more than a bushel of potatoes, and several fowls, all of which he said he had purloined from the plantations in the neighbourhood.

This encampment was in a level open wood, and it appeared surprising to me that its occupant had not been discovered and conveyed back to his master before this time. I told him that I thought he ran great risk of being taken up by remaining here, and advised him to break up his lodge immediately, and pursue his journey, travelling only in the night time. . . . I remained with this man two or three hours, and ate dinner of fowls dressed after his rude fashion.

. . . At the end of the cloudy weather, I felt much refreshed and strengthened, and resumed my journey in high spirits, although I now began to feel the want of shoes—those which I wore when I left my mistress having long since been worn out, and my boots were now beginning to fail so much, that I was obliged to wrap straps of hickory bark about my feet, to keep the leather from separating, and falling to pieces. It was now, by my computation, the month of November, and I was yet in the state of South Carolina. I began to consider with myself, whether I had gamed or lost, by attempting to travel on the roads; and, after revolving in my mind all the disasters that had befallen me, determined to abandon the roads altogether, for two reasons:—the first of which was, that on the highways, I was constantly liable to meet persons, or to be overtaken by them; and a second, no less powerful, was, that as I did not know what roads to pursue, I was oftener travelling on the wrong route than on the right one.

Setting my face once more for the north-star, I advanced with a steady, though slow pace, for four or five nights, when I was again delayed by dark weather, and forced to remain in idleness nearly two weeks; and when the weather again became clear, I was arrested, on the second night, by a broad and rapid river, that appeared so formidable, that I did not dare to attempt its passage, until after examining it in daylight. On the succeeding night, however, I crossed it by swimming—resting at some large rocks near the middle. After gaining the north side of this river, which I believed to be the Catawba, I considered myself in North Carolina, and again steered towards the north. . . .

■

3.8. Description of a Maroon Camp (1861)

Not all enslaved people who escaped bondage necessarily sought freedom in a northern state or in Canada. Some took advantage of remote locations within the slave system itself and formed independent maroon settlements like the one described in this excerpt. Though marronage occurred in all slave states/colonies, evidence of maroon activity is most abundant in South Carolina's history. ::

Runaways—Last Tuesday a party of gentlemen from this place went in search of runaways who were thought to be in a swamp two miles from here. A trail was discovered which, winding about much, conducted the party to a knoll in the swamp on which corn, squashes, and peas were growing and a camp had been burnt. Continuing the search, another patch of corn, etc., was found and a camp from which several negroes fled, leaving two small negro children, each about a year old. . . . There were several guns fired at the negroes who fled from the camp but none proved effectual. The camp seemed well provided with meal, cooking utensils, blankets, etc. The party returned, having taken the two children, twelve guns and one axe. Means should immediately be taken for the capture of these runaways, as they are probably lurking about this place.

Marion Star, June 18, 1861.

■

3.9. Susie King Taylor Remembers the Thirty-third USCT (1902)

Susie King Taylor (1848–1912) was born a slave in Georgia. She learned to read and write in Savannah and taught at a school for freedmen on St. Simon's Island from April to October 1862. There, she met and married her husband, Edward King, a noncommissioned officer in the First South Carolina Volunteers (later the Thirty-third USCT), and for three years she moved with his regiment as laundress and nurse. The First South Carolina was the first officially recognized black regiment of the Union Army. Formed largely from escaped South Carolina slaves in late 1862, the unit saw its first combat on January 26, 1863, and helped capture Fort Gregg on Morris Island in Charleston Harbor (the engagement described at the end of this excerpt) in September 1863. ::

The latter part of August, 1862, Captain C. T. Trowbridge[24] . . . came to St. Simon's Island from Hilton Head, by order of General Hunter,[25] to get all the men possible to finish filling his regiment which he had organized in March, 1862.[26] He had heard of the skirmish on this island, and was very much pleased at the bravery shown by these men. He found me at Gaston Bluff teaching my little school, and was much interested in it. When I knew him better I found him to be a thorough gentleman and a staunch friend to my race.

Captain Trowbridge remained with us until October, when the order was received to evacuate, and so we boarded the Ben-De-Ford, a transport, for Beaufort, S.C. When we arrived in Beaufort, Captain Trowbridge and the men he had enlisted went to camp at Old Fort, which they named "Camp Saxton." I was enrolled as laundress.

The first suits worn by the boys were red coats and pants, which they disliked very much, for, they said, "The rebels see us, miles away."

The first colored troops did not receive any pay for eighteen months, and the men had to depend wholly on what they received from the commissary, established by General Saxton.[27] A great many of these men had large families, and as they had no money to give them, their wives were obliged to support themselves and children by washing for the officers of the gunboats and the soldiers, and making cakes and pies which they sold to the boys in camp. Finally, in 1863, the government decided to give them half pay, but the men would not accept this. They wanted "full pay" or nothing. They preferred rather to give their services to the state, which they did until 1864, when the government granted them full pay, with all the back pay due. . . .

Susie King Taylor, *Reminiscences of My Life in Camp with the 33rd United States Colored Troops* (Boston: Published by the Author, 1902), 15–17, 22–28, 31–34.

Fort Wagner being only a mile from our camp, I went there two or three times a week, and would go up on the ramparts to watch the gunners send their shells into Charleston (which they did every fifteen minutes), and had a full view of the city from that point. Outside of the fort were many skulls lying about; I have often moved them one side out of the path. The comrades and I would have quite a debate as to which side the men fought on. Some thought they were the skulls of our boys; others thought they were the enemy's; but as there was no definite way to know, it was never decided which could lay claim to them. They were a gruesome sight, those fleshless heads and grinning jaws, but by this time I had become accustomed to worse things and did not feel as I might have earlier in my camp life.

It seems strange how our aversion to seeing suffering is overcome in war,— how we are able to see the most sickening sights, such as men with their limbs blown off and mangled by the deadly shells, without a shudder; and instead of turning away, how we hurry to assist in alleviating their pain, bind up their wounds, and press the cool water to their parched lips, with feelings only of sympathy and pity.

... Colonel Higginson had left us in May of this year, on account of wounds received at Edisto. All the men were sorry to lose him. They did not want him to go, they loved him so. He was kind and devoted to his men, thoughtful for their comfort, and we missed his genial presence from the camp.

The regiment under Colonel Trowbridge did garrison duty, but they had troublesome times from Fort Gregg, on James Island, for the rebels would throw a shell over on our island every now and then. Finally orders were received for the boys to prepare to take Fort Gregg, each man to take 150 rounds of cartridges, canteens of water, hard-tack, and salt beef. This order was sent three days prior to starting, to allow them to be in readiness. I helped as many as I could to pack haversacks and cartridge boxes.

The fourth day, about five o'clock in the afternoon, the call was sounded, and I heard the first sergeant say, "Fall in, boys, fall in," and they were not long obeying the command. Each company marched out of its street, in front of their colonel's headquarters, where they rested for half an hour, as it was not dark enough, and they did not want the enemy to have a chance to spy their movements. At the end of this time the line was formed with the 103d New York (white) in the rear, and off they started, eager to get to work. It was quite dark by the time they reached Pawnell Landing. I have never forgotten the goodbys of that day, as they left camp. Colonel Trowbridge said to me as he left, "Good-by, Mrs. King, take care of yourself if you don't see us again." I went with them as far as the landing, and watched them until they got out of sight, and then I returned to the camp. There was no one at camp but those left on picket and a few disabled soldiers, and one woman, a friend of mine, Mary Shaw, and it was lonesome and sad, now that the boys were gone, some never to return. . . . About four o'clock, July 2, the charge was made. The firing could be plainly heard in camp. I hastened down to the landing and remained there until eight o'clock that morning. When the wounded arrived, or rather began to arrive, the first one brought in was Samuel Anderson of our company. He was badly wounded. Then others of our boys, some with their legs off, arm gone, foot off, and wounds of all kinds imaginable. They had to wade through creeks and marshes, as they were discovered by the enemy and shelled very badly. A number of the men were lost, some got fastened in the mud and had to cut off the legs of their pants, to free themselves. The 103d New York suffered the most as their men were very badly wounded.

My work now began. I gave my assistance to try to alleviate their sufferings. I asked the doctor at the hospital what I could get for them to eat. They wanted soup, but that I could not get; but I had a few cans of condensed milk and some turtle eggs, so I thought I would try to make some custard. I had doubts as to my success, for cooking with turtle eggs was something new to me, but the adage has it, "Nothing ventured, nothing done," so I made a venture and the result was a very delicious custard. This I carried to the men, who enjoyed it very much. My services were given at all times for the comfort of these men. I was on hand to assist whenever needed. I was enrolled as company laundress, but I did very little of it, because I was always busy doing other things through camp, and was employed all the time doing something for the officers and comrades. . . .

■

3.10. Robert Smalls Captures the CSS *Planter* (1862)

Robert Smalls was born a slave in Beaufort but was sent to Charleston and hired out by his master at age twelve. There, he labored as a dockworker and eventually as a pilot, and he gained a reputation for his knowledge of Charleston Harbor. When the Civil War broke out, Smalls was assigned to the Confederate gunboat the Planter. *Left unattended by his white officers on May 12, 1862, Smalls and seven other enslaved crewmen, with his family stowed aboard, piloted the* Planter *past the unsuspecting sentries on the harbor and reached the Union blockade beyond range of Confederate guns. He turned the* Planter *over to the US Navy, handed over a code book of secret Confederate signals, and revealed the placement of mines in the area. Smalls served throughout the rest of the war as a pilot for the federal forces and eventually became the first black captain of a vessel. He went on to a long postwar political career representing South Carolina. ::*

The Rebellion Record: A Diary of American Events, vol. 5, ed. Frank Moore (New York: G. P. Putnam, 1863), 132.

"Robert Smalls and the CSS *Planter* (May 1862)," *Harper's Weekly,* June 14, 1862, p. 372.

Sɪʀ: I inclose a copy of a report from Commander E. G. Parrott, brought here last night by the late rebel steam-tug Planter, in charge of an officer and crew from the *Augusta*. She was the armed dispatch and transportation steamer attached to the engineer department at Charleston, under Brigadier-General Ripley, whose barge, a short time since, was brought out to the blockading fleet by several contrabands.[28]

The bringing out of this steamer, under all the circumstances, would have done credit to any one. At four o'clock in the morning, in the absence of the captain, who was on shore, she left her wharf close to the government office and headquarters, with Palmetto and Confederate flags flying, passed the successive forts, saluting as usual by blowing her steamwhistle. After getting beyond the range of the last gun, she quickly hauled down the rebel flags and hoisted a white one.

The *Onward* was the inside ship of the blockading fleet in the main channel, and was preparing to fire when her commander made out the white flag. The armament of the steamer is a 32-pounder, or pivot, and a fine 24-pounder howitzer. She has, besides, on her deck, four other guns, one 7-inch rifled, which were to have been taken the morning of the escape to the new fort on the middle ground. One of the four belonged to Fort Sumter, and had been struck in the rebel attack on the fort on the muzzle. Robert, the intelligent slave and pilot of the boat, who performed this bold feat so skillfully, informed me of this fact, presuming it would be a matter of interest to us to have possession of this gun. This man, Robert Smalls, is superior to any who have come into our lines— intelligent as many of them have been. His information has been most interesting, and portions of it of the utmost importance.

The steamer is quite an acquisition to the squadron by her good machinery and very light draught. The officer in charge brought her through Saint Helena Sound, and by the inland passage down Beaufort river, arriving here at ten o'clock last night.

On board the steamer when she left Charleston were eight men, five women and three children.

I shall continue to employ Robert as a pilot on board the Planter for the inland waters, with which he appears to be very familiar. I do not know whether, in the views of the government, the vessel will be considered a prize; but, if so, I respectfully submit to the department the claims of this man Robert and his associates.[29]

Very respectfully, your obedient servant,
S. F. Dupont[30]

■

3.11. Charlotte Forten Teaches Freedmen on the Sea Island (1864)

Charlotte Forten (1837–1914) was from a prominent black abolitionist household in Philadelphia. She was the first black teacher to come South as part of the Port Royal Experiment, and her published correspondence with Northern reformers and essays in national publications helped bring those efforts to the attention of Northern readers. ::

. . . The first day at school was rather trying. Most of my children were very small, and consequently restless. Some were too young to learn the alphabet. These little ones were brought to school because the older children—in whose care their parents leave them while at work—could not come without them. We were therefore willing to have them come, although they seemed to have discovered the secret of perpetual motion, and tried one's patience sadly. But after some days of positive, though not severe treatment, order was brought out of chaos, and I found but little difficulty in managing and quieting the tiniest and most restless spirits. I never before saw children so eager to learn, although I had had several years' experience in New-England schools. Coming to school is a constant delight and recreation to them. They come here as other children go to play. The older ones, during the summer, work in the fields from early morning until eleven or twelve o'clock, and then come into school, after their hard toil in the hot sun, as bright and as anxious to learn as ever.

Of course there are some stupid ones, but these are the minority. The majority learn with wonderful rapidity. Many of the grown people are desirous of

Charlotte Forten, "Life on the Sea Islands," Parts I and II, *The Atlantic* 13 (May–June 1864), 587–96, 666–76.

learning to read. It is wonderful how a people who have been so long crushed to the earth, so imbruted as these have been,—and they are said to be among the most degraded negroes of the South,—can have so great a desire for knowledge, and such a capability for attaining it. One cannot believe that the haughty Anglo-Saxon race, after centuries of such an experience as these people have had, would be very much superior to them. And one's indignation increases against those who, North as well as South, taunt the colored race with inferiority while they themselves use every means in their power to crush and degrade them, denying them every right and privilege, closing against them every avenue of elevation and improvement. Were they, under such circumstances, intellectual and refined, they would certainly be vastly superior to any other race that ever existed.

After the lessons, we used to talk freely to the children, often giving them slight sketches of some of the great and good men. Before teaching them the "John Brown" song, which they learned to sing with great spirit, Miss T. told them the story of the brave old man who had died for them. I told them about Toussaint, thinking it well they should know what one of their own color had done for his race. They listened attentively, and seemed to understand. . . .

Harry, the foreman on the plantation, a man of a good deal of natural intelligence, was most desirous of learning to read. He came in at night to be taught, and learned very rapidly. I never saw any one more determined to learn. We enjoyed hearing him talk about the "gun- shoot,"—so the people call the capture of Bay Point and Hilton Head. They never weary of telling you "how Massa run when he hear de fust gun." . . .

They are willing to make many sacrifices that their children may attend school. One old woman, who had a large family of children and grandchildren, came regularly to school in the winter, and took her seat among the little ones. She was at least sixty years old. Another woman—who had one of the best faces I ever saw—came daily, and brought her baby in her arms. It happened to be one of the best babies in the world, a perfect little "model of deportment," and allowed its mother to pursue her studies without interruption. . . .

Daily the long-oppressed people of these islands are demonstrating their capacity for improvement in learning and labor. What they have accomplished in one short year exceeds our utmost expectations. Still the sky is dark; but through the darkness we can discern a brighter future. We cannot but feel that the day of final and entire deliverance, so long and often so hopelessly prayed for, has at length begun to dawn upon this much-enduring race. An old freedman said to me one day, "De Lord make me suffer long time, Miss. 'Peared like we nebber was gwine to git troo. But now we's free. He bring us all out right at las'." In their darkest hours they have clung to Him, and we know He will not forsake them. . . .

■

3.12. The Terrible Massacre at Fort Wagner (1864)

Charlotte Forten was also a friend of Robert Gould Shaw, commanding officer of the Fifty-fourth Massachusetts Infantry Regiment, and was present when the Fifty-fourth stormed Fort Wagner on July 18, 1863. Nearly half of these soldiers were killed, captured, or missing after the battle, but, as Forten writes, the men of the Fifty-fourth were lauded for their heroism under fire. Despite this defeat, the valor demonstrated by the regiment encouraged the Union Army to further mobilize African American troops. ::

. . . We had met [Colonel Robert Gould Shaw][31] a few nights before, when he came to our house to witness one of the people's shouts. . . . A few days afterwards we saw his regiment on dress-parade, and admired its remarkably fine and manly appearance. After taking supper with the Colonel we sat outside the tent, while some of his men entertained us with excellent singing. Every moment we became more and more charmed with him. How full of life and hope and lofty aspirations he was that night! How eagerly he expressed his wish that they might soon be ordered to Charleston! "I do hope they will give us a chance," he said. It was the desire of his soul that his men should do themselves honor,—that they should prove themselves to an unbelieving world as brave soldiers as though their skins were white. . . . We never saw him afterward. In two short weeks came the terrible massacre at Fort Wagner. . . . During a few of the sad days which followed the attack on Fort Wagner, I was in one of the hospitals of Beaufort, occupied with the wounded soldiers of the Fifty-Fourth Massachusetts. The first morning was spent in mending the bullet-holes and rents in their clothing. What a story they told! Some of the jackets of the poor fellows were literally cut in pieces. It was pleasant to see the brave, cheerful spirit among them. Some of them were severely wounded, but they uttered no complaint; and in the letters which they dictated to their absent friends there was no word of regret, but the same cheerful tone throughout. They expressed an eager desire to get well, that they might "go at it again." Their attachment to their young colonel was beautiful to see. They felt his death deeply. One and all united in the warmest and most enthusiastic praise of him. He was, indeed, exactly the person to inspire the most loyal devotion in the hearts of his men. And with everything to live for, he had given up his life for them. Heaven's best gifts had been showered upon him, but for them he had laid them all down. I think they truly appreciated the greatness of the sacrifice. May they ever prove

Charlotte Forten, "Life on the Sea Islands," (Part I) *The Atlantic* 13 (June 1864), 666–76.

worthy of such a leader! Already, they, and the regiments of freedmen here, as well, have shown that true manhood has no limitations of color. . . .

■

3.13. Sherman Consults African American Leaders Ahead of Special Field Order No. 15 (1865)

On January 16, 1865, General William Tecumseh Sherman (1820–1891) issued his Special Field Order No. 15, which confiscated as Union property a strip of coastline from Charleston to the St. John's River in Florida and redistributed the 400,000 acres to freed African American families in forty-acre plots. This order came just four days after discussions that Sherman and Secretary of War Edwin Stanton held with twenty African American leaders in Savannah (at least three of whom were born or lived in South Carolina). The idea for massive land redistribution was not new, but Sherman's plan took shape only after this meeting with black leaders. Special Field Order No. 15 was later overturned by President Andrew Johnson. ::

Headquarters of Maj.-Gen. Sherman,
City of Savannah, Ga., Jan. 12, 1865—8 P.M.

On the evening of Thursday, the 12th day of January, 1865, the [twenty] persons of African descent met by appointment to hold an interview with Edwin M. Stanton, Secretary of War, and Major-Gen. Sherman, to have a conference upon matters relating to the freedmen of the State of Georgia, to-wit:

. . . Garrison Frazier[32] being chosen by the persons present to express their common sentiments upon the matters of inquiry, makes answers to inquiries as follows:

First: State what your understanding is in regard to the acts of Congress and President Lincoln's proclamation,[33] touching the condition of the colored people in the Rebel States.

Answer—So far as I understand President Lincoln's proclamation to the Rebellious States, it is, that if they would lay down their arms and submit to the laws of the United States before the first of January, 1863, all should be well; but if they did not, then all the slaves in the Rebel States should be free henceforth and forever. That is what I understood.

Second—State what you understand by Slavery and the freedom that was to be given by the President's proclamation.

Answer—Slavery is, receiving by *irresistible power* the work of another man, and not by his *consent.* The freedom, as I understand it, promised by the proclamation, is taking us from under the yoke of bondage, and placing us where

New York Daily Tribune, February 13, 1865.

we could reap the fruit of our own labor, take care of ourselves and assist the Government in maintaining our freedom.

Third: State in what manner you think you can take care of yourselves, and how can you best assist the Government in maintaining your freedom.

Answer: The way we can best take care of ourselves is to have land, and turn it and till it by our own labor–that is, by the labor of the women and children and old men; and we can soon maintain ourselves and have something to spare. And to assist the Government, the young men should enlist in the service of the Government, and serve in such manner as they may be wanted. (The Rebels told us that they piled them up and made batteries of them, and sold them to Cuba; but we don't believe that.) We want to be placed on land until we are able to buy it and make it our own.

Fourth: State in what manner you would rather live—whether scattered among the whites or in colonies by yourselves.

Answer: I would prefer to live by ourselves, for there is a prejudice against us in the South that will take years to get over; but I do not know that I can answer for my brethren. . . .

Fifth: Do you think that there is intelligence enough among the slaves of the South to maintain themselves under the Government of the United States and the equal protection of its laws, and maintain good and peaceable relations among yourselves and with your neighbors?

Answer—I think there is sufficient intelligence among us to do so.

Sixth—State what is the feeling of the black population of the South toward the Government of the United States; what is the understanding in respect to the present war—its causes and object, and their disposition to aid either side. State fully your views.

Answer—I think you will find there are thousands that are willing to make any sacrifice to assist the Government of the United States, while there are also many that are not willing to take up arms. I do not suppose there are a dozen men that are opposed to the Government. I understand, as to the war, that the South is the aggressor. President Lincoln was elected President by a majority of the United States, which guaranteed him the right of holding the office and exercising that right over the whole United States. The South, without knowing what he would do, rebelled. The war was commenced by the Rebels before he came into office. The object of the war was not at first to give the slaves their freedom, but the sole object of the war was at first to bring the rebellious States back into the Union and their loyalty to the laws of the United States. Afterward, knowing the value set on the slaves by the Rebels, the President thought that his proclamation would stimulate them to lay down their arms, reduce them to obedience, and help to bring back the Rebel States; and their not doing so has now made the freedom of the slaves a part of the war. It is my opinion that there is not a man in this city that could be started to help the Rebels one inch, for that would be suicide. There were two black men left with the Rebels because they had taken an active part for the Rebels, and thought something might befall them if they stayed behind; but there is not another man. If the prayers that have gone up for the Union army could be read out, you would not get through them these two weeks.

Seventh: State whether the sentiments you now express are those only of the colored people in the city; or do they extend to the colored population through the country? and what are your means of knowing the sentiments of those living in the country?

Answer: I think the sentiments are the same among the colored people of the State. My opinion is formed by personal communication in the course of my ministry, and also from the thousands that followed the Union army, leaving their homes and undergoing suffering. I did not think there would be so many; the number surpassed my expectation.

Eighth: If the Rebel leaders were to arm the slaves, what would be its effect?

Answer: I think they would fight as long as they were before the bayonet, and just as soon as soon as they could get away, they would desert, in my opinion.

Ninth: What, in your opinion, is the feeling of the colored people about enlisting and serving as soldiers of the United States? and what kind of military service do they prefer?

Answer: A large number have gone as soldiers to Port Royal to be drilled and put in the service; and I think there are thousands of the young men that would enlist. There is something about them that perhaps is wrong. They have suffered so long from the Rebels that they want to shoulder the musket. Others want to go into the Quartermaster's or Commissary's service.

Tenth: Do you understand the mode of enlistments of colored persons in the Rebel States by State agents under the Act of Congress?[34] If yea, state what your understanding is.

Answer: My understanding is, that colored persons enlisted by State agents are enlisted as substitutes, and give credit to the States, and do not swell the army, because every black man enlisted by a State agent leaves a white man at home; and, also, that larger bounties are given or promised by State agents than are given by the States. The great object should be to push through this Rebellion the shortest way, and there seems to be something wanting in the enlistment by State agents, for it don't strengthen the army, but takes one away for every colored man enlisted.

Eleventh: State what, in your opinion, is the best way to enlist colored men for soldiers.

Answer: I think, sir, that all compulsory operations should be put a stop to. The ministers would talk to them, and the young men would enlist. It is my opinion that it would be far better for the State agents to stay at home, and the enlistments to be made for the United States under the direction of Gen. Sherman.

In the absence of Gen. Sherman, the following question was asked:

Twelfth: State what is the feeling of the colored people in regard to Gen. Sherman; and how far do they regard his sentiments and actions as friendly to their rights and interests, or otherwise?

Answer: We looked upon Gen. Sherman prior to his arrival as a man in the Providence of God specially set apart to accomplish this work, and we unanimously feel inexpressible gratitude to him, looking upon him as a man that should be honored for the faithful performance of his duty. Some of us called upon him immediately upon his arrival, and it is probable he would not meet the Secretary with more courtesy than he met us. His conduct and deportment toward us characterized him as a friend and a gentleman. We have confidence in Gen. Sherman, and think that what concerns us could not be under better hands. This is our opinion now from the short acquaintance and interest we have had. . . .

Some conversation upon general subjects relating to Gen. Sherman's march then ensued, of which no note was taken.

War Department, Adjt. Gen.'s Office
Washington, February 1, 1865;

I do hereby certify that the foregoing is a true and faithful report of the questions and answers made by the colored ministers and church members of Savannah in my presence and hearing, at the chambers of Major General Sherman, on the evening of Thursday, January 12, 1565. The questions of General Sherman and the Secretary of War were reduced to writing and read to the persons present. The answers were made by the Rev. Garrison Frazier, who was selected by the other ministers and church members to answer for them. The answers were written down in his exact words, and read over to the others, who one by one expressed his concurrence or dissent as above set forth
E. D. Townsend, Ass't Adj't Gen.

Beecher said that Secretary Stanton had remarked that it was the first time in the history of this nation when the representatives of this Government had gone to these poor, debased people to ask "What they wanted for themselves." "What do you want for your own people?" was the question which had been put to them; and the speaker concluded that it was upon the basis of this conference that General Sherman had formed his recent order, in relation to the freedmen of his Department, which has been so severely criticised at the North, but for

"'Marching On!'—The Fifty-fifth Massachusetts Colored Regiment Singing
John Brown's March in the Streets of Charleston, February 21, 1865,"
Harper's Weekly, March 18, 1865, p.165.

which, now that the acts are known, he should be still further honored and admired. Beecher concluded by stating that General Grant had been heard, in the
presence of several distinguished officers, to give the opinion that, for picket
and guard duty, the negroes made the best soldiers in the world. He had not
tested them in the matter of endurance, the quality displayed by our troops in
the terrible succession of battles, called the battle of the Wilderness, but could
otherwise answer for their military capabilities, and, on the whole, be considered them equal to any soldiers in the world.

■

3.14. Freed Slaves Parade in Charleston (1865)

*At the close of the Civil War, former slaves responded in a variety of ways to their
new freedom. In the account reproduced here, African Americans in Charleston organized a parade to celebrate their emancipation. Thousands of marchers enacted
their personal conceptions of freedom and citizenship through dramatic tableaux,
banners, and music in ways similar to the public demonstrations of Northern white
workers before the war.* ::

New-York Daily Tribune, Tuesday, April 4, 1865.

There was the greatest procession of loyalists in Charleston last Tuesday that the city has witnessed for many a long year. The present generation has never seen its like. For these loyalists were true to the Nation without any qualifications of State rights, reserved sovereignties, or other allegiances; they gloried in the flag, they adored the Nation, they believed with the fullest faith in the ideas which our banner symbols and the country avows its own. It was a procession of colored men, women and children, a celebration of their deliverance from bondage and ostracism; a jubilee of freedom, a hosannah to their deliverers.

The celebration was projected and conducted by colored men. It met on the Citadel green at noon. Upward of ten thousand persons were present, colored men, women and children, and every window and balustrade overlooking the square was crowded with spectators. This immense gathering had been convened in 24 hours, for permission to form the procession was given only on Sunday night, and none of the preliminary arrangements were completed till Monday at noon.

. . . The procession began to move at one o'clock under the charge of a committee and marshalls on horseback, who were decorated with red, white and blue sashes and rosettes.

First came the marshals and their aid[e]s, followed by a band of music; then the 21st Regiment[35] in full form; then the clergymen of the different churches, carrying open Bibles; then an open car, drawn by four white horses, and tastefully adorned with National flags. In this car there were 15 colored ladies dressed in white, to represent the 15 recent Slave States. Each of them had a beautiful bouquet to present to Gen. Saxton after the speech which he was expected to deliver. A long procession of women followed the car. Then followed the children of the Public Schools, or part of them; and there were 1,800 in line, at least. They sang during the entire length of the march:

> John Brown's body lies a moulding in the grave,
> John Brown's body lies a moulding in the grave,
> John Brown's body lies a moulding in the grave,
> His soul is marching on!
> Glory! Glory! Glory! Hallelujah!
> Glory! Glory! Glory! Hallelujah!
> *We* go marching on!

This verse, however, was not nearly so popular as one which it was intended should be omitted, but rapidly supplanted all the others, until at last all along the mile or more of children, marching two abreast, no other sound could be heard than

We'll hang Jeff. Davis on a sour apple tree!
We'll hang Jeff. Davis on a sour apple tree!
We'll hang Jeff. Davis on a sour apple tree!
As we go marching on!

. . . Very few of these children had ever been at school before; not one of them had ever walked in a public procession; they had had only one hour's drill on their playground; and yet they kept in line, closed up, and were under perfect control and orderly up to the last. They only ceased to sing in order that they might cheer Gen. Saxton, Col. Woodford,[36] various groups of Union officers or sailors, or one or two Northern men whom they recognized as their friends. Gen. Saxton and lady were in a carriage at one street where the procession passed, and Col. Woodford and lady at another; and one continuous cheer greeted them, mingled with cheers for an officer whom they supposed to be Gen. Hatch.[37] The colored people know all these officers as their friends. Gen. Saxton is their favorite everywhere in the Department, and they have all learned that Gen. Hatch and Col. Woodford gave them equal rights in the public schools, an advantage which they prize next to freedom.

After the children came the various trades. First, the fishermen, with a banner bearing an emblematical device, and the words, "The Fishermen welcome you, Gen. Saxton." Second, a society with the banner, "The Union South." Third, carpenters, masons, teamsters, drovers, coopers, bakers, paper-carriers, barbers, blacksmiths, wood-sawyers, painters, wheelwrights, and the fire companies. The carpenters carried their planes and other tools; the masons their trowels; the teamsters their whips; the coopers their adzes; the bakers' crackers hung around their necks; the paper-carriers a banner, and each a copy of *The Charleston Courier;* the barbers their shears; the blacksmiths their hammers; the wood-sawyers their sawbucks; the painters their brushes; the wheel-wrights a large wheel; and the fire companies, ten in number, with their banners, their hosemen with their trumpets.

The most original feature of the procession was a large cart, drawn by two dilapidated horses with the worst harness that could be got to hold out, which followed the trades. On this cart there was an auctioneer's block, and a black man, with a bell, represented a negro trader, a red flag waving over his head; recalling the days so near and yet so far off, when human beings were made merchandise of in South Carolina. This man had himself been bought and sold several times and two women and a child who sat on the block had also been knocked down at public auction in Charleston. As the cart moved along, the mock-auctioneer rang his bell and cried out: *"How much am I offered for this good cook?" "She is an 'xlent cook, ge'men." "She can make four kinds of mock-turtle soup, from beef, fish or fowls." "*200's bid." "Two hundred?" "200's bid." "250,"*

"300," "350," "400," "450," "Who bids? who bids? 500." And so he went on imitating in sport the infernal traffic of which many of the spectators had been the living victims. Old women burst into tears as they saw this tableau, and forgetting that it was a mimic scene, shouted wildly, *Give me back my children! Give me back my children!* The wringing of hands seen on the sidewalks caused more than one looker-on to curse the policy that would even suggest the possibility that the wretches who had bought and sold loyal men might be or ought to be readmitted to the rights of citizenship. But there are people here who would even recommend that these persons alone should be regarded as citizens! There is no officer in all the United States who could stand up before the storm of righteous indignation which a fearless record of the lives of the oathtakers here would arouse. And that chronicle of crime is being made here. If ever they attempt to put down the true loyalists here, this record will be sent to THE TRIBUNE.

Behind the auction-car 60 men marched, tied to a rope, in imitation of the gangs who used often to be led through these streets on their way from Virginia to the sugar-fields of Louisiana. All of these men had been sold in the old times.

Then came the hearse, a comic feature which attracted great attention, and was received with shouts of laughter. There was written on it with chalk.

"Slavery is Dead."
"Who Owns Him?"
"No One."
"Sumter Dug His Grave on the 13th of April, 1861."

. . . Various societies were represented. The procession was more than two miles and a-half in length, and officers said that it marched in better military style than the great procession on the 6th of March in New-York. There was no drunkness, no riotous disposition, no insolent airs, no rudeness.

The banners bore among other mottoes, these sentences:

"We know no caste or color."
"The spirit of John Brown still lives."
"Liberty and Union, one and inseparable."
"Our past the Block, our future the School."
"We know no master but ourselves."
"We are filling the last ditch."
"Our reply to slavery, Colored Volunteers."
"Free Homes, Free Schools, One Country and One Flag."

. . . The great procession took one hour and twenty minutes to pass any point. On the return to the citadel where a stand was prepared for Gen. Saxton and the other speakers, there were at least 10,000 persons assembled. There were 4,200 men in the procession by count, exclusive of the military, the women and the children.

... Rev. Mr. French led in singing a doxology, and the great assembly dispersed in an orderly manner after enthusiastic and prolonged cheers for Gen. Saxton, the Yankees, the Star Spangled Banner, and a final, tumultuous and long continued three times three for Abraham Lincoln.

The fears so lately expressed that an outpouring of the colored people would produce a riot is thus shown to be unfounded. "Fear the slave who breaks his chain, free the slave and fears are vain," is a truth which these modern Rip Van Winkles who take the oath here and think that they are Union men do not yet begin to suspect, far less to believe.

CHAPTER 4

"All men are born free and equal"

THE ERA OF RECONSTRUCTION

■

4.1. South Carolina "Black Codes" (1865)

White legislators in South Carolina, seeking to retain control over the freedmen in the immediate wake of the Civil War, drafted special laws limiting the freedom of African Americans. The state's "Black Codes" were the most comprehensive in the South. Though the legislation did acknowledge a few rights of African Americans that had not been legally recognized previously, the overall effect of the laws was so patently restrictive that they were soon nullified by the federal military commander in the state. Their publication provoked an outcry in the North. In response, Congress appointed a special Joint Committee on Reconstruction to investigate conditions in the South and to determine whether the states of the former Confederacy were entitled to be represented in either house of Congress. ::

An Act Preliminary to the Legislation
Induced by the Emancipation of Slaves

Whereas the Convention of this State, by the Constitution lately ratified, did recognize the emancipation of slaves and declare that "neither slavery nor involuntary servitude, except as a punishment for crime, shall ever be re-established in this State," and did direct that, for each District in the State, there should be established an Inferior Court, to be styled "the District Court, which Court shall have jurisdiction of all civil causes wherein one or both of the parties are persons of color, and of all criminal causes wherein the accused in a person of color;" therefore . . .

Acts and Joint Resolutions of the General Assembly of the State of South Carolina, Passed at the Sessions of 1864–1865 (Columbia,S.C.: Julian A. Selby, 1866), 271–304.

III. All free negroes, mulattoes and mestizoes, all freedmen and freed-women, and all descendants through either sex of any of these persons, shall be known as persons of color, except that every such descendant, who may have of Caucasian blood seven-eights or more shall be deemed a white person.

IV. The Statutes and regulations concerning slaves are now inapplicable to persons of color; and although such persons are not entitled to social or political equality with white persons, they shall have the right to acquire, own and dispose of property; to make contracts; to enjoy the fruits of their labor; to sue and be sued; and to receive protection under the law in their persons and property.

V. All rights and remedies respecting persons or property, and all duties and liabilities under laws, civil and criminal, which apply to white persons, are extended to persons of color, subject to the modifications made by this Act and the other Acts before mentioned. . . .

An Act to Establish and Regulate the Domestic Relations of Persons of Color, and to Amend the Law in Relation to Paupers and Vagrancy

. . .

Husband and Wife

. . . I. The relation of husband and wife amongst persons of color is established.

II. Those who now live as such, are declared to be husband and wife. . . .

IV. Every colored child, heretofore born, is declared to be the legitimate child of his mother, and also of his colored father, if he is acknowledged by such a father. . . .

Parent and Child

XII. The relation of parent and child, amongst persons of color, is recognized, confers all the rights and remedies, civil and criminal, and imposes all the duties that are incident thereto by law. . . .

Contracts for Service

XXXV. All persons of color who make contracts for service or labor, shall be known as servants, and those with whom they contract, shall be known as masters. . . .

XL. Contracts between masters and servants may be set aside for fraud, notwithstanding they have been approved. . . .

Rights of Master as Between Himself and his Servant

L. When the servant shall depart from the service of the master without good cause, he shall forfeit the wages due to him. The servant shall obey all lawful orders of the master or his agent, and shall be honest, truthful, sober, civil and diligent in his business. The master may moderately correct servants who have made contracts, and are under eighteen years of age. . . .

House Servants and Others Not in Husbandry

... LXIX. Servants and apprentices employed as house servants in the various duties of the household, and in all the domestic duties of the family, shall, at all hours of the day and night, and on all days of the week, promptly answer all calls and obey and execute all lawful orders and commands of the family in whose service they are employed....

LXX. It is the duty of this class of servants to be especially civil and polite to their masters, their families and guests, and they shall receive gentle and kind treatment.

Mechanics, Artisans and Shop-Keepers

LXXII. No person of color shall pursue or practice the art, trade or business of an artisan, mechanic or shopkeeper, or other trade, employment or business (besides that of husbandry, or that of a servant under a contract for service or labor,) on his own account and for his own benefit, or in partnership with a white person, or as agent or servant of any person, until he shall have obtained a license therefor from the Judge of the District Court . . . and upon payment, by the applicant, to the Clerk of the District Court, of one hundred dollars, if a shopkeeper or pedlar, to be paid annually, and ten dollars, if a mechanic, artisan, or to engage in any other trade, also to be paid annually....

Vagrancy and Idleness

... XCVI. All persons who have not some fixed and known place of abode, and some lawful and reputable employment; those who have not some visible and known means of a fair, honest and reputable livelihood; all common prostitutes; those who are found wandering from place to place, vending, bartering or peddling any articles or commodities, without a license from the District Judge, or other proper authority; all common gamblers; persons who lead idle or disorderly lives, or keep or frequent disorderly or disreputable houses or places; those who, not having sufficient means of support, are able to work and do not work; those who (whether or not they own lands, or are lessees or mechanics,) do not provide a reasonable and proper maintenance for themselves and families; those who are engaged in representing, publicly or privately, for fee or reward, without license, any tragedy, interlude, comedy, farce, play or other similar entertainment, exhibition of the circus, sleight-of-hand, wax works, or the like; those who, for private gain, without license, give any concert or musical entertainment, of any description; fortune-tellers; sturdy beggars; common drunkards; those who hunt game of any description, or fish on the land of others, or frequent the premises, contrary to the will of the occupants, shall be deemed vagrants, and be liable to the punishment hereinafter prescribed.

XCVII. Upon information, on oath, of another, or upon his own knowledge, the District Judge, or a Magistrate, shall issue a warrant for the arrest of any person of color known or believed to be a vagrant, within the meaning of this Act . . . on conviction, the defendant shall be liable to imprisonment, and to hard labor, one or both, as shall be fixed by the verdict, not exceeding twelve months.

XCVIII. The defendant, if sentenced to hard labor after conviction, may, by order of the District Judge or Magistrate, before whom he was convicted, be hired for such wages as can be obtained for his services, to any owner or lessee of a farm, for the term of hard labor to which he was sentenced, or be hired for the same labor on the streets, public roads or public buildings. The person receiving such vagrant shall have all the rights and remedies for enforcing good conduct and diligence at labor that are herein provided in the case of master and servant. . . .

■

4.2. Address of the State Colored Convention to the White Inhabitants of South Carolina (1865)

Economic and political power in the South remained in the hands of the shaken but not fully vanquished former slaveholders well into 1866. With the apparent support of the President Johnson, this class attempted to reestablish its antebellum authority and subjugate African Americans, re-creating as nearly as possible the former system of chattel slavery. However, African American leaders acted collectively to press for and secure the freedom and rights of the emancipated slaves. The address reprinted here, written by Richard H. Cain,[1] was one of several public papers issuing from a convention of black South Carolinians who met in Charleston in late 1865 to similar effect. ::

Charleston, Nov. 25, 1865
A State Convention of the colored people of South Carolina met in Charleston on Monday of last week, closing its labors this morning. Delegates were in attendance from all parts of the State. Representative men were present—men whose sentiments would have commanded respect even in the North. Their deliberations have been marked by a degree of sagacity, calmness and earnest sincerity which has surprised their friends, and commanded the respect of even the most skeptical. . . . A candid world is bound to acknowledge its proceedings as the gravest exhibition of progressive ideas the State has ever known. . . .

Address of the State Convention to the
White Inhabitants of the State of South Carolina

Fellow-Citizens: We have here assembled as delegates representing the colored people of the State of South Carolina, in the capacity of a State Convention,

New York Daily Tribune, November 29, 1865.

to confer together and to deliberate upon our intellectual, moral, industrial, civil and political condition, and particularly our condition as affected by the great changes which have recently taken place in this State and throughout this whole country, to declare our sentiments, and to devise ways and means which may, through the blessing of God, tend to our improvement, elevation, and progress, fully believing that our cause is one which commends itself to the hearts of all good men throughout the civilized world; that it is the sacred cause of truth and righteousness; that it particularly appeals to those professing to be governed by that faith which teaches that "Whatsoever ye would that men should do unto you, do ye even so to them."

These principles we conceive to embody the great duty of man to his fellow man; and as men we only ask to be included in the practical application of this principle. We feel that the *justness* of our cause is a sufficient apology for our cause at this time.

Heretofore we have had no avenues opened to us or our children. We have had no firesides that we might call our own—none of those incentives to work for the development of our minds and the aggrandizement of our race in common with other people. The measures which have been devised for the development of white men, women and children have been denied to us. The laws which have made white men powerful have degraded us, because we were black and because we were reduced to the condition of chattels. But now that we are freemen—now that we are elevated, by the Providence of God, to manhood, we have resolved to stand up, and like men, speak and act for ourselves. We fully recognize the truth of the maxim. "The gods help those who help themselves."

In making this appeal to you, we adopt the language of the immortal Declaration of Independence: that "all men are created equal," and that "life, liberty, and the pursuit of happiness," are the right of all; that taxation and representation should go together; that governments are ordained to protect, and not to subvert, the rights of men, that the Constitution of the United States was framed to establish justice, to promote the general welfare, and to secure the blessing of liberty to all the people of the land; that resistance to tyrants is obedience to God, are all American principles and maxims, and, taken together, they form the constructive elements of the American Government.

We think we fully comprehend and duly appreciate the principles and measures which compose this platform; and all we desire or ask for is to be placed in a position that we could conscientiously and legitimately defend, with you, those principles against the surges of despotism to the last drop of our blood. We have not come together in battle array to assume a boastful attitude and to talk loudly of high-sounding principles, or of unmeaning platitudes; nor do we pretend to any great boldness; for we remember your former wealth, and greatness, and we know our poverty and weakness; and although we feel keenly our wrongs, still we come together, we trust, in a spirit of meekness and of patriotic good-will toward all the people of the State. But yet it is some consolation to know, (and it inspires us with hope when we reflect) that our cause is not alone the cause of four millions of black men in this country, but we are intensely alive to the fact that it is also the cause of millions of oppressed men in other "parts of God's beautiful earth," who are now struggling to be free in the fullest sense of the word and God and nature are pledged to their triumph. We are American by birth, and we assure you that we are Americans in feeling, and in spite of all the wrongs which we have so long and silently endured in this country, we can yet exclaim, with a full heart, "O, America, with all thy faults we love thee still!"

. . . Thus we would address you—not as Rebels and enemies, but as friends and fellow countrymen, who desire to dwell among you in peace, and whose destinies are interwoven and linked with those of the whole American people, and hence must be fulfilled in this country. As descendants of a race feeble and long-oppressed, we might with propriety appeal to a great and magnanimous people like the American for special favor and encouragement, on the principle that the strong should aid the weak, and that the learned should teach the unlearned. But it is for no such purpose that we raise our voices to the people of South Carolina on this occasion. We ask for no special privileges, or peculiar favors. We ask only for *even-handed justice,* for the removal of such positive obstructions and disabilities as past and recent legislation has thrown in our way and heaped upon us. Without any just cause or provocation on our part, we, by the action of your Convention[2] and Legislature, have, with few exceptions, been virtually excluded—

First: from the rights of citizenship, which you cheerfully accord to strangers, notwithstanding we have been born and reared in your midst, and were faithful while your greatest trials were upon you, and have done nothing since which could justly merit your disapprobation.

Second: We are denied the right of giving our testimony in the Courts of the State, in consequence of which our persons and property are subject, the former to every species of violence and insult, and the latter to fraud and spoliation without redress.

Third: We are also, by the present laws, not only denied the right of citizenship—the inestimable right of choosing who shall rule over us in the land of our birth, but by the so-called "Black Code" we are deprived of the rights which are vouch-safed to the lowest white profligate in the country—the right to engage in any legitimate business save under such unjust restraints as are imposed upon no other class of people in the State.

Fourth: You have, by legislative action, placed barriers in the way of our improvement in the arts and sciences. You have given us little or no encouragement to engage in agricultural pursuits, by refusing to sell us lands, while you are organizing societies to bring foreigners into the country. The clear intent of which is to thrust us out, or reduce us to a serfdom intolerable to us, and as you will find in the end, ruinous to your own prosperity.

Fifth: Your public journals wickedly charge us with destroying the products of the country since we have been made free, when they know that the country, and the products thereof, were destroyed by a desolating war of four years, in which we had no hand. How unjust to charge upon the innocent and helpless the very crimes which yourselves have committed, and which brought down ruin upon your own heads!

Sixth: We simply ask that we shall be recognized as *men;* that there be no obstructions placed in our way; that the same laws which govern *white men* shall govern *black men;* that we have the right of trial by a jury of our *peers;* that schools be established for the education of *colored children* as well as *white,* and that the advantages of both colors shall, in this respect, be *equal;* that no impediments be put in the way of our acquiring homesteads for ourselves and our people; that, in short, we be dealt with as others are—in equity and justice.

Seventh: We claim that we deserve the confidence and good will of all classes of men. We ask that the same opportunities be extended to us that freemen have a right to demand at the hands of their fellow-citizens. We desire the growth and prosperity of this State, and the well-being of *all* men, and we would be found ever struggling to elevate ourselves and add to the glory of the national character. We trust that the day is not far distant when you will acknowledge that our progress in social, intellectual, moral, and religious development entitles us to the highest commendation and respect, and that we shall be worthy to occupy with the best in the land positions of trust and power; when we shall realize the great truth that "all men are endowed, by their Creator with certain inalienable rights" and that although complexions may differ, "a man's a man for a' that."[3]

■

4.3. Freedmen's Bureau Marriage Rules (1866)

Slave marriages did not have legal standing, nor did they protect families from the abuses and caprice of slave owners. Upon emancipation, one of the first actions many enslaved couples took was to have their marriage relations formalized. General O. O. Howard, commissioner of the Freedman's Bureau, issued orders to his assistant commissioners on the conditions for solemnizing and recording former slave marriages. ::

General Order No. 14
Hd. Qrs. Asst. Commissioner
Bureau R.F. & A.L. South Carolina
Charleston, 1866

Marriage Rules

Section 1: Parties Eligible to Marriage

1. All male persons of the age of eighteen and having never been married; and all females of the age of fourteen or sixteen, and having never been married, shall be eligible to marriage.

2. All persons having been married, who shall furnish satisfactory evidence of either the marriage or divorce, or death of all former companions, will be eligible to marriage again.

3. All married persons producing satisfactory evidence of separation from their companions against their wishes, and for cases not under their control for a period of two years, and that they have no evidence that they are alive; or if alive, that they will ever forcibly be restored to them, may marry again.

Section 2: Parties Authorized to Grant Permits for Marriages

1. Ordained ministers of the Gospel are authorized to give permits of marriage.

2. Any un-ordained preacher of the Gospel with two male members of his church, whom he may select, or, if he forfeit, two such male members as his church may appoint shall constitute a committee authorized to grant permits for marriage, provided in all cases, satisfactory evidence be furnished.

First—that the parties are both of lawful age and that neither has never been married.

Second—that if either, or both have been married, that such party has complied with the conditions of Section 1, rules 2 & 3.

Magistrates and any other persons authorized by the State to grant permits of marriage, or to solemnize the same are requested to conform their action, so far as may be practicable, to the rules herein adopted.

Marriages to be legal must be solemnized by:

First. Ordained ministers of the Gospel, or

Second. Such Civil Magistrates as are authorized by the laws of the State.

Section 3: Commission for Dissolving Marriage Agreements

1. A Commission for dissolving marriage agreements may be formed as follows: The parties desiring a separation shall first jointly choose a minister of some church, who shall act as chairman. Each party shall then select a man to serve with him, and these three persons so chosen shall constitute the commission.

2. If only one party sue for a separation, the other party being absent, or if present, refusing to take any action in the appointment of the commission, then the party suing shall select the minister as before provided, and action shall also choose a man to act with him. The minister thus chosen shall select a third man to constitute the commission. The said applicant shall in all cases furnish to the commission evidence of notification of the proceeding to the other party when present, or if absent, that reasonable effort has been made to notify such party of the proceedings in the case.

3. The Commission may at the request of either party, or of any one of its own members, select two other persons to serve in the Commission.

4. The Commission after hearing the complaints & evidence offered by the party or parties complaining shall give its decision, which shall be accepted as final, and the parties shall be required to comply therewith.

5. It is further provided that any church having provisions, rules and regulations of its own adoption for dissolving marriage agreements may be applied to, by any parties, and the decision of the church, in all such cases shall be accepted and complied with by the parties.

Section 4: Causes for Dissolving Marriage Agreements

1. For adultery or for fornication proven against either party.

2. If after a willful and protracted absence a former wife refuses, upon application made by the husband, to renew her marriage relations with him, he may ask for a release from said wife, by a Commission which shall be formed as provided for in Section 3, Rule 2. If after due notice given by the Commission to the wife so refusing, she fail to show any moral or legal objection as provided for in these regulations to the renewal of her former marriage relations with him; the Commission shall grant to the man a release from all his obligations to her as his wife, and for the support of all her children by him.

3. If a man refuses to renew his marriage relations with a former wife, she may appeal to a Commission, which shall be formed as provided for in Section 3, Rule 2. If the husband fail to prove any moral or legal objection to the renewal of their marriage relations, then the Commission shall grant her a release from all her obligation to him as her husband.

4. The Commission shall be further authorized to give such direction for the custody and support of any children of parties so separated as under the particular circumstances may seem proper.

5. No future marriages, duly solemnized, may be dissolved by the provisions of these rules except for either adultery or fornication clearly proven. It being understood in all cases, that the party proved guilty of adultery or fornication (either of these crimes) for which the divorce shall have been granted, shall not be eligible to marriage again.

Section 5: First Marriages and Re-Unions

1. The marriage of all parties being together as husband and wife at the time of obtaining their freedom, or solemnized since obtaining it, will be acknowledged as legal and binding.

2. All parties whose marriage was only a mutual agreement between themselves, with no public form of ceremony, are required to have their marriage confirmed by a Minister or Magistrate, and obtain a certificate of the same.

3. No parties having agreed to enter the marriage relation will be allowed to live together as husband and wife until their marriage has been legally solemnized.

4. All parties claiming to have been married but separated by the War or other causes and having no certificate of their marriage must obtain from some ordained Minister or Magistrate a permit for their reunion before they will be allowed to live together as husband and wife.

Duties of Husbands to Former Wifes

1. A wife when restored by freedom to her husband, if he be living with another, shall be received by him as his lawful wife except for moral causes as provided in Section 4, Rule 1.

2. If a man living without a wife find two wives restored to him by freedom, the one having children by him and the other not, he shall take the mother of his children as his lawful wife unless he show cause as provided in Section 4, Rule 1.

3. If a man living without a wife shall refuse to renew the marriage relation with a former wife restored by freedom who may desire such renewal, there being no moral or legal objection to the same proven by him, he shall be held responsible for the support of such wife and also of all his children by her so long as they remain minor.

4. The man failing for want of cause proven to obtain a release from renewing his marriage relations with a former wife, will be allowed to marry another woman so long as such wife may live, or until for just cause, she shall have married another.

5. Every man marrying a woman having children shall be responsible for their protection and support so long as they are minors, or until their marriage provided they have no other means of support.

Section 6: Certificates of Marriage and Separation

1. Ministers shall furnish each couple married by them with a certificate giving the name, age and residence of each party, with the date of the marriage.

2. Certificates shall be given to both persons, if present, whose marriage

agreement is dissolved. Such certificates shall be signed by the Chairman of the Commission.

3. There being no provision by the State for recording certificates of marriages dissolved, it is recommend that all Commissions keep an accurate and carefully preserved record of the same.

4. Ordained ministers are authorized to give certificates to parties married since obtaining their freedom if they have no official evidence of the same, provided such parties furnish satisfactory evidence of their marriage. Returns of all such certificates for public record will be required as in all other cases.

5. Every Freedman having only one name is required to assume a "title" or family name. It may be the name of any other person. When once assumed, it must always thereafter be used and no other. . . .

■

4.4. Cardozo's Speech Advocating Land Redistribution (1868)

Francis L. Cardozo (1836–1903) was born free in Charleston and later attended the University of Glasgow. He was named principal of the Avery Institute in Charleston after the Civil War and also entered into politics as a delegate to the state Constitutional Convention in 1868. Later during Reconstruction, he was elected South Carolina secretary of state and state treasurer. The speech printed here is from the 1868 Convention, where he notably advocated the redistribution of lands and opposed the "stay law," an act to protect large plantations from being seized and sold for debt. ::

. . . I regard any stay law as unjust and unconstitutional. It is unjust to the creditors. Let every man who contracts a debt, pay for it. If he is an honest man he will pay his debts at any sacrifice. In our country it is unfortunate, as Americans, that we have a character by no means enviable as repudiators. Look at the attempt to repudiate the national debt. As an American, I protest against any further repudiation whatever, either in the form of a stay law or illegal legislation. I deem it inappropriate for us to touch the matter at all. We are sent here to form a Constitution. To travel outside of our proper province, will probably be to incur odium, displeasure and dissatisfaction. I wish to confine the action of this Convention to its proper sphere. The first question that arises is, what claim have these debtors on our sympathies more than creditors? Are the debtors greater in number than the creditors? If we legislate in favor of any, will it be doing the greatest good to the greatest number? I maintain it will not. It is a class measure. This will be but the beginning. We will be burdened with

Proceedings of the Constitutional Convention of South Carolina, Held at Charleston, S.C., Beginning January 14th and Ending March 17, 1868, vol. 1 (Charleston, S.C.: Denny and Perry, 1868), 116–18.

applications, and the burden will be upon those who introduced the measure, not upon those who refused to legislate for other special favorite classes. I ask not only what are the claims of the debtors, but also what are the nature of these sales? Was it the transfer of real estate? I think everyone here will say no. Nine tenths of the debts were contracted for the sale of slaves. I do not wish we should go one inch out of the way to legislate either for the buyer or the seller. They dealt in that kind of property, they knew its precarious tenure, and therefore let them suffer. When the war commenced every rebel sold his property to give money to a common cause. And their slaves were sold for the same object, to maintain a war waged for the purpose of perpetually enslaving a people. That was the object. The ladies of the South stripped themselves of their jewels, and the men sold their lands and their slaves for that object. Now, let them suffer for it. As the gentleman from Charleston[4] very ably said, "they have cast the die, let them take their chances." There is also another reason, and one of the strongest, why the Convention should not take any action on the subject, but postpone it indefinitely. One of the greatest bulwarks of slavery was the infernal plantation system, one man owning his thousand, another his twenty, and another fifty thousand acres of land. This is the only way by which we will break up that system and I maintain that our freedom will be of no effect if we allow it to continue. What is the main cause of the prosperity of the North? It is because every man has his own farm and is free and independent. Let the lands of the South be similarly divided. I would not say for one moment they should be confiscated, but if sold to maintain the war, now that slavery is destroyed, let the plantation system go with it. We will never have true freedom until we abolish the system of agriculture which existed in the Southern states. It is useless to have any schools while we maintain this stronghold of slavery as the agricultural system of the country. The gentleman has said that if these plantations are sold now, they would pass into the hands of a few mercenary speculators. I deny it and challenge a single proof to sustain the assertion. On the contrary I challenge proof to show that if the plantations are not sold, the old plantation masters will part them. If they are sold, though a few mercenary speculators may purchase some, the chances are that the colored man and the poor man would be the purchasers. I will prove this, not by mere assertion, but by facts. About one hundred poor colored men of Charleston met together and formed themselves into a Charleston Land Company. They subscribed for a number of shares at $10 per share, one dollar payable monthly. They have been meeting for a year. Yesterday they purchased six hundred acres of land for $6,600 that would have sold for $25,000 or $50,000 in better times. They would not have been able to buy it had not the owner through necessity been compelled to sell. This is only one instance of thousands of others that have oc-curred in this city and state. I look upon it, therefore, as the natural result of the war that this system of large plantations, of no service to the owner or anybody else, should be abolished. I think Providence has not only smiled upon every effort for abolishing this hideous form of slavery, but that since the war it has given unmistakable signs of disapprobation wherever continued, by blasting the cotton crops in that part of the country. Men are now beginning not to plant cotton but grain for food, and in doing so they are establishing a system of small farms, by which not only my race, but the poor whites and ninety-nine hundredths of the other thousands will be benefited. The real benefit from this legislation would inhere to not more than thirty thousand landholders against the 700,000 poor people of the State. If we are to legislate in favor of a class at all, any honest man, any man who has the interest of the people at heart will legislate in favor of the great number. In speaking against the landholders, and in taking this position I do not cherish one feeling of enmity against them as a class or individuals. But this question takes a larger range and is one in which the whole country is involved. I can never sacrifice the interests of nine or ten millions to the interests of 300,000, more especially when the 300,000 initiated the war and were the very ones who established and infernal Negro code and want to keep their lands until better times. They do not want that a nigger or a Yankee shall ever own a foot of their land. Now is the time to take the advantage. Give them an opportunity, breathing time, and they will reorganize the same old system they had before the war. I say, then, just as General Grant said when he had Lee hemmed in around Petersburg, now is the time to strike, and in doing so we will strike for our people and posterity, and the truest interest of our country.

■

4.5. The South Carolina Constitution (1868)

Because many South Carolina whites had either been disfranchised because of their participation in the rebellion or avoided the election in an attempt to forestall a new constitutional convention, delegates to the convention of 1868 were largely African Americans and nonnative whites. Accordingly, the document they adopted was a radical departure from the conservative constitution of 1865 and previous versions and was a model of racial inclusion and democratic ideals. ::

We, the People of the State of South Carolina, in Convention—assembled, Grateful to Almighty God for this opportunity, deliberately and peaceably of entering into a explicit and solemn compact with each other, and forming a

The Constitution of South Carolina, Adopted April 16, 1868, and the Acts and Joint Resolutions of the General Assembly, Passed at the Special Session of 1868, Together with the Military Orders Therein Reenacted (Columbia, S.C.: John W. Denny, 1868).

new Constitution of civil Government for ourselves and posterity, recognizing the necessity of the protection of the people in all that pertains to their freedom, safety and tranquility, and imploring the direction of the Great Legislator of the Universe, do agree upon,—ordain and establish the following Declaration of the Rights and Form of Government as the Constitution of the Commonwealth of South Carolina.

ARTICLE I.

Declaration of Rights.

Section 1. All men are born free and equal—endowed by their Creator with certain inalienable rights, among which are the rights of enjoying and defending their lives and liberties, of acquiring, possessing and protecting property, and of seeking and obtaining their safety and happiness.

Section 2. Slavery shall never exist in this State; neither shall involuntary servitude, except as a punishment for crime, whereof the party shall have been duly convicted.

Section 3. All political power is vested in and derived from the people only; therefore they have the right, at all times, to modify their form of government in such manner as they may deem expedient, when the public good demands.

Section 4. Every citizen of this State owes paramount allegiance to the Constitution and Government of the United States, and no law or ordinance of this State in contravention or subversion thereof can have any binding force.

Section 5. This State shall ever remain a member of the American Union, and all attempts, from whatever source, or upon whatever pretext, to dissolve the said Union, shall be resisted with the whole power of the State. . . .

Section 31. All elections shall be free and open, and every inhabitant of this Commonwealth possessing the qualifications provided for in this Constitution shall have an equal right to elect officers and be elected to fill public office.

Section 32. No property qualification shall be necessary for an election to or the holding of any office, and no office shall be created, the appointment to which shall be for a longer time than good behavior. After the adoption of this Constitution, any person who shall fight a duel, or send or accept a challenge for that purpose, or be an aider or abettor in fighting a duel, shall be deprived of holding any office of honor or trust in this State, and shall be otherwise punished as the law shall prescribe. . . .

Section 34. Representation shall be apportioned according to population, and no person in this State shall be disfranchised or deprived of any of the rights or privileges now enjoyed, except by the law of the land or the judgment of his peers. . . .

ARTICLE VIII.

Right of Suffrage.

Section 1. In all elections by the people the electors shall vote by ballot.

Section 2. Every male citizen of the United States, of the age of twenty-one years and upwards, not laboring under the disabilities named in this Constitution, without distinction of race, color, or former condition, who shall be a resident of this State at the time of the adoption of this Constitution, or who shall thereafter reside in this State one year, and in the County in which he offers to vote sixty days next preceding any election, shall be entitled to vote for all officers that are now, or hereafter may be, elected by the people, and upon all questions submitted to the electors at any elections; Provided, That no person shall be allowed to vote or hold office who is now or hereafter may be disqualified therefor by the Constitution of the United States, until such disqualification shall be removed by the Congress of the United States; Provided, further, That no person, while kept in any alms house or asylum, or of unsound mind, or confined in any public prison, shall be allowed to vote or hold office. . . .

Section 8. The General Assembly shall never pass any law that will deprive any of the citizens of this State of the right of suffrage, except for treason, murder, robbery, or dueling, whereof the person shall have been duly tried and convicted. . . .

ARTICLE X.

Education.

. . .

Section 3. The General Assembly shall, as soon as practicable after the adoption of this Constitution, provide for a liberal and uniform system of free public schools throughout the State, and shall also make provision for the division of the State into suitable school districts. There shall be kept open at least six months in each year one or more schools in each school district. . . .

Section 9. The General Assembly shall provide for the maintenance of the State University, and, as soon as practicable, provide for the establishment of an Agricultural College. . . .

Section 10. All the public schools, colleges and universities of this State, supported in whole or in part by the public funds, shall be free and open to all the children and youths of the State, without regard to race or color. . . .

ARTICLE XIII.

Militia.

Section 1. The militia of this State shall consist of all able-bodied male citizens of the State between the ages of eighteen and forty-five years, except such persons as are now, or may hereafter be, exempted by the laws of the United States, or who may be adverse to bearing arms, as provided for in this Constitution; and shall be organized, armed, equipped and disciplined as the General Assembly may by law provide.

Section 2. The Governor shall have power to call out the militia to execute the laws, repel invasion, repress insurrection, and preserve the public peace.

Section 3. There shall be an Adjutant and Inspector-General elected by the qualified electors of the State, at the same time and in the same manner as other State officers, who shall rank as a Brigadier-General, and whose duties and compensation shall be prescribed by law. The Governor shall appoint, by and with the advice and consent of the Senate, such other staff officers as the General Assembly may direct. . . .

■

4.6. Reports of Outrages Committed by Whites Against Freedmen (1866–1868)

Among the many tasks for which the Freedman's Bureau was responsible were investigating and maintaining records of "outrages" perpetrated by whites against freedmen. ::

Report of Outrages Committed by Whites Against Freedmen in the Bureau District of Greenville, S.C. During the Month of December 1866

Name of offender: David Alison (Laurens District). *Name of Person injured:* Sally Charles. *Date of outrage:* Dec. 13th 1866. *Place Where committed:* Robert Scott's on the road from Greenville C. H. to Laurens, near the border line of Greenville & Laurens districts. *Nature of injury:* tying, beating 30 blows with a hickory with & driving from the neighborhood. *Remarks:* case just reported to this office. Referred Dec. 29th for investigation to Doct. Dunhlin Moore, Magistrate Greenville Dist. No report received. . . .

By whom committed: Calhoun Nichols, white. *On whom committed:* Clara Anderson, colored. *Place:* Greenville, S. C. *Outrage committed:* assault & battery. *Remarks:* Calhoun Nichols, a mere boy, was, May 25.67, quarreling with Clara Anderson, a colored girl, because she would not call him "Mr. Nichols," he, however, calling her "Clara." Both were engaged in cleaning a church in Greenville. Clara Anderson persisted in calling him "Calhoun," whereupon he

Records of the Assistant Commissioner for the State of South Carolina, Bureau of Refugees, Freedmen, and Abandoned Lands, 1865–1870, National Archives Publication M869, Roll 34, "Reports of Murders and Outrages."

struck her. I had him arrested and bought before a Magistrate, but in consideration of his youth and the fact that he begged Clara Anderson's pardon, paid her ten dollars damages and the Magistrate's costs, I allowed the case to be dropped, warning him however that he had no right to call other people, not in his employ, by their Christian names and require them to address him as a Master. . . .

Report of Outrages Committed by Whites Against
Freedmen in Abbeville District, SO. CA.
During the Month of June 1868

Name of offender: T. E. Bowie, acting constable, & Saml. Mundy, John H. Mundy, George Lomax & Andrew Stevenson. *Date of outrage:* 30th May 68, 10 o'clock P. M. *Persons injured:* Rachel Foster & Randal her son, a minor. *Nature of injury:* under an unlawful warrant issued by James McCaslan J. P. by direction of Mr. Hartar, broke into her house and by force of arms took her son back to Mr. Stevenson who claimed to be his employer. *Where committed:* Abbeville Dist. *Remarks:* released the boy from contract with Mr. Stevenson, unwittingly signed by him without the cognizance of his mother. Outrage referred to the civil authorities and not heard since heard from. . . .

Report of Outrages Committed by Whites Against
Freedmen in Abbeville County, SO. CA.
During the Month of July 1868

. . . *Name of offender:* Alfred Blackwell. *Date of outrage:* 22nd July. *Person injured:* Lizzie Blackwell. Nature of injury: choked and otherwise abused her. *Where committed:* Abbeville District. *Remarks:* referred to Squire Giles & not yet heard from.

Name of offender: Mr. C. L. Cason. *Date of outrage:* 19th July. *Person injured:* Jr. McIntosh. Nature of injury: beat him severely & sent him to jail on charge of attempt at rape on sister. *Where committed:* Abbeville District. *Remarks:* Warrant issued against Cason by Squire McCord on failure of Squire Sharp because Plaintiff had no land & could not give white security to prosecute. . . .

Name of offender: John Godman. *Date of outrage:* 20th July. *Person injured:* Elsie Ritchie. Nature of injury: beat her severely. *Where committed:* Abbeville District. *Remarks:* referred to Squire Tarrant & not yet heard from. . . .

Name of offender: Geo. Marvin. *Date of outrage:* 15th July. *Person injured:* Foley Huckerby. Nature of injury: beat her. *Where committed:* Abbeville District. *Remarks:* returned to Squire Giles who had refused to act. . . .

Name of offender: John Ridge. *Date of outrage:* 12th July. *Person injured:* Chas. Plumber. Nature of injury: beat him about ½ hour. *Where committed:* Abbeville District. *Remarks:* referred to Squire Jas. McCaslan & not heard from. . . .

Law Diploma of Richard Henry Greener, first African American professor at the University of South Carolina as well as the first black graduate of its Law School (1876). Courtesy of the University of South Carolina University Archives.

Report of Outrages Committed by Whites Against Freedmen In Abbeville County, SO. CA.
During the Month of August 1868

... *Name of offender:* Nat Haynes. *Date of outrage:* 13th July. *Person injured:* Geo. Alexander. Nature of injury: assaulted him for being a Republican. *Where committed:* Abbeville County. *Remarks:* dropped by Plaintiff. ...

Name of offender: Caroline Mays. *Date of outrage:* 17th Aug. *Person injured:* Sallie Moore. Nature of injury: assault & battery. *Where committed:* Abbeville C. H. *Remarks:* <u>Plaintiff</u> placed under recognizance by Squire McCord, but warrant <u>not served</u> on Defendant.

Name of offender: Geo. Miller. *Date of outrage:* 22nd Aug. *Person injured:* Geo. Webb. Nature of injury: in his absence tore down the house occupied under contract for the year. *Where committed:* Abbeville County. *Remarks:* referred to Squire Sharp & not heard from. . . .

Report of Outrages Committed by Whites Against Freedmen In Abbeville County, SO. CA. During the Month of September 1868

Name of offender: Blackwell, Wm. Harman & 10 others unknown. *Date of outrage:* 19th April. *Person injured:* Henry Moore, Nelson Martin, Moses Martin, Josh Wardlaw. *Nature of injury:* broke into their houses at night, smashed their guns, stripped, whipped & shot at them &c. because they were Radicals. *Where committed:* Abbeville County. *Remarks:* Case of Wardlaw ref'd to Squire McCord some time ago & nothing done. Others sent to Squire J. McCaslan who has not as yet done anything. Offenders said to live in Edgefield. . . .

Name of offender: Robin Gilmore. *Date of outrage:* 16th Sept. *Person injured:* Lavinia White. Nature of injury: beat her & she being with child tried to strike her on the abdomen with a hoe. *Where committed:* Abbeville County. *Remarks:* referred to Squire J. McCaslan and not heard from. . . .

Name of offender: Wm. Talbert. *Date of outrage:* 4th Sept. *Person injured:* Jeff Buchanan. Nature of injury: shot him dead in field. *Where committed:* Abbeville County. *Remarks:* no complaint from relatives & no action taken that is known of.

Name of offender: John Thompson & Thos. Quarles. *Date of outrage:* 9th Sept. *Person injured:* Mans Calhoun. Nature of injury: locked him in store and gave him over 100 lashes. *Where committed:* Abbeville C. H. *Remarks:* no complaint. . . .

Report of Outrages Committed by Whites Against Freedmen In Abbeville County, SO. CA. During the Month of November 1868

Name of offender: Boozer, Tom Arnold, Gus Aiken & Bill Monday. *Date of outrage:* Novbr. 2nd. *Person injured:* name not known. Nature of injury: broke into his house at night & violently destroyed Republican Tickets which he had for distribution next day. *Where committed:* near Cokesburg. *Remarks:* case in the hands of the Dept. State Constable.

Name of offender: K. K. K. *Date of outrage:* October 28th. *Person injured:* Frank Talbert. Nature of injury: was stopped on the road at night & made to swear that he would vote the Democratic ticket. *Where committed:* neighborhood of "Childs Box." *Remarks:* reported to Dep. State Constable for the county. . . .

Name of offender: K. K. K. *Date of outrage:* (blank). *Person injured:* innumerable. Nature of injury: have been lying out in the woods since some time before the election to save being murdered in their beds, their houses having in the mean time been frequently visited at night for that purpose. *Where committed:* Long Cane, Gold Mine & outer regions. *Remarks:* reported to Dep. State Constable for the county.

Name of offender: Dr. Moses Taggart, Joe Cannaday, John Butler, Geo. Hughes, Harvey Ragan, Jim Briscoe, —— Collison & many others names unknown. *Date of outrage:* Novbr. 3rd. *Person injured:* Anthony Marshall, Washington Green, Dick Brady, Wade Hamilton, Jackson Griffin, Reuben Watson, Allen Goode. *Nature of injury:* Anthony Marshall killed, Green, Brady, Hamilton, Griffin & Watson wounded, Goode beaten, at a riot instigated by Taggart & participated in by the others, whereby the Freedmen were prevented from voting on that place. *Where committed:* White Hall. *Remarks:* reported to Dep. State. Constable for the County. Reported also to Hd. Qts. with the exception of the names of Griffin & Watson, not previously reported....

Name of offender: various parties. *Date of outrage:* Oct. & Nov. *Person injured:* innumerable. *Nature of injury:* were prevented from voting by violence & threats of violence—it being in most instances publicly declared that death would be visited on any one who attempted to vote the Republican ticket. *Where committed* (blank). *Remarks:* the names of all parties as far as known handed in to the Dep. St. Constable....

■

4.7. Robert Brown Elliott on the Civil Rights Bill (1874)

Between stints in the state General Assembly, Robert Brown Elliott (1842–1884) won election to Congress in 1870. His most memorable speech in Washington, reprinted here, was in defense of a civil rights bill proposed by Senator Charles Sumner of Massachusetts. Elliott was responding directly to Alexander Stephens, former vice president of the Confederacy, an outspoken white supremacist. Observers agreed that the black politician got the better of the Georgian. ::

While I am sincerely grateful for this high mark of courtesy that has been accorded to me by this House, it is a matter of regret to me that it is necessary at this day that I should rise in the presence of an American Congress to advocate a bill which simply asserts equal rights and equal public privileges for all classes

Reprinted in *Masterpieces of Negro Eloquence: The Best Speeches Delivered by the Negro from the Days of Slavery to the Present Time,* ed. Alice Moore Dunbar (New York: Bookery, 1914), 667–88.

of American citizens. I regret, sir, that the dark hue of my skin may lend a color to the imputation that I am controlled by motives personal to myself in my advocacy of this great measure of national justice. Sir, the motive that impels me is restricted by no such narrow boundary, but is as broad as your Constitution. I advocate it, sir, because it is right. . . .

The Negro, true to that patriotism and love of country that have ever marked and characterized his history on this continent, came to the aid of the Government in its efforts to maintain the Constitution. To that Government he now appeals; that Constitution he now invokes for protection against outrage and unjust prejudices founded upon caste.

But, sir, we are told by the distinguished gentleman from Georgia (Mr. Stephens)[5] that Congress has no power under the Constitution to pass such a law, and that the passage of such an act is in direct contravention of the rights of the States. I cannot assent to any such proposition. The Constitution of a free government ought always to be construed in favor of human rights. Indeed, the thirteenth, fourteenth, and fifteenth amendments, in positive words, invest Congress with the power to protect the citizen in his civil and political rights. Now, sir, what are civil rights? Rights natural, modified by civil society. . . .

Are we then, sir, with the amendments to our constitution staring us in the face; with these grand truths of history before our eyes; with innumerable wrongs daily inflicted upon five million citizens demanding redress, to commit this question to the diversity of legislation? . . .

But the Slaughter-house cases!—The Slaughter-house cases![6]

The honorable gentleman from Kentucky,[7] always swift to sustain the failing and dishonored cause of proscription, rushes forward and flaunts in our faces the decision of the Supreme Court of the United States in the Slaughterhouse cases, and in that act he has been willingly aided by the gentleman from Georgia. Hitherto, in the contests which have marked the progress of the cause of equal civil rights, our opponents have appealed sometimes to custom, sometimes to prejudice, more often to pride of race, but they have never sought to shield themselves behind the Supreme Court. But now for the first time, we are told that we are barred by a decision of that court, from which there is no appeal. If this be true we must stay our hands. The cause of equal civil rights must pause at the command of a power whose edicts must be obeyed till the fundamental law of our country is changed.

Has the honorable gentleman from Kentucky considered well the claim he now advances? If it were not disrespectful I would ask, has he ever read the decision which he now tells us is an insuperable barrier to the adoption of this great measure of justice?

In the consideration of this subject, has not the judgment of the gentleman from Georgia been warped by the ghost of the dead doctrines of States-rights?

Has he been altogether free from prejudices engendered by long training in that school of politics that well-nigh destroyed this Government?

Mr. Speaker, I venture to say here in the presence of the gentleman from Kentucky, and the gentleman from Georgia, and in the presence of the whole country, that there is not a line or word, not a thought or dictum even, in the decision of the Supreme Court in the great Slaughter-house cases, which casts a shadow of doubt on the right of Congress to pass the pending bill, or to adopt such other legislation as it may judge proper and necessary to secure perfect equality before the law to every citizen of the Republic. Sir, I protest against the dishonor now cast upon our Supreme Court by both the gentleman from Kentucky and the gentleman from Georgia. In other days, when the whole country was bowing beneath the yoke of slavery, when press, pulpit, platform, Congress and courts felt the fatal power of the slave oligarchy, I remember a decision of that court which no American now reads without shame and humiliation.[8] But those days are past; the Supreme Court of to-day is a tribunal as true to freedom as any department of this Government, and I am honored with the opportunity of repelling a deep disgrace which the gentleman from Kentucky, backed and sustained as he is by the gentleman from Georgia, seeks to put upon it. . . .

The amendments in the Slaughter-house cases one and all, are thus declared to have as their all-pervading design and ends the security of the recently enslaved race, not only their nominal freedom, but their complete protection from those who had formerly exercised unlimited dominion over them. It is in this broad light that all these amendments must be read, the purpose to secure the perfect equality before the law of all citizens of the United States. What you give to one class you must give to all, what you deny to one class you shall deny to all, unless in the exercise of the common and universal police power of the State, you find it needful to confer exclusive privileges on certain citizens, to be held and exercised still for the common good of all.

Such are the doctrines of the Slaughter-house cases—doctrines worthy of the Republic, worthy of the age, worthy of the great tribunal which thus loftily and impressively enunciates them. . . .

Now, sir, recurring to the venerable and distinguished gentleman from Georgia (Mr. Stephens) who has added his remonstrance against the passage of this bill, permit me to say that I share in the feeling of high personal regard for that gentleman which pervades this House. His years, his ability, and his long experience in public affairs entitle him to the measure of consideration which has been accorded to him on this floor. But in this discussion I cannot and will not forget that the welfare and rights of my whole race in this country are involved. When, therefore, the honorable gentleman from Georgia lends his voice and influence to defeat this measure, I do not shrink from saying that it is not from him that the American House of Representatives should take lessons in matters touching human rights or the joint relations of the State and national governments. While the honorable gentleman contented himself with harmless speculations in his study, or in the columns of a newspaper, we might well smile at the impotence of his efforts to turn back the advancing tide of opinion and progress; but, when he comes again upon this national arena, and throws himself with all his power and influence across the path which leads to the full enfranchisement of my race, I meet him only as an adversary; nor shall age or any other consideration restrain me from saying that he now offers this Government which he has done his utmost to destroy, a very poor return for its magnanimous treatment, to come here and seek to continue, by the assertion of doctrines obnoxious to the true principles of our Government, the burdens and oppressions which rest upon five millions of his countrymen who never failed to lift their earnest prayers for the success of this Government when the gentleman was seeking to break up the union of these States and to blot the American Republic from the galaxy of nations.

Sir, it is scarcely twelve years since that gentleman shocked the civilized world by announcing the birth of a government which rested on human slavery as its corner-stone.[9] The progress of events has swept away that pseudo-government which rested on greed, pride, and tyranny; and the race whom he then ruthlessly spurned and trampled on is here to meet him in debate, and to demand that the rights which are enjoyed by its former oppressors—who vainly sought to overthrow a Government which they could not prostitute to the base uses of slavery—shall be accorded to those who even in the darkness of slavery kept their allegiance true to freedom and the Union. Sir, the gentleman from Georgia has learned much since 1861; but he is still a laggard. Let him put away entirely the false and fatal theories which have so greatly marred an otherwise enviable record. Let him accept, in its fullness and beneficence, the great doctrine that American citizenship carries with it every civil and political right which manhood can confer. Let him lend his influence with all his masterly ability, to complete the proud structure of legislation which makes this nation worthy of the great declaration which heralded its birth and he will have done that which will most nearly redeem his reputation in the eyes of the world, and best vindicate the wisdom of that policy which has permitted him to regain his seat upon this floor.

To the diatribe of the gentleman from Virginia (Mr. Harris)[10] who spoke yesterday, and who so far transcended the limits of decency and propriety as to announce upon this floor that his remarks were addressed to white men alone, I shall have no word of reply. Let him feel that a Negro was not only too magnanimous to smite him in his weakness, but was even charitable enough to grant him the mercy of his silence. I shall, sir, leave to others less charitable the unenviable and fatiguing task of sifting out of that mass of chaff the few grains

"Teaching the Freedmen," from J. T. Trowbridge, *The South: A Tour of Its Battlefields and Ruined Cities, a Journey through the Desolated Places, and Talks with the People* (Hartford, Conn.: L. Stebbins, 1866), 338.

of sense that may, perchance deserve notice. Assuring the gentleman that the Negro in this country aims at a higher degree of intellect than that exhibited by him in this debate, I cheerfully commend him to the commiseration of all intelligent men the world over—black men as well as white men.

Sir, equality before the law is now the broad, universal, glorious rule and mandate of the Republic. No State can violate that. Kentucky and Georgia may crowd their statute-books with retrograde and barbarous legislation; they may rejoice in the odious eminence of their consistent hostility to all the great steps of human progress which have marked our national history since slavery tore down the stars and stripes on Fort Sumter; but, if Congress shall do its duty, if Congress shall enforce the great guarantees which the Supreme Court has declared to be the one pervading purpose of all the recent amendments, then their unwise and unenlightened conduct will fall with the same weight upon the gentlemen from those States who now lend their influence to defeat this bill, as upon the poorest slave who once had no rights which the honorable gentlemen were bound to respect. . . .[11]

Technically, this bill is to decide upon the civil status of the colored American citizen; a point disputed at the very formation of our present form of government, when by a short-sighted policy, a policy repugnant to true republican government, one Negro counted as three-fifth of a man. The logical result of this mistake of the framers of the Constitution strengthened the cancer of slavery, which finally spread its poisonous tentacles over the southern portion of the body politic. To arrest its growth and save the nation we have passed through the harrowing operation of intestine war, dreaded at all times, resorted to at the last extremity, like the surgeon's knife, but absolutely necessary to extirpate the disease which threatened with the life of the nation the overthrow of civil and political liberty on this continent. In that dire extremity the members of the race which I have the honor in part to represent—the race which pleads for justice at your hands to-day,—forgetful of their inhuman and brutalizing servitude at the South, their degradation and ostracism at the North, flew willingly and gallantly to the support of the national Government.

Their sufferings, assistance, privations, and trials in the swamps and in the rice-fields, their valor on the land and on the sea, form a part of the ever-glorious record which makes up the history of a nation preserved, and might, should I urge the claim, incline you to respect and guarantee their rights and privileges as citizens of our common Republic. But I remember that valor, devotion, and loyalty are not always rewarded according to their just deserts, and that after the battle some who have borne the brunt of the fray may, through neglect or contempt, be assigned to a subordinate place, while the enemies in war may be preferred to the sufferers.

The results of the war, as seen in reconstruction, have settled forever the political status of my race. The passage of this bill will determine the civil status, not only of the Negro, but of any other class of citizens who may feel themselves discriminated against. It will form the cap-stone of that temple of liberty, begun on this continent under discouraging circumstances, carried on in spite of the sneers of monarchists and the cavils of pretended friends of freedom, until at last it stands, in all its beautiful symmetry and proportions, a building the grandest which the world has ever seen, realizing the most sanguine expectations and the highest hopes of those who, in the name of equal, impartial, and universal liberty, laid the foundation-stone.

■

4.8. Benjamin McElmarray's Testimony Regarding the Ellenton Riot (1877)

A September 15, 1876, robbery of a white woman by two black men led to five days of skirmishing in and around Ellenton, South Carolina, between a white mob and black forces intent on protecting one of the accused from lynching. The riots resulted in the deaths of one or two whites and as many as a hundred African Americans, including

Testimony as to the Denial of the Elective Franchise in South Carolina at the Elections of 1875 and 1876, Taken under the Resolution of the Senate of December 5, 1876, vol. 3 (Washington, D.C.: Government Printing Office, 1877), 231–32.

state legislator Simon Coker. The following testimony is taken from a deposition given to the U.S. district attorney for South Carolina ordered by the U.S. Senate following the disputed election of 1876. ::

Benjamin Mcelmarray, duly sworn, deposes and says: I live near Ellenton,[12] about three miles below, and about a quarter of a mile from Point Comfort. . . . I was at Ellenton on Saturday, September 16, and I saw Allen Williams, Ed. Williams, Jim Bush, and Pig Bush, and they told me about the two men assaulting Mrs. Harlay. . . . Allen Williams said they were going to kill all the niggers until they got to the right one. They had killed one already. Later in the evening, Bob Dunbar, William Hankerson, Charlie Evans, and Lewis, the telegraph-operator at Ellenton, and Dave Crossland went off with their guns and rode toward Augusta on horseback, and we never heard any more of them until Sunday, at church, at Union Bridge. I was home, and they sent for me to come up to old man Dunbar's, as they were killing the colored people. I, Bryant Council, Jake Foreman, Edward Scott, Joe Scott, Ellis Wright, David Bush, Jerry Weathersby, Wilkins Hamilton, Basil Bryant, and a good many more went . . . to Union Bridge. Basil said he had had his gun taken from him by the whites that day. About two hours of sun, Charlie Evans, William Hankerson, and Lewis came along, and Basil asked if they reckoned he would get his gun; but before they answered, Lewis said, "Go ahead, boys; Butler[13] is coming in here tonight, and is going to play hell with the niggers," and then they went on and didn't say another word to us. Lewis was behind the other men in a buggy. They had crossed Union Bridge and were going toward the station. Then came along Elmore Ashley, and five men with him whom I didn't know. They were on horseback and every one had guns. Elmore had a sixteen-shooter. They stopped and talked with us for a little while. About this time news come to us from Rouse's Bridge that the whites had shot Henry Campbell, and some of the men started to take the guns from Ashley's men; but Ashley stated that he had given them his gun to look at, and Bryant Council took it away from the colored man and gave it back to Ashley, and told him and his party they had better go on, and told them to hurry out of the way. They went on pretty fast. A gun was fired by one of our boys. Wilkins Hamilton fired, but I don't think it was fired at them.

The white men had got over two hundred yards away when the gun was fired. They had gone across the bridge to the station. About that time young Bob Dunbar came to the bridge from the direction the other party come, and I heard Jim Bush call out "that the niggers were killing Elmore Ashley up yonder." There were about 50 or 60 armed white men came in this crowd. They filled the road for four or five hundred yards. Bob Dunbar was at the head of them and Dave Crossland, George Newman, Wish McDaniels, were with him. These were the only men I recognized in the company, Robert Dunbar called out to his men to charge, and then came on to the bridge and started to fire, and the second or third shot killed Bryant. The colored people were on this side the bridge and started to fire. They were all scared and had nothing but bird-shot in their guns. There were six or seven guns fired. Both the white and colored people ran in opposite directions. Wilkins Hamilton was wounded at the bridge Sunday night; he was shot through the fleshy part of the leg; it was with a ball. Next day I was at Ellenton Station when Coker[14] was there. . . . I think there were about 200 people there, colored. We had all got together to consult; some had guns and some were drilling. Coker come up and told them they were going against their own selves, because some were talking about fight-ing. He told them to break up and go home, and they all took him at his word and they broke up. He said the United States would come against them if they found them with weapons going to fight the white people. I went home, and in the evening I went down to mind Basil Bryant's body, to take care of it from the hogs. I was lying upon a log with my bat over my face; I heard some one say close up, and I looked and saw the road full of armed and mounted white men; I jumped and ran and they fired on me. I should think there were about 500. They never said a word to me before they fired, and by the time I started to run they fired on me, but didn't hit me. They were about one hundred yards from me; I heard the balls whistle past me. I didn't recognize any of the party; hadn't time. I got away into the woods and the white men went toward Ellenton Station.

This was about two and a half hours of sun on Monday evening. I saw them after this shooting at colored men on the railroad. I was watching them. I saw them shoot, and saw the colored men run. . . . There was a large crowd shooting, but I didn't know any of them. I got on the upper side of them, near House's Bridge, and heard them shooting, but laid up pretty close. I got round home, and found they had killed my brother and two others David Bush is my brother. Warren Kelsey and Sam Brown, a deaf and dumb boy, were the others. I saw their bodies and looked at them. They were shot through and through. David Bush was shot in the back of his neck and in his eye. Warren Kelsey was shot all to pieces. I staid about all day Tuesday, but saw nothing more. These boys were shot on this side, before they got to the bridge. They were home getting dinner. It was at Henry Kelsey's house, which is right on the road, about one hundred yards from it. It is about one and a half miles round the road to Union Bridge from there. On this side the bridge, about a quarter of a mile from where Doctor Cannon lives. I didn't see the dead bodies of those killed round the station, only that of John Kelsey after it was removed from the station. I helped to bury them. We buried them all in one grave on Wednesday, the day the Yankees came to the station. Didn't know anything about the killing of Coker.

CHAPTER 5

"Each tomorrow will find us farther than today"

BLACK LIFE IN THE NEW SOUTH

■

5.1. Black Republicans Visit President-Elect (1881)

Following the Compromise of 1877, African Americans in South Carolina endured intimidation, outright violence, and segregation that was not only demeaning but that severely curtailed their participation in the economic, social, and political life of their communities. In 1881 a delegation of African American leaders led by the South Carolinian Robert B. Elliott appealed to President-Elect James Garfield to support legal equality and the just administration of government. ::

As representatives of the colored Republicans of the States of Virginia, North Carolina, South Carolina, Georgia, Florida, and Texas, we have come in their behalf and in our names to congratulate you on your triumphant election, to the high and responsible office of President of the United States, and to assure you that as their prayers during the exciting political contest which has so happily eventuated in your success, were fervently uttered in your behalf as the standard bearer of the Republican party, so shall they still pray that you may be girded by the Divine wisdom in securing to all American citizens the blessing of equal laws and just administration. Cheered by the many brave utterances which you have in the past made on our behalf, and recognizing the valuable services you have hereto rendered in the cause of our emancipation and enfranchisement, we have also come to present to you a brief statement of our condition in the South, not in a spirit of dictation, but in the belief that a fair representation of our case can best be made by those of us who are compelled to endure grievous wrongs for mere opinion's sake. Although clothed with

The (Chicago) Inter Ocean, January 15, 1881.

the rights of citizenship by the provisions of the Constitution of the United States and recognised as such by legislative enactments and judicial decisions, yet still, in all the Southern States we are but citizens in name, and not in fact. Our right to participate in elections for the choice of public officers is not only questioned, but, in many localities, absolutely denied us by means of armed violence, fraud and intimidation. In many of the Southern States, sir, the rights of majorities are illegally and wantonly subverted by the imperious will of unscrupulous minorities, for no other reason than this; these majorities consist of men, who, free and enfranchised by the laws of the land, prefer to remain loyal to the country of which they are citizens, and steadfast in the support of that political party which saved the life of the nation and to the charge of which can most safely be entrusted the duty of preserving the results accomplished by the late war. The methods resorted to by our political opponents in the South, to deprive us of rightful satisfaction in public affairs, have been so often stated to the public and are so well known to you, that it is unnecessary that we should enter upon a detailed statement of them on this occasion. Suffice it, that by the infamous use of tissue ballots, by the deliberate falsification of registry books and election returns, by forcible exclusion from the polls by armed mobs, by murder and general system of terrorism, and by the refusal in many instances to hold elections at precincts where the majority of the voters are Republicans, elections have been rendered a mere farce. The support of the State governments have been made to derive their powers, not from the consent of the governed, but from the arbitrary will of arbitrating minorities. We are powerless, sir, to redress these wrongs through the machinery of the State courts; for, to all intents and purpose, they are organized against us, the juries oftentimes being composed, not only of those who sympathize with the violators of the law, but frequently consisting, in part, of the active participants in these wrong-doings; and, indeed, when we turn even to the Federal courts for the vindication of our rights, we find that these wrongs are suffered to pass unchallenged, and the perpetrators of them go unwhipped of justice because, under the present jury laws, enacted by a Democratic Congress, the aiders and abettors in these crimes sit in the jury box to pass judgment on them. . . .

Another difficulty under which we labor is the want for proper educational facilities for our children, arising in many instances, not so much from the unwillingness as from the inability of the State governments to meet the educational demands of their inhabitants. In view of these difficulties, and recognizing as we do the further fact that our citizenship con only be rendered permanently effective by a general diffusion of education among our people, we would respectfully urge the importance of creating a national system of education for the toiling masses, under the supervision and control of the Federal Government, instead of leaving the enlightenment of the youth of the country

"Emancipation Day" (c. 1905). From the collections of the
South Carolina Historical Society; 30-21-03A (vertical file).

solely dependent upon the changeful policies of political parties, or the inadequate resources of State government, to the end that it may justly be said of our
country that it not only enfranchises all, but educates all.

While It is far from our purpose or intention to indicate or express any preferences as between Republicans for appointment to office, we nevertheless
deem it our duty in the interest of those whom we have the honor to represent,
as well as in the interest of the Republican party at large, to call attention to
the character of Federal appointments in the South in the past, and respectfully urge that the system of placing in public position men not only in want
of sympathy with the principles and improvements of the Republican party,
but who use those positions to obstruct and hinder, the enforcement of laws
passed for the protection of rights of American citizens; men who, though
calling themselves Republicans, are of no fixed or well-defined political sentiments; men who are all things to all men, and nothing to any, and are totally
without a following, and represent nobody but themselves, be no longer set
over us as representatives of the Federal Government. Such appointments, sir,
instead of strengthening the Republican party in the south, have been a positive source of weakness. Sir, we are not unmindful of the truth which cannot

be too often repeated, the privileges which have been too often conferred upon us as citizens have imposed upon us, as such citizens, weighty responsibilities, which can neither be abated or slighted. We fully appreciate the fact that to enjoy our liberty we should use every effort to prove ourselves worthy of liberty, and that to be good citizens we must be intelligent and useful citizens: but we cannot fail to remember, also, that rights and duties are correlatives, and that the performance of duties, as good and law-abiding citizens, should entitle us to receive and enjoy rights and immunities in common with all other classes of American citizens. In accordance, at least, with the measure of our deserts. We beg to assure you General, that it is to us a matter of deep regret that we should have at all visited you as representatives of a distinctive element, in the body politics, believing in the sublime words or the declaration of independence, that all men are created equal, and rejoicing also in the fact that, through the efforts of the Republican party, whose standard-bearer you were in the last campaign, the teachings of the fathers have been translated into the Constitution. We can but hope that the time is not far distant when they shall be rendered a living reality, as well in practice as in theory, by all classes or American citizens, domiciled in every State and Territory of this Union. But until that time shall be present with us, until class distinction retires against us, until the accident of our complexions shall have ceased to furnish an excuse for the INFLICTION OF INJURIES upon us. . . .

We devoutly pray that your administration may be crowned with most abundant success, and that through your efforts as Chief Magistrate we shall have a country that shall lift all and oppress none.

■

5.2. Robert Smalls Warns against Disfranchisement at the Constitutional Convention (1895)

The South Carolina Constitution of 1895 was the culmination of a long process of attempts to disfranchise African Americans in South Carolina. The convention oversaw many changes to the state's foundational document, but the most significant changes concerned the right to vote, effectively disfranchising most South Carolina African Americans (and many poor whites). Robert Smalls was one of the few African American delegates to the convention, and his was one of the most prominent voices in opposition to the new restrictions. ::

I was born and raised in South Carolina, and to-day I live on the very spot on which I was born, and I expect to remain here as long as the great God allows

From Robert Smalls, *Speeches at the Constitutional Convention* (Charleston, S.C.: Enquirer Print, 1896), 6–11.

me to live, and I will ask no one else to let me remain. I love the State as much as any member of this Convention, because it is the garden spot of the South.

Mr. President, this Convention has been called for no other purpose than the disfranchisement of the Negro. Be careful and bear in mind that the elections which are to take place early next month in very many of the States are watching the action of this Convention, especially on the suffrage question.

Remember that the Negro was not brought here of his own accord. I found by reference to a history in the Congressional Library in Washington . . . that in 1619, in the month of June a Dutch man-of-war landed at Jamestown, Va., with 15 sons of Africa aboard, at the time Miles Kendall was deputy Governor of Virginia. He refused to allow the vessel to be anchored in any of her harbors. But he found out after his order had been sent out that the vessel was without provisions, and the crew was in a starving condition. He countermanded his order, and supplied the vessel with the needed provisions in exchange for 14 Negroes. It was then that the seed of slavery was planted in the land. . . .

We served our masters faithfully and willing and as we were made to do 244 years. In the last war you left them home. You went to the war, fought and came back home, shattered to pieces worn-out, one legged and found your wife and family being properly cared for by the Negroes you left behind. Why should you now seek to disfranchise a race that has been so true to you?

. . . Since Reconstruction times 53,000 have been killed in the South, and not more than three white men have been convicted and hung for these crimes. I want you to be mindful of the fact that the good people of the North are watching this Convention upon this subject. I hope you will make a Constitution that will stand the test. I hope that we may be able to say when our work is done that we have made as good a Constitution as the one we are doing away with.

The Negroes are paying taxes in the South on $263,000,000 worth of property. In South Carolina according to the census the Negroes pay tax on $12,500,000 worth of property. That was in 1890. You voted down without discussion merely to lay on the table, a proposition for a simple property and educational qualification. What do you want? You tried the infamous eight-box and registration laws until they were worn to such a thinness that they could stand neither the test of the law nor of public opinion. In behalf of the 600,000 Negroes in the State and the 132,000 Negro voters all that I demand is that a fair and honest election law be passed. We care not what the qualifications imposed are: all that we ask is that they be fair and honest and honorable, and with these provisos we will stand or fall by it. You have 102,000 white men over 21 years of age; 13,000 of these cannot read nor write. You dare not disfranchise them; and you know that the man who proposes it will never be elected to another office in the State of South Carolina. But whatever Mr. Tillman can do, he can make nothing worse than the infamous eight-box law, and I have no praise for the Conservatives, for they gave the people that law. Fifty eight thousand Negroes cannot read nor write. This leaves a majority of 14,000 white men who can read and write over the same class of Negroes in this State. We are willing to accept a scheme that provides that no man who cannot read nor write can vote, if you dare pass it. . . .

To embody such a provision in the election law would be to mean that every white man would interpret it aright and every Negro would interpret it wrong. I appeal to the gentleman from Edgefield[1] to realize that he is not making a law for one set of men. Some morning you may wake up to find that the bone and sinew of your country is gone. The Negro is needed in the cotton field and in the low country rice fields, and if you impose too hard conditions upon the Negro in this State there will be nothing else for him to do but to leave. What then will you do about your phosphate works? No one but a Negro can work them: the mines that pay the interest on your State debt. I tell you the Negro is the bone and sinew of your country and you cannot do without him. I do not believe you want to get rid of the Negro, else why did you impose a high tax on immigration agents who might come here to get him to leave?

Now, Mr. President, we should not talk one thing and mean another. We should not deceive ourselves. Let us make a Constitution that is fair, honest and just. Let us make a Constitution for all people, one we will be proud of and our children will receive with delight. . . .

Mr. President, strange things have happened and I have been shocked in my life, but the greatest surprise of my life was when the distinguished lawyer from Barnwell, Mr. Aldrich,[2] introduced a Constitution in this Convention that was taken verbatim et literatim from the Constitution and of '65 and the black code of '66, which deprived every Negro from holding an office in this State, notwithstanding that Constitution and black code were rejected by Congress. That Constitution caused the passage of the act of reconstruction by Congress and made it necessary for the Constitutional Convention of 1868, which gave to you the best Constitution of any one of the Southern States. Let us make a Constitution Mr. President, that will demand the respect of mankind everywhere, for we are not above public opinion. While in Washington a committee of capitalist came over from England hunting for timber land in which to invest. One of South Carolina's Representatives in Congress called upon those gentlemen and informed them that there were large tracts of land in Beaufort Country, in the Township of Bluffton, for sale. They inquired for the name of the State, and when they were informed that the timber lands were in South Carolina they answered: "You need not go any further, as our instructions were, before we left England, not to invest money in a State where life and property was not secure under the law."

In God's name let us make a Constitution that will receive the approval of everybody—the outside world as well as those at home. . . .

■

5.3. The Lynching of Postmaster Frazier Baker (1898)

The incidence of lynching reached its peak in the United States in the 1890s, yet few of these crimes resulted in punishment or even trial for the perpetrators. However, the lynching of Lake City postmaster Frazier Baker attracted national attention, and a federal grand jury in Charleston did indict the lynchers. The case resulted in a mistrial, with the all-white jury unable to reach a verdict. ::

Lake City, South Carolina—George Washington's birthday was ushered in in this section on Tuesday morning, at 1 o'clock with the most revolting crime ever perpetrated. . . . Postmaster Baker, an Afro-American of this little town, and his family at the time stated above were burned out of their home, the postmaster and a babe in arms killed, his wife and three daughters shot and maimed for life, and his son wounded.

Mr. Baker was appointed postmaster three months ago. Lake City is a town of 500 inhabitants, and the Afro-American population in the vicinity is large. There was the usual prejudiced protest at his appointment. Three months ago as the postmaster was leaving the office at night in company with several men of our class, he was fired on from ambush. Since then he moved his family into a house in which he also established the post office.

Last week Tuesday night a body of scoundrels (white) who were concealed behind buildings and fences in the neighborhood, riddled the building with shot and rifle bullets. They shot high and no one was hurt. It was simply an effort to intimidate him. A short time before Senators Tillman and McLauren[3] . . . had asked the postmaster general to remove Mr. Baker because of his color and the request had been refused. The refusal was wired here. Mr. Baker did not remove his family and gave no evidence of being frightened. Being a government official he felt confident of protection from Washington.

At 1 o'clock Tuesday morning a torch was applied to the post office and house. Back, just within the line of light, were over a hundred white brutes— murderers—armed with pistols and shotguns. By the time the fire aroused the sleeping family, consisting of the postmaster, his wife, four daughters, a son and an infant at the breast, the crowd began firing into the building. A hundred bullet holes were made through the thin boarding and many found lodgment in members of the family within.

Cleveland Gazette, February 26, 1898.

"Hoeing Rice, South Carolina, U.S.A." (1904). Magic Lantern slide, author's collection.

"A Southern Baptism, Aiken, South Carolina" (c. 1906). Postcard, author's collection.

The postmaster was the first to reach the door and he fell dead just within the threshold, being shot in several places. The mother had the baby in her arms and reached the door over her husband's body, when a bullet crashed through its skull, and it fell to the floor. She was shot in several places. Two of the girls had their arms broken close to the shoulders and will probably lose them. Another of the girls is fatally wounded. The boy was also shot.

Only two of the seven occupants of the house escaped with slight injuries. The bodies of Mr. Baker and the infant were cremated in the building. All mail matter was destroyed. A coroner's jury was impaneled Tuesday evening. It visited the charred remains and adjourned until today. Nothing will be done to apprehend the infernal brutes and murderers. . . .

■

5.4. Our Returned Negro Soldiers (1919)

Even though black soldiers had enthusiastically committed to the war effort, fought, and died on European battlefields in World War I, discrimination and violence still awaited them on their return home. The editorial reprinted here from the Charleston Messenger *examines the issue of African American discontent and points to a new, developing ideology in the black community—a more outspoken advocacy of dignity and a refusal to submit quietly to Jim Crow.* ::

It is such a pity that we have to put the word 'Negro' before soldiers. But, seeing we are in a country that puts a premium on the color of a person's skin instead of his or her worth, we must be content with present conditions.

While he was away, in common with people of the other race, those of us who were left behind economized and stinted ourselves that our black boys might be as comfortable as the circumstances of war would permit.

They did their duty at home and abroad, and now they have returned. To what have they come? Did they find a grateful country? How were they treated while in foreign lands? Let some returned Negro soldier tell the tale. We have spoken to those who have been overseas, and who only got as far as training camps. Have spoken to commissioned, "non-coms," as well as privates. Let them speak for themselves.

Perhaps there might have been some officers and privates who were able to "pass" who did not feel the curse of America's hobby. The others felt the full weight upon their defenseless heads. However, they are back from the field of carnage. Instead of the expected "well done" they confidently and rightfully

Charleston Messenger, October 18, 1919, reprinted in Robert T. Kerlin, *The Voice of the Negro 1919* (New York: Dutton, 1920), 37–38.

expected, what greeted them on every side? Let them tell. On every side he is met with the statement, "niggers, as you were."

What does that mean? Any one familiar with conditions in America knows that meant that those soldier boys who fought as bravely as the bravest were to be lynched for the least offense, deprived of civil rights, insulted on the streets, simply because they were helpless; made to ride in filthy railroad cars; compelled to live in unsanitary sections of cities.

There is scarcely a day that passes that newspapers don't tell about a Negro soldier lynched in his uniform. Why do they lynch Negroes, anyhow? Have they not all the machinery of the law in their hands? With a white judge, a white jury, white public sentiment, white officers of the law, it is just as impossible for a Negro accused of crime, or even suspected of crime, to escape the white man's vengeance or his justice as it would be for a fawn to escape that wanders accidentally into a den of hungry lions. So why not give him the semblance of a trial?

Instead of race prejudice being modified, as some of us fondly hoped, it has become intensified. The riot that started in Washington started by attacks on Negro soldiers, and from them it was only a step to killing innocent, defenseless Negroes. No one condemns a criminal Negro any sooner than we do, but we are not prepared to say that all Negroes are criminals; nor do we believe that all the criminals are Negroes. Most of the criminals caught and lynched or punished are Negroes, we will admit, but is not something wrong in that respect?

The returned Negro soldier, as a whole, is contented with simple justice. He feels himself a man like other men, and naturally he feels that if his country saw fit to compel him to fight for it, that country, in turn, ought to at least be grateful and give him a man's chance in the race of life.

The relatives of returned Negro soldiers were beaten and killed on the streets of Washington, right in front of the White House, under the dome of the Capitol of the greatest Republic on earth—a Republic that went to war to beat down injustice, and make the world safe for democracy. Has the head of the nation uttered one word of condemnation of the mob? If so, we have failed to see it.

■

5.5. The Kind of Democracy the Negro Race Expects (1918)

William Pickens (1881–1954) was a prolific speaker on the direction of black education in the United States. Born in South Carolina, he was educated at Talladega College and Yale before undertaking a career in academia. Pickens was also involved

William Pickens, *The Kind of Democracy the Negro Race Expects* (Baltimore: Herald Printing Company, 1918).

with the NAACP from its inception. The speech reproduced here, delivered on different occasions during and after World War I, reflected his challenge to the United States to envision a democracy inclusive of African Americans even as it promoted the concept of inclusion around the world. ::

Democracy is the most used term in the world today. But some of its uses are abuses. Everybody says "Democracy"! But everybody has his own definition. By the extraordinary weight of the presidency of the United States many undemocratic people have had this word forced upon their lips but have not yet had the right ideal forced upon their hearts. I have heard of one woman who wondered with alarm whether "democracy" would mean that colored women would have the right to take any vacant seat or space on a street car, even if they had paid for it. That such a question should be asked, shows how many different meanings men may attach to the one word democracy. This woman doubtless believes in a democracy of me-and-my-kind, which is no democracy. The most autocratic and the worst caste systems could call themselves democratic by that definition. Even the Prussian junker[4] believes in that type of democracy; he has no doubt that he and the other junkers should be free and equal in rights and privileges. Many have accepted the word democracy merely as the current password to respectability in political thinking. The spirit of the times is demanding democracy; it is the tune of the age; it is the song to sing. But some are like that man who belonged to one of the greatest political parties: after hearing convincing arguments by the stump-speaker of the opposite party, he exclaimed: "Wa-al, that fellow has convinced my judgment, but I'll be d—d if he can change my vote!"

It is in order, therefore, for the Negro to state clearly what he means by democracy and what he is fighting for.

First. Democracy in Education. This is fundamental. No other democracy is practicable unless all of the people have equal right and opportunity to develop according to their individual endowments. There can be no real democracy between two natural groups, if one represents the extreme of ignorance and the other the best of intelligence. The common public school and the state university should be the foundation stones of democracy. If men are artificially differentiated at the beginning, if we try to educate a "working class" and a "ruling class," forcing different race groups into different lines without regard to individual fitness, how can we ever hope for democracy in the other relations of these groups? . . . The Negro believes in democracy of education as first and fundamental: that the distinction should be made between individual talents and not between color and castes.

Second. Democracy in Industry. The right to work in any line for which the individual is best prepared, and to be paid the standard wage. This is also fundamental. In the last analysis there could be very little democracy between multi-millionaires and the abject poor. There must be a more just and fair distribution of wealth in a democracy. And certainly this is not possible unless men work at the occupations for which they are endowed and best prepared. There should be no "colored" wages and no "white" wages; no "man's" wage and no "woman's" wage. Wages should be paid for the work done, measured as much as possible by its productiveness. No door of opportunity should be closed to a man on any other ground than that of his individual unfitness. . . . For every man to serve where he is most able to serve is public economy and is to the best interest of the state. This lamentable war that was forced upon us should make that plain to the dullest of us. Suppose that, when this war broke out, our whole country had been like Mississippi . . . where a caste system was holding the majority of the population in the triple chains of ignorance, semi-serfdom and poverty. Our nation would be now either the unwilling prey or the golden goose for the Prussian. . . . The Negro asks American labor in the name of democracy to get rid of its color caste and industrial junkerism.

Third. Democracy in State. A political democracy in which all are equal before the laws; where there is one standard of justice, written and unwritten; where all men and women may be citizens by the same qualifications, agreed upon and specified. We believe in this as much for South Africa as for South Carolina, and we hope that our American nation will not agree with any government, ally or enemy, that is willing to make a peace that will bind the Africa Negro to political slavery and exploitation.

Many other evils grow out of political inequality. Discriminating laws are the mother of the mob spirit. . . . The first move therefore against mob violence and injustice in the petty courts is to wipe out discriminating laws and practices in the higher circles of government. The ignorant man in Tennessee will not rise in ideal above the intelligent man in Washington.

Fourth. Democracy without Sex-preferment. The Negro cannot consistently oppose color discrimination and support sex discrimination in democratic government. This happened to be the opinion also of the First Man of the Negro race in America,—Frederick Douglass. The handicap is nothing more nor less than a presumption in the mind of the physically dominant element of the universal inferiority of the weaker or subject element. It is so easy to prove that the man who is down and under, deserves to be down and under. In the first place, he is down there, isn't he? And that is three-fourths of the argument to the ordinary mind; for the ordinary mind does not seek ultimate causes. The argument against the participation of colored men and of women in self-government is practically one argument. . . . Enfranchisement would spoil a good field-hand,—or a good cook. Black men were once ignorant,— women were once ignorant. Negroes had no political experience—women had no such experience. The argument forgets that people do not get experience on the outside. But the American Negro expects a democracy that will accord the right to vote to a sensible industrious woman rather than to a male tramp.

Fifth. Democracy in Church. The preachings and the practices of Jesus of Nazareth are perhaps the greatest influence in the production of modern democratic ideas. The Christian church is, therefore, no place for the caste spirit or for snobs. And the colored races the world over will have even more doubt in the future than they have had in the past of the real Christianity of any church which hold out to them the prospect of being united in heaven after being separated on earth.

Finally. The great colored races will in the future not be kinder to a sham democracy than to a "scrap-of-paper" autocracy. The private home, private right and private opinion must remain inviolate; but the commonwealth, the public place and public property must not be appropriated to the better use of any group by "Jim-Crowing" and segregating any other group. By the endowments of God and nature there are individual "spheres"; but there are no such widely different racial "spheres." Jesus' estimate of the individual soul is the taproot of democracy, and any system which discourages the men of any race from individual achievement, is no democracy. To fix the status of a human soul on earth according to the physical group in which it was born, is the gang spirit of the savage which protects its own members and outlaws all others.

For real democracy the American Negro will live and die. His loyalty is always above suspicion, but his extraordinary spirit in the present war is born of his faith that on the side of his country and her allies is the best hope for such democracy. And he welcomes, too, the opportunity to lift the "Negro question" out of the narrow confines of the Southern United States and make it a world question. Like many other questions our domestic race question, instead of being settled by Mississippi and South Carolina, will now seek its settlement largely on the battlefields of Europe.

■

5.6. Colored Teachers in Charleston Schools (1921)

In 1918 only one of Charleston's three public schools for black children employed black teachers. NAACP officials in Charleston demanded that the school system replace white teachers in black schools with black educators. A massive petition drive in 1919 forced Charleston officials to concede, and NAACP membership in the city swelled from fewer than 30 individuals before the campaign to 1,300 afterward. ::

The Crisis 22 (June 1921): 60.

It is not widely known that, up to 1920 the colored public schools of Charleston, South Carolina, were manned by southern white teachers. There was no objection to these teachers simply because of their race. White teachers from New England and the North have done unforgettable pioneer work for the establishment of Negro education and the finest point of contact between the races today are many of the white teachers who still remain in southern colored schools.

But the teachers in Charleston schools were not simply white; they were white people who maintained their standing as "southern" whites; that is, they believed in the inevitable inferiority of all Negroes, in the "supremacy" of the white race, in absence of all social contact between teacher and taught, in discrimination against Negroes and in limited Negro education.

Such a situation was intolerable and black Charleston writhed under it for years. However, it was not easy to get rid of the anomaly. In the first place, colored people did not want to put themselves on record as willing to increase discriminatory statutes on the law books of South Carolina. Again they were afraid that any organized movement against white teachers, and especially white women, would bring upon them enmity and retaliation from the white community; despite the fact that the white teachers in colored schools got the same pay as those in white schools, the annual per capita expenditure on enrolled white pupils was $35.70, and on colored $2.55! If now the Board of School Commissioners became offended and colored teachers were forced on them what greater discrepancy might not appear? Finally Negroes were not at all sure for many years that they themselves wanted colored teachers!

Their resentment therefore simmered on with many abortive movements for a long time. In 1910 Charleston bad a Negro school population of 5,329, of whom only 65 per cent were reported in school and many of these in private schools. For this population there were up to 1919, three colored public schools with 53 white teachers and principals. Only two colored teachers were employed in the whole system, and these in order to comply with a bequest made by colored troops during the Civil War.[5]

In January, 1919, colored Charleston led by the local branch of the NAACP, determined that it was time for the white teachers to go at any cost. Their attitude toward the colored children was humiliating to the last degree. Under their tutelage the children were learning to despise themselves and their race and to regard white folks as their natural masters.

On January 18, the colored people sent a petition to the Governor, the Superintendent of Education, and the legislature, saying:

"We, the citizens of the Negro race and parents of pupils of the aforesaid race in attendance as pupils of the public schools of Charleston, do, through our committee . . . most respectfully petition for assistance and relief from the uncalled for, unnecessary, unusual, abnormal conditions that surround and control the management, instruction and teaching of the children of the aforesaid race in the public schools of the city of Charleston.

"Fifty-six years after freedom the Negroes of the city of Charleston are denied the right to teach Negro children by Negroes in the free public schools of Charleston; and,

"*Whereas,* We need relief from this unnecessary, unusual, abnormal condition; and,

"*Whereas,* We have thousands of educated men and women—who are prepared and worthy to teach the children of the aforesaid race in the city of Charleston; and,

"*Whereas,* Under the existing law of the free public schools of the State of South Carolina, it is impossible for teachers of the Negro race to teach children of the Negro race in the free public schools in the city of Charleston; and,

"*Whereas,* Negro teachers do teach children in every other city of this state, and in every city in every one of the thirteen old slave-holding States in the Union:

"*We, therefore,* most humbly petition and pray to each and every one of you in authority to have Section No. 1780 of the Civil Code of 1912 amended so as to read: That it shall be unlawful for a person of the white race to teach in the free public schools of South Carolina provided and set aside for the children of the Negro race."

The chairman of the committee, the Honorable Thomas E. Miller,[6] a colored man who was once a member of Congress from South Carolina, was sent to Columbia to lay this petition before the Legislature. . . . A joint hearing was arranged by the House Committee on Education and the colored committee went up to Columbia.

Meantime, however, they had been busy. Sixteen mass meetings had been called in the city and the members of the Charleston Branch had been called upon to make a city wide canvas. They were told to "spread the information broadcast to all parents of colored pupils that it is necessary for them to go on record as being desirous of having colored teachers in the public schools of this city, and that simply holding that desire and not being willing to signify by their signatures lends no assistance. Warn them against petitions requesting the retention of white teachers."

Hundreds helped in the canvass, and over five thousand signatures of heads of families representing three-fourths of the colored population of Charleston, were secured. A typed copy of these cards, certified to by a judge of the city court, was sent to Columbia.

It must, of course, be remembered that in South Carolina with a population (1910) of 835,843 Negroes and 679,161 whites, there is not a single Negro representative in the Legislature. Moreover, the census reported (1910) 357,822 Negroes, 10 years of age and over, who could read and write. The Negroes therefore represented a totally disfranchised group appealing to whites, and their only resource was strategy. That strategy consisted in skillfully driving a wedge between the up-state poor whites and the aristocrats of Tidewater.

The hearing before the House committee turned into an interesting joint debate. Three members of the Charleston Board of Commissioners were present and the colored committee with Congressman Miller as spokesman. The chairman of the committee on education gave each side thirty minutes. As the debate progressed the small minority who had been favorable to the bill, rapidly and visibly began to change to a large majority. . . .

As a last shot the white Charlestonians said that this colored committee did not really represent the colored folk of Charleston and that they were a set of highbrows and mulattoes trying to do what the real Negro of Charleston did not want done. Thereupon Mr. Miller, bending over with the weight of the satchel, presented the certificates representing some 25,000 of Charleston's 35,000 colored population. This really settled the matter.

The Charleston delegation saw that their cause was lost and immediately they proposed a compromise which would enable them to do what the Negroes wished without being compelled by law. This was exactly what the Negroes preferred because they were themselves unwilling to make it legally impossible for white persons to teach in the Negro public schools. . . .

■

5.7. Negro Farmers in South Carolina (1929)

South Carolina farmers did not share in the wave of prosperity enjoyed by many other Americans in the 1920s, and the decade was particularly hard on black agriculturalists. Many left farming and moved from the countryside into cities in South Carolina, and many others left the state altogether. Those who remained struggled to survive, though officials optimistically noted increasing rates of land ownership by African Americans as well as their willingness to avail themselves of the latest advances in agricultural science. ::

The census of 1920 gives information about colored farmers in South Carolina showing that they own farm land to the extent of 1,146,396 acres. This is an average of nearly 63 acres to the farm. The values of the farm property owned by Negroes were placed at $59,839,583 in 1920; at $22,112,291 in 1910. . . .

"Report of Mr. H.E. Daniels, state supervisor of Smith-Lever Extension Agents for Negro Farmers in South Carolina," in Asa H. Gordon, *Sketches of Negro Life and History in South Carolina,* 2nd ed. (Columbia: University of South Carolina Press, 1971), 169–72. Reprinted courtesy of the University of South Carolina Press.

The estimate of the Department of Commerce published October, 1926, gives the total number of Negro farmers as 90,678, a loss of nearly 20,000 since 1920. These 20,000 contain certainly some owners—how many no one really knows. If we estimate it at 16 per cent, it would mean that about 3,400 farmers have lost their farms. Considering the deflation of values and the depression of farming since 1920, it would not surprise us if 16 per cent have had to give up their homes and farms, and sometimes lose heavily in money, as well as suffer the disappointment of blighted hope and foiled ambition. It is rather cause for rejoicing that 85 per cent or more have been able to weather the storm and difficulties during the past five years. If we accept the shrinkage in farm owners as around 2,200 to 3,400, we should then have a loss of Negro farm tenants of 16,000 to 17,500. It is probably quite safe to say that the number of Negro farm tenants has decreased from 16,000 to 18,000, and now stands at about 71,000.

Those of us who know how hard the life on the farm has been, how low the standard of living, how poor the rewards of farm labor for the years since 1920, cannot feel sorry that those 20,000 farmers have left the farms. Wherever they and their families have gone, they have probably been at least as well off, most probably much better off, at least for food and clothes, and shelter, than if they had stayed on the farm. Their going has probably brought some relief to themselves and to their families. It has relieved the pressure on those who have remained. Work at the North, work in Florida, work on railroads' and public roads, has been a great blessing to many of our colored farmers, who would have almost starved on the farm. Let us hope others will follow them, rather than any of those should, in the present unsettled condition of agriculture, come back to the farm.

The important question is, what is being done among the 90,578 farmers who remain, and for their wives and children, who together constitute a farm population of 528,292—nearly one-third the people of the state? Practically one-half of the agriculture of the state is in their hands. If they prosper, everybody else prospers. If they suffer, everybody else suffers.

In all agricultural efforts everywhere the two matters of outstanding importance are: (1) the relation of the farmer to his land. Does he own or rent it? (2) the relation of the farmer to science. Does he know the results of scientific experiment? Can he secure them and put them into practice?

In the matter of ownership of farm land, the record of the Negro in South Carolina is worthy of all praise. To have come in less than two generations of freedom from nearly nothing to ownership of 1,000,000 acres, worth $35,000,000 to $40,000,000 is a mighty achievement—heroic indeed, when the obstacles are considered. The Negro is like every other human being—he desires to own the land he toils over—but the way to ownership has not always been easy.

The Federal Land Bank system lends money to persons who own farms, or are about to become owners, to assist in the purchase and improvement of farms, and to replace debts already contracted for those purposes, with a debt on the more favorable terms of a longer period of payment and a lower interest rate. The system has been of incalculable benefit to farmers generally in the United States, and the Negro farmer in South Carolina has benefited by it to some extent. The farmers who borrow from the Federal Land Banks are organized into associations, of which there are twelve for Negroes.

I do not say it is easy for a colored farmer to borrow from the Federal Land Bank. That source of credit is the largest single source, and the point I want to make is, that colored farmers have used and are using it, in hundreds of instances through their own associations. Probably no one has ever added up the full amount of their borrowings from the Land Bank, but I feel sure that it will total not less than a half million dollars. How much they have borrowed from state banks and individuals for the purpose of buying farms, I do not know. But it will amount to several millions, probably to eight or even ten millions. Of course their lives are made bitter by this debt. The Bible says, "The borrower is servant unto the lender,"[7] and our sad experience tells us it is the truth. Yet upon the whole, the bitter hardship of years of toil and self-denial is sweetened by hope that some happy day the home or farm will be free from debt. The road to ownership is not easy; it is a stiff uphill climb, but a good company is traveling that way, and there are helping hands in the friendly banks and bankers. Industrious thrifty Negro farmers need not be afraid to set out upon it. "In due season ye shall reap, if ye faint not."[8] In general, my conclusion is, that it is easier now than it ever has been before for a colored farmer to own his farm.

The Negro farmer in South Carolina has a far better opportunity today to learn the science of farming than he has ever had. Farmers' bulletins are his for the asking. If he can read. All the treasure houses of scientific knowledge are wide open to him. Farm papers are cheap. I asked a good colored farmer how many farm papers he took, and he answered "four." That man has built as good a barn as I know in his country, has a large two-story house, and has for years kept careful accounts on his farm. He is a careful, in many respects a scientific, farmer.

There has been steady growth among Negro farmers in producing cash crops and food and feed supplies resulting from contact with extension workers and organization. We may close this statement with an example of the progress Negro farmers are making in cash crops and food and feed supplies as a result of the contact they have had with extension workers.

Sam Glover, R. F. D. No. 2, Orangeburg, S. C, by advice and assistance from the extension workers, began demonstration in 1916 on a farm of twenty-five acres of land in a low state of cultivation, with one horse and no livestock of any consequence. He lived in a house worth about $300; his first demonstration was three acres of corn and peas and the results were very gratifying.

The following year it was increased to ten acres in cotton, five acres in corn and five acres in small grain, resulting in good yields. The next year he added twenty-five acres to his farm and the entire farm was then run as demonstration. Following constant advice and assistance from extension workers on the ideas of soil building, crop rotation and pedigreed seed, today he owns 125 acres of land in a high state of cultivation with a modem home worth $3,000; two Jersey cows; fifteen head of swine, including two brood sows and one pure bred boar; three head of horses; improved farm implements; one automobile; 460 bushels corn; wheat sufficient for 1928; has sold eighteen bales of cotton; has eight tons of hay for sale above what is necessary to carry him through 1928. His wife and daughter sold $330 worth of vegetables, chickens, eggs and butter in 1927. The entire farm with modern improvements is valued at $8,000.

He has a life insurance policy with the Metropolitan Life Insurance Company for $3000. One of his daughters graduated from State College and is now teaching in the rural schools of Orangeburg County, carrying out the lessons learned at the State College in developing rural people. He has also three children in State College at present as a result of contact with extension workers; has a bank account, if no misfortune befalls him, to insure his 1928 crop without debt.

What is true of Sam Glover's progress is equally true of a large number of Negro farmers in South Carolina, who have come in contact with Negro extension workers.

■

5.8. The Goal (1926)

Benjamin Mays (1894–1984) was born near Epworth, South Carolina, to former slaves. As an educator, college president, and civil rights activist, Mays influenced generations of young African American leaders, including Dr. Martin Luther King Jr., who called Mays his "spiritual and intellectual father." He delivered the speech reprinted here at the Older Boys' Conference held at Benedict College in Columbia in 1926. ::

Were I to talk to you about the physical goal, that little white line that contending teams defend and fight to cross; were I to speak of the home plate in baseball, that little rubber cushion that every runner seeks to touch; you would

Benjamin Mays, "The Goal: Address Delivered at Older Boys' Conference," in Asa H. Gordon, *Sketches of Negro Life and History in South Carolina*, 2nd ed. (Columbia: University of South Carolina Press, 1971), 203–11. Reprinted courtesy of the University of South Carolina Press.

readily and clearly understand what I mean by the goal. In fact, the football goal can be seen with the naked eye. It can be touched with the physical hand. No doubt, you have seen Benedict College defend that white line as the Allies defended Verdun; perhaps you have seen Allen University fight as though the sky would fall if they crossed not the goal. You must have heard the cheers, the roars, and the yells of the grand stand, urging its team to victory. Surely you have seen the excited multitude go wild with enthusiasm as someone made a "touchdown." These things are too familiar to be further explained.

But this goal of life, this goal that you have asked me to speak about, is not so easily defined. It cannot be seen with the naked eye; neither can it be touched with the physical hand. It cannot be thoroughly demonstrated; thus, if I do not make clear to you just what the goal of life is, you must sympathize. The task is just too difficult, that's all.

Were I white, and held a professor's chair in the University of South Carolina; were you white, and represented the best white schools of this commonwealth; my task would not be so difficult. We would then be clothed in that skin that gives perpetual protection. We would represent that group that presumes to hold the destiny of this nation in its hand, and to whom the doors of opportunity are never closed. Were this true, I would define the goal without limitations. I would recommend that you aspire to be governor of your native state. I would point the way to the president's chair. As it is, Americans though we be, I must speak to you not as an American to Americans but as a Negro to Negroes. It is this regrettable fact that makes the goal most difficult for me to define.

Yes, we are Americans; we are South Carolinians; we are Negroes; and I make no apologies for being any. I am proud to be an American citizen. Neither do I make any apologies for being a South Carolinian. I tell that everywhere I go. I cannot and would not apologize for being a Negro. We have a great history; we have a greater future. Be this as it may, there can be no denying that the rules of this game, though laid down for Americans, we must play with handicaps and restrictions. It is this thing that makes the goal difficult for me to define. Nevertheless, whatever the restrictions are, we have a rendezvous with South Carolina; we have a rendezvous with America; we must not fail that rendezvous.

Though the game of life may be compared with a football game, in many respects, the two games differ. For example in the football game, we know when the goal is crossed. In life's game, the goal is never crossed. The goal we set for this generation will not be the goal for the next generation. The goal of our fathers is not ours. Already, my father and I live in two separate worlds. His creed is not my creed; his ideals are not my ideals; and his philosophy of life differs widely from my philosophy of life. Forty years from today, a youth reading my speech will perhaps call it "old timey" and out of date. Thus the goal moves on. The goal of life . . . is never overtaken. . . .

Thus life's goal is an ideal. It lures us onward and upward and makes it possible for successive generations to stand on the shoulders of the generations that precede; the real goal, however, is never reached. This is as it should be. When the ideal is reached, it ceases to be an ideal. When the ideal is reached, satisfaction comes; when satisfaction comes, stagnation appears; and when stagnation appears, death is at hand. I pity the satisfied youth. . . .

Do your bit in order that those who come after you may enjoy a larger freedom and receive a greater heritage. Not only is this the goal of Negro youth, it is the goal of America. It was the goal of the Pilgrim Fathers. They suffered; they bled; they died. They did it in order that those who followed would enjoy a larger religious freedom. It was the goal of those who fought in the Revolutionary War. They fought that we might enjoy a larger political freedom. It was the goal of America in the great World War. We fought that the world might enjoy the freedom of democracy. It was the goal of the Negro, Crispus Attucks, the first to shed his blood that America might be free. It was the goal of the immortal Abraham Lincoln who freed four million slaves. It was the goal of those black boys who fought and died in Flanders Field. They did it, partly in the hope that discrimination, segregation and lynching would soon disappear. It was the goal of our enslaved parents, for they prayed and endured the lash in order that their children might some day be freed. Your sitting here tonight is an answer to their prayers, their toils, and their sacrifices. Young men, the goal of life is something like this.

Only a few years separate you from me. As you see, I am a young man. Yet I will live in vain, if I do not live and so act that you will be freer than I am—freer intellectually, freer politically, and freer economically. I must make it possible for you to become citizens of the world. I owe it to you to make fine, wholesome, racial contact; sell my personality to white men who do not believe in us, in order that you may enjoy what I will never enjoy.

May my right hand forget its cunning, and my tongue cleave to the roof of my mouth, if I do not make it possible for my unborn son to live more completely than I am now living. I owe it to my silver-haired mother who picked cotton in the cold winter days on the hills of South Carolina in order that I might go to school. I was seventeen years old before I was able to stay in school more than four months a year. The school in my section ran only three or four months yearly. A longer term would not have helped for the farm was calling me. God grant that my unborn son may share a larger freedom and a richer heritage than I enjoy. . . .

I must hasten on to something more definite. As I have already indicated, Lincoln, with one stroke of his pen, broke the chains of physical slavery; but there is another chain that Lincoln could not break. This chain is not physical; it is mental. The Negro, though freed by Lincoln, emerged from slavery with a slave's psychology, an inferiority complex. In the main, he thought like a slave; he acted like a slave; he crouched, cringed, and cowered like a slave. To him the white man was God, and sixty-three years is a comparatively short time in which to breed out this inferiority complex.

How could it be otherwise? For more than two hundred years the Negro was in physical slavery. The white man did his thinking. The white man acted for him. The white man even gave him his form of religion. Excepting the free Negro, he did not develop any sense of responsibility for he had no need to. His duty was to obey and carry out the dictates of his master. It was inevitable, then, that along with the physical slavery there was being developed a slave's psychology. Lincoln did not, and Lincoln could not break the mental chains.

During the period of slavery the Negro to a large extent learned to disrespect the personality of the Negro. He had no confidence in his fellow slaves, and his white masters encouraged this distrust. There was no opportunity for cooperation, and as long as the slave system worked well, there was no need of co-operation. Thus, in the main, the Negro emerged from slavery with little or no confidence in himself and with little or no confidence in his brother in black.

You would be surprised to know that there are intelligent Negroes today who do not believe in the inherent possibilities of the Negro race. They have unconsciously, perhaps, accepted the erroneous, unscientific propaganda that the Negro is inherently inferior. They have accepted this philosophy in spite of the fact that the best scientists of the world have agreed that there is no such thing as an inferior race; that there is an equal amount of inherent potentiality and power in all races. It is clear that inferiority is not a racial trait; it is an individual trait. The intelligence tests prove this to be a fact. For the most brilliant white child, there can be found a Negro child equally brilliant; and for the most stupid colored child, there can be found a white child equally as stupid.

Of course, we do not deny that, on the whole, the white man and the Negro parent stand on two different planes— two different levels of civilization. Neither do we deny that on the whole, the white man has attained more culture than the Negro has attained; we have already indicated that this is due to environmental factors rather than to inherent qualities.

As a result of this psychology and lack of training on the part of the average Negro parent, the Negro youth has suffered. He has not received the stimulus from his parents and teachers that the white child has received. Too often the Negro child has been led to believe that he cannot do the things that the white

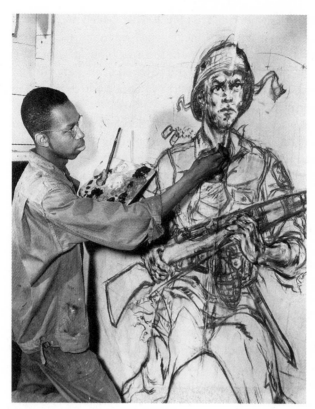

World War II soldier
from South Carolina
(c. 1942). From the
John H. McCray
Papers, courtesy of
the South Caroliniana
Library, University
of South Carolina,
Columbia.

child does. This clips his ambition, crushes his genius, and often a great mind goes undeveloped.

This is a challenge to Negro teachers. Help the Negro boy find himself. Encourage ability wherever you find it—be it in art, science or industry. Drive home the fact that the old Palmetto State is expecting him to make his contribution to civilization—his contribution in agriculture, in industry, in the arts and sciences—in fact, in every phase of human endeavor.

Young men, you must strive to be an agriculturist, not a Negro agriculturist—just an agriculturist! Strive to be a doctor, not a Negro doctor—just a doctor! Seek to serve your state, not as a Negro but as a man. Aspire to be great—not among Negroes, but among men! God knows I want to be a great teacher; not a Negro teacher—just a great teacher. I want no racial adjective modifying it. I want to preach the gospel of peace, good will, justice, and brotherhood—not to Negroes and for Negroes, but to men and for men. I want to act so that each tomorrow will find us farther than today—not the Negro race, the human race. It seems to me that this is our goal.

■

5.9. Modjeska Monteith Simkins Challenges Governor over White Supremacy (1944)

Modjeska Monteith Simkins (1899–1922) was one of South Carolina's leading public health and civil rights reformers. She wrote the following letter to Governor Olin Johnson after he called a special session of the General Assembly in 1944 in an attempt to circumvent a U.S. Supreme Court ruling in Smith v. Allwright *that declared all-white primaries illegal. Johnson declared that "after these statutes are repealed, we will have done everything in our power to guarantee white supremacy in our primaries."*

The Honorable Olin D. Johnson[9]
Governor of South Carolina
The State Capitol
Columbia, South Carolina.

My Dear Sir:
According to certain of your public statements which have been brought into high relief very recently in connection with the Special Session of the General Assembly of South Carolina, you hold that the mere fact of being born of white parents transcends all other human values,—that all white men and all white women are superior to all men and women of color simply because they are not born white. And there are thousands in South Carolina who think as you do. But it happens that I do not agree in the least with you and your constituency on this thing you call "white supremacy."

With the assistance of your adherents, however, you should be able to give a precise definition of what you term "white supremacy," and to present logical and indisputable date to substantiate whatever you think it is. I do not believe, on the other hand, that you will be able to present authentic information to prove your claims.

Consequently, since in South Carolina at the present time you are the most outstanding exponent and advocate of the "white supremacy" concept, I am hereby challenging you to public debate on the subject *Resolved: The Concept of "White Supremacy" Is Sound—Biblically, Historically, and Scientifically.* In your presentation, I am challenging you to prove, unequivocally and conclusively, that you are superior to me to say nothing of the hundreds of Negroes and other nationally and internationally renowned persons of color.

Modjeska Monteith Simkins to Olin D. Johnson, April 17, 1944, Modjeska Monteith Simkins Papers, South Carolina Political Collections, University of South Carolina.

The least publicity on the prospective debate would draw a discerning audience. While the composite reactions of the audience would give each of us some idea of the impressions made, there must be special judges. You may choose one judge; I shall choose one, and we must agree on a third. Better still, you may choose two and I will choose one. If you desire, you may select any person of your choice as a colleague. In that case, I shall choose a second.

The debate may be held in any public assembly hall in Columbia, preferably in the hall of the General Assembly on an evening during your special session.

The time has come for a showdown on the "white supremacy" issue. Demagoguery, haranguing, supposition, and emotionalism must be pitted against the logic, commonsense, science, and the teachings of Jesus Christ. I remember, by the way, that you are a good Baptist—a member of the First Baptist Church here in Columbia. Therefore, Dr. Campbell, whom I believe to be a brilliant theologian, may be willing to assist you with your biblical data.

Now, I am awaiting an early if not an immediate reply to my challenge—just as soon as you can possibly arrange your schedule. But if I receive no answer by midnight of April 22, or if you reply that you will not accept the challenge, it could be considered as conclusive proof that you and your fellow-travelers realize that you have been bluffing yourselves all along.

It could also be considered as clear evidence that you conceded that "white supremacy" is a myth for which, therefore, neither sensible nor scientific bases can be found. Such an admission made either by your disregard of this challenge or by your expressed refusal to accept it would place you in an embarrassing situation, My dear Governor, for many besides the two of us would learn of your refusal to defend your favorite concept, as fanatically as you have done before, when it is challenged by an intelligent, educated person.

Very sincerely yours,

Mrs. Andrew W. Simkins

■

5.10. Southern Schrecklichkeit (1946)

World War II veteran Isaac Woodward, while still in uniform following his honorable discharge from the Army, was attacked and blinded by state police in Batesburg (now Batesburg-Leesville) in 1942. The NAACP publicized the story, and the event sparked a national outcry. Woody Guthrie recorded "The Blinding of Isaac Woodward" in response, and President Truman directed the Justice Department to investigate the case. Though Woodward's assailant was not convicted, the case was a factor in Truman's decision to establish the Civil Rights Commission in 1947 and to submit the first comprehensive civil rights bill to Congress in 1948. ::

The Crisis 53, no. 9 (September 1946): 276–77.

The Isaac Woodward Case: Southern police contempt for human decency and dignity where Negroes are concerned is made clear in the case of the brutal blinding of Isaac Woodard, twenty-seven-year old Negro veteran, by Batesburg, S.C., police. The wholly unnecessary and unbelievably fiendish beating and blinding of Woodward took place hardly more than three hours after the veteran's discharge from a mobilization center.

Woodard, who spent fifteen months in the Philippines and New Guinea with the 429th Port Battalion, served in the Army from October 13, 1942, to February 12, 1946, when he received an honorable discharge from Camp Gordon, Ga.

After his discharge from Camp Gordon, Woodard took a Greyhound bus in Atlanta, Ga., for Winnsboro, S. C., where he was to pick up his wife for a trip to New York to visit his parents. Somewhere between Atlanta and Aiken, S. C., Woodard got into an altercation with the driver over a "comfort stop." When the bus reached Batesburg, the driver had Woodard arrested for creating a disturbance. Neither the driver nor the police gave him a chance to explain, and when they got him to the jail the police pummelled and beat Woodard until he was unconscious, crunching out his eyes with the end of a billy.

Next morning Woodard was taken before the local judge and offered the choice of a $50 fine or thirty days on the road. But having only $40 cash and his mustering out check of $694.73, which he refused to sign, Woodward was taken back to the jail where the cops made clumsy attempts to treat his now sightless eyes. The police later took him to the veterans' hospital at Columbia, S. C., where he stayed from February 13 to April 13, 1946, until he was released in custody of his sisters.

The Association[10] has demanded that the Department of Justice investigate the beating and blinding of Woodard and that the guilty parties be prosecuted to the full extent of the law. On July 15, Howard C. Peterson, assistant secretary of war, notified the NAACP that Woodard's case is "now under study by the governor of South Carolina, the Veterans' Administration, and the Department of Justice."

Mr. Peterson adds that "by reason of the fact that Woodard was a civilian at the time of this unfortunate incident and no longer a member of the Army & or under military contract, the case does not come within jurisdiction of the War Department."

On July 24, at an Association sponsored meeting of veterans' organizations in the Wendell Willkie Memorial building,[11] a reward of $1,000 was posted for any person or persons supplying information that will lead to the apprehension and conviction of the policemen responsible for the outrageous attack upon Woodard. On August 10 Woodard was admitted to membership in the Blinded Veterans Association at organization headquarters, 80 Warren Street,

New York City. The NAACP has already had the American Red Cross file an application for full compensation for Woodard with the Veterans Administration.

In the meantime funds are pouring into the national office to aid Woodard. Ethel S. Epstein, former labor secretary under LaGuardia, enclosed a check for $250. Employees of the Dell Publishing company in New York have also contributed funds for the blinded veteran. Joe Louis, heavyweight boxing champion, sponsored a benefit for Woodard at the Lewisohn Stadium on August 16. Contributions to date total $2,118.89.

The public is warned that the NAACP is the only organization authorized and retained by Isaac Woodard to handle any matters connected with his case.

CHAPTER 6

"We Shall Overcome"

THE AFRICAN AMERICAN REVOLUTION
IN THE PALMETTO STATE

■

6.1. I'll Overcome Some Day (1900)

The anthem of the civil rights movement, "We Shall Overcome," was based on the gospel song "I'll Overcome Some Day," which was itself based in part on slave songs of the 1800s. In 1945 striking black tobacco workers in Charleston sang the song as they marched the picket lines, and by the end of the strike, in March 1946, they had replaced the "I" of the refrain with "We" to reflect their group solidarity. An activist visiting Charleston to assist the strikers heard the song, and she taught it to others when she returned to the Highlander Folk School in Tennessee, a social justice leadership training center and hub of civil rights reformers. From there, the song spread to become the most recognizable anthem of the movement. ::

This world is one great battlefield,
With forces all arrayed;
If in my heart I do not yield
I'll overcome some day.
I'll overcome some day,
I'll overcome some day,
If in my heart I do not yield,
I'll overcome some day.
Both seen and unseen powers join
to drive my soul astray,
But with God's word a sword of mine,

"I'll Overcome Some Day," in *New Songs of the Gospel* (Philadelphia: Hall-Mack, 1900), 27.

I'll overcome some day.
I'll overcome some day,
I'll overcome some day,
But with God's word a sword of mine,
I'll overcome some day.
A thousand snares are set for me,
And mountains in my way;
If Jesus will my leader be,
I'll overcome some day.
I'll overcome some day,
I'll overcome some day,
If Jesus will my leader be,
I'll overcome some day.
I fail so often when I try
My Savior to obey;
It pains my heart and then I cry,
Lord, make me strong some day.
Lord, make me strong some day,
Lord, make me strong some day,
It pains my heart and then I cry,
Lord, make me strong some day.
My mind is not to do the wrong,
But walk the narrow way;
I'm praying as I journey on,
To overcome some day.
To overcome some day.
To overcome some day.
I'm praying as I journey on,
To overcome some day.
Tho' many a time no signs appear,
Of answer when I pray,
My Jesus says I need not fear,
He'll make it plain some day.
I'll be like him some day.
I'll be like him some day.
My Jesus says I need not fear,
I'll be like him some day.

■

6.2. The Progressive Democratic Party Urges Boycott of Democratic Polling Places (1946)

John Henry McCray and other black South Carolina civil rights leaders founded the Progressive Democratic Party in 1944 to encourage African Americans to register to vote and to contest the validity of the white Democratic Party. Regular Democrats had organized themselves as a "private club" in order to exclude black participation in its primaries, effectively disfranchising black voters. ::

FROM: John H. McCray, Chairman, The Progressive Democratic Party, Columbia

TO: Party Members and all other Believers in Human Rights for ALL MEN

SUBJECT: *Immediate and Continued Boycott of All Business Places That Harbor Enrollment and Voting Facilities of the S.C. Democratic Party*

Perhaps the most commonly known principle of military strategy is "The BEST DEFENSE is a STRONG OFFENSE." "STRATEGY" means a plan or scheme for defeating an enemy—for gaining some advantage.

Plans exhibiting THE MOST EFFECTIVE STRATEGY must be employed constantly to gain advantage in the fight for political equality in this state which, of course, taxes all Negroes in full measure to help pay its obligations although they do not help elect the officials. Men who think at all will tell you that *"TAXATION WITHOUT REPRESENTATION"* is just as tyrannical in 1946 as it was when George the Third of England pulled the same villainous trick on the Thirteen Colonies.

It has been suggested by an outstanding South Carolinian that Negroes should employ the strategy of BOYCOTTING EVERY PLACE used by the South Carolina ("White Supremacy") Democratic Party for enrollment and voting purposes. I have discussed this matter with several prominent persons including Mr. O.E. McKaine,[1] member of the Advisory Board of the Southern Negro Youth Congress[2] and of the field staff of the Southern Congress for Human Welfare;[3] and Mrs. Andrew W. Simkins, also a member of the advisory board of the SNYC and who is also closely connected with the Southern Conference for Human Welfare, the Southern Regional Council,[4] and the Civil Rights Congress[5] as well as the NAACP.

John H. McCray to Party Members, August 1946, Black History–Civil Rights Minority Issues—1970s to Present, Vertical File, courtesy of the South Caroliniana Library, University of South Carolina, Columbia.

All persons contacted are in full accord with the suggestion. They declare that any person who supports the "white supremacy" primary in any way is an ENEMY OF AMERICAN DEMOCRACY whether he realizes it or not—and that like other enemies of the full enjoyment of human rights anywhere in the world—must be made to pay for his un-Democratic acts. Further, they declare that not only does the South Carolina Democratic Party conspire against the Constitution of the United States and the Mandates of the highest Court of the Land,[6] but that it further besmears itself by condoning the ungentlemanly and insulting remarks continuously made against Negroes by certain aspirants for nomination as party candidates, although not a single Negro is expected to vote for or against any candidate.

In order to carry out the BOYCOTT suggestion, we must find out at once in every precinct in South Carolina the place of business that houses the primary polling places. These places are very likely to be listed in many daily and weekly papers over this weekend. Look for these lists and notify others. We shall also seek every list possible and send them out to party leaders. If you do not find the lists—GO YOURSELF AND GET OTHERS TO GO OUT TUESDAY, AUGUST 13, AND FIND OUT WHERE THE POLLS ARE. Wherever they are—in drug stores—grocery stores—in places where automobiles are sold or repaired—in whatever place of business they are—DECIDE YOURSELF AND AND URGE EVERY OTHER NEGRO NEVER TO ENTER THOSE PLACES AGAIN EXCEPT POSSIBLY IN CASES OF EXTREME EMERGENCY, OR THEY MAY BE JUDGES TRAITOROUS.

If you are running accounts at any of those voting places, pay up and take your business elsewhere. To keep up the fight and make it hotter as time goes by, leave every place from now on where either the enrolment or the voting of the "white supremacy primary" takes place. If you find that tax-supported places like schools are used, get your mind made up to take out injunctions the next time it occurs. We must MEAN BUSINESS. In business MONEY TALKS! MAKE IT YELL!!!

We must contend that who is not for us is AGAINST US. And we must fight them with whatever strategy that is legal, manly, and womanly. The above suggestion is that and MORE. It will bear good fruit! Let's carry it out to a "T".

■

6.3. Majority Opinion in *Elmore v. Rice* (1947)

In 1947 George Elmore (1905–1993) filed a class-action lawsuit to test the legality of the South Carolina Democratic Party's organizing itself as a "private" white-only club that prohibited African Americans from participating in its primaries. In a state with a nearly nonexistent Republican Party, this procedure essentially disfranchised

72 F. Supp. 516 (E.D.S.C. 1947)

black voters and guaranteed Democratic victory. Judge J. Waites Waring's landmark ruling opened primaries to all South Carolina voters. ::

. . . Plaintiff, George Elmore, is a duly and legally qualified elector under the Constitution and laws of the United States and of the State of South Carolina and is subject to none of the disqualifications for voting thereunder. This suit is brought by him to test the legality of the action of the defendants in not permitting him and other qualified Negro electors to vote in the Democratic Party's Primary held on August 13, 1946, in Richland County, which Primary was held for the purpose of nominating candidates on the Democratic ticket for the House of Representatives of the United States, and for various State offices. The rules of the Democratic Party restrict voting in its primaries to white persons. The plaintiff, George Elmore, is a Negro. . . .

In South Carolina for many years the Democratic Party has conducted primary elections for the choice of municipal, county, state and federal officers. It is a matter of common knowledge that for a great many years the Democratic Party has completely controlled the filling of offices in the State of South Carolina. For the purpose of this case and as shown by the stipulations, certain dates are fixed, and it is agreed that since 1900 every Governor, member of the General Assembly, United States Representative and United States Senator for the State of South Carolina, elected by the people of this State in the General Elections, was the nominee of the then existing Democratic Party of South Carolina, and that during the past 25 years the Democratic Party of South Carolina has been the only political party in this State to hold State-wide primaries for the nomination of candidates for Federal and State offices . . . the Democratic Primary in South Carolina was regulated and controlled by direct State action and was an integral part of the election laws of the State. . . . And in 1944 with the decision in Smith v. Allwright[7] . . . it was clearly evident that the Democratic Party in South Carolina, as then constituted and acting under the statutes enacted by its State, no longer had the right to limit its members to whites and to exclude Negroes.

And this was clearly recognized by the officers and those in charge of the Democratic Party, as well as State and Federal officials, who were the same in many cases. As a matter of fact, the then Governor of the State of South Carolina, Olin D. Johnston (now United States Senator from this State), issued a proclamation calling for an Extraordinary Session of the General Assembly of South Carolina to convene on April 14, 1944. In that proclamation . . . he stated one of the specific purposes of the session was for "the purpose of safeguarding our elections, the repealing of all laws on the statute books pertaining to Democratic Primary elections." The General Assembly convened and received a message from the Governor in which he elaborated the purpose for which the extraordinary session was called and urged that it be limited "to the consideration of matters pertaining to elections and election laws." . . . Among other things, the Governor also said:

. . . "I regret that this ruling by the United States Supreme Court has forced this issue upon us, but we must meet it like men. I further regret that certain agitators within and without South Carolina are taking advantage of this situation to create strife and dissension at the present time. These agitators are not friends of either race, but they are creating strife and dissension to further their own selfish gain.

"History has taught us that we must keep our white Democratic primaries pure and unadulterated so that we might protect the welfare and homes of all the people of our State. . . .

"The Attorney General's Office, with the assistance of the Solicitors of this State, have been working diligently for several days upon the matter of finding all primary laws upon the statute books that must be repealed so that we might have a free, white Democratic primary which can nominate its candidates free and untrammeled without legislative sanction.

"After these statutes are repealed, in my opinion, we will have done everything within our power to guarantee white supremacy in our primaries of our State insofar as legislation is concerned. Should this prove inadequate, we South Carolinians will use the necessary methods to retain white supremacy in our primaries and to safeguard the homes and happiness of our people.

"White supremacy will be maintained in our primaries. Let the chips fall where they may!"

Thereafter, at this extraordinary session, lasting from April 14 to April 20, 1944, the General Assembly repealed a large number of statutes (approximately 150) all relating to State regulation of primaries and their organization and government or to elections held thereunder. The work seems to have been completely and thoroughly done insofar as I am informed. Every trace of statutory regulation of party primaries was expunged from the statutes of this State. . . .

The stipulations in this case show that in the Democratic Primary of August 1946 (the one in which plaintiff was denied the right to vote) there were cast for the office of Governor of the State 290,223 votes, whereas in the General Election in November of that year the votes for that same office amounted to only 26,326. It is further shown that since 1900, every Governor, and all members of the General Assembly, and also all United States Representatives and United States Senators, elected by the people of South Carolina in the General Elections, were the nominees of the then existing Democratic Party of the State; and that during the past 25 years the Democratic Party is the only political party in this State which has held statewide primaries for the nomination of candidates for Federal and State offices. . . .

[I]n these United States the time has passed for a discussion of whether we should have universal suffrage.... The Constitution and laws of the United States provide for it and forbid discrimination because of race or creed. A free ballot to be freely exercised by all the citizens is the established American way of government. In the argument in this case, frequent reference was made to the desirability or undesirability of whites and blacks voting in the same primary, and it was suggested that the Negroes have a separate primary from the whites. It was further suggested that the parties in South Carolina are substantially the same as private clubs; and that a private club has a right to choose its membership and the members to determine with whom they wish to associate. Of course that is true of any private club or private business or association, but private clubs and business organizations do not vote and elect a President of the United States, and the Senators and members of the House of Representatives of our national congress; and under the law of our land, all citizens are entitled to a voice in such selections. It has been stated, and I believe it is a fact, that South Carolina is the only State which now conducts a primary election solely for whites....

When the General Assembly, answering the call of Governor Johnston, met in extraordinary session, it was wholly and solely for the purpose of preventing the Negro from gaining a right to vote in the primaries as granted under the doctrine of the Smith v. Allwright case. There was no concealment as to the reason for this call.... For too many years the people of this Country, and perhaps particularly of this State, have evaded realistic issues. In these days when this Nation and the Nations of the world are forced to face facts in a realistic manner, and when this country is taking the lead in maintaining the democratic process and attempting to show to the world that the American government and the American way of life is the fairest and best that has yet been suggested, it is time for us to take stock of our internal affairs....

It is time for South Carolina to rejoin the Union. It is time to fall in step with the other states and to adopt the American way of conducting elections.

I am of the opinion that the present Democratic Party in South Carolina is acting for and on behalf of the people of South Carolina; and that the Primary held by it is the only practical place where one can express a choice in selecting federal and other officials. Racial distinctions cannot exist in the machinery that selects the officers and lawmakers of the United States; and all citizens of this State and Country are entitled to cast a free and untrammelled ballot in our elections, and if the only material and realistic elections are clothed with the name "primary", they are equally entitled to vote there.

The prayer of the complaint for a declaratory judgment will therefore be granted by which it will be adjudged that the plaintiff and others similarly situated are entitled to be enrolled and to vote in the primaries conducted by the

Democratic Party of South Carolina, and the defendants and their successors in office will be enjoined from excluding qualified voters from enrollment and casting ballots by reason of their not being persons of the white race. Appropriate findings of fact and conclusions of law and an order carrying the foregoing into effect will be entered.

■

6.5. The Negro in America Today (1954)

Alan Paton (1903–1988) was a South African author and anti-apartheid activist. His first novel, Cry, the Beloved Country *(1948), explored the tragedies of racial injustice and exposed South Africa's system of apartheid to the world. In 1954 Paton was asked by* Collier's *Magazine to travel to the American South to observe and to interview Southerners about their own system of racial segregation His thoughts on South Carolina appear in this excerpt. ::*

I had the privilege of an interview with Governor James Francis Byrnes of South Carolina. I have a great respect for governors, especially one who had been a Justice of the Supreme Court, Director of War Mobilization and Secretary of State. The governor is seventy-five years of age, but does not look it.

Governor Byrnes justified segregation to me on the ground of "natural orders." Nature, he said, had her categories, and individuals from the one were not found in the other. In the shoals of blackfish one never encountered a . . . (here I lost the word, but I hope that it might have been a whiting). He said that this talk of "conflict in the soul of the South" was nonsense. It was the Negro of mixed blood who was the unhappy man—who, because he belonged to no order, fought unceasingly for the removal of any differentiation whatsoever. And the National Association for the Advancement of Colored People was his instrument.

I asked the governor about the U.S. Army posts in the South, where no segregation was permitted. How could such practice be tolerated by a state whose own practices were diametrically opposed? He replied that if these were the policies of the Army, there was nothing more to be said; but the Army would be expected to respect the segregation policies of the state when it went off the post.

In this reply one sees clearly the final yielding of the South: the state will not ultimately oppose the United States. . . .

On March 25, 1954, the governor addressed the South Carolina Education Association. His closing words were: "We must earnestly pray that Almighty God will give to those who lead us the wisdom to know what is right and the courage to do the right."

Alan Paton, "The Negro in America Today," *Collier's* (October 15, 1954), 52–66.

It is impossible to mock at such words. The very use of them shows that the user knows that he and his state are caught up in a conflict of right and wrong. I have no doubt that Governor Byrnes would declare himself to be on the side of the angels—were he not afraid that the angels might be on the side of the Negroes. Perhaps that seems impossible to him, at this time, at his age, after all he has said. Still, he has counseled all the people of South Carolina to keep cool and calm, and has not said a word about the militia. . . .

. . . I visited School District No. 22, Clarendon County, South Carolina, and talked to William Ragin, of Route 2, Box 4, Summerton. He bought his farm in 1942, one hundred acres at $100 per acre. Today he owns everything on it, and owes no man anything. William Ragin is a small, spare man, with a way of smiling as though he knows of some pleasant thing private to himself.

Mr. Ragin was one of the small band of NAACP members who started the court case that culminated in the Supreme Court decision outlawing school segregation.[8] They went from house to house asking the parents of more than 1,000 Negro children to sign a petition claiming their children were denied the equal protection of the laws. Most of the people were afraid to sign, but eventually 25 did. Of these, some dropped out "when the steam got up." They were told they would lose their land or their jobs or suffer in other ways, if they kept their names on the petition. (The moving spirit of the group, the Reverend Mr. Joseph A. De Laine[9] [sic], by way of foretaste, lost his house; it burned or was burned to the ground—which, no one discovered. The fire engine came out, but finding that the house was beyond the city limits, it turned back again.)

The first court hearing was in Charleston, in 1951. Over the proceedings hung a grim weight of white disapproval, but the petitioners held on. They lost this first battle, but it was at this time that Judge J. Waites Waring presented a dissenting opinion in which he said that if segregation was wrong then the place to stop it was in the first grade and not in graduate colleges; segregation was per se inequality.

Mr. Ragin followed the case right up to Washington, but it was a different Washington from what he had once known. "I made it my business to eat in one of those places that I couldn't eat in before."

A small clean-looking boy rode up.

"That's the boy in the case," said Mr. Ragin. "That's Glenn."

I asked the boy if he knew anything about the case, but he shook his head.

"He was only six when it started," explained Mr. Ragin, "but he knows they built a new piece on the school."

"And your white neighbors, Mr. Ragin?"

"Well, some don't speak to me, and some speak as though nothing had happened, and one or two told me privately that they hoped we'd win."

"My father taught me to have no hate in me for anybody," he said. "But he said I was an American and I had to stand up for my rights."

He smiled reminiscently.

"He used to say to me, be a man, my son, because no one else can be a man for you...."

I went to see Glenn Ragin's school. It is one of the better colored schools of South Carolina, and it has this new piece Mr. Ragin spoke of. The state is spending more and more money on public schools; the cost goes up by leaps and bounds.

In 1944 South Carolina schools cost $16,000,000.

In 1949 they cost $34,000,000.

In 1954 they will cost $65,000,000.

In justice, it must be said that most of this increase is going to Negro schools. Governor Byrnes, speaking to the South Carolina Education Association last March, stated that Negro schools had been given two thirds of a sum of $94,000,000 allocated for use over a period of years as part of a far-reaching building program; that meant an expenditure of $106 for each white pupil and $271 for each Negro pupil. "We are forced to do in a few years what our fathers and grandfathers should have done in the past seventy- five years," the governor said.

I was able to visit one of the Negro schools in Clarendon County that had not yet benefited from the new dispensation. It was moving enough to see its forlorn state, its broken windows, its pathetic equipment, its sagging foundations. But more moving to me was the sight of the Stars and Stripes and under it these words:

> I pledge allegiance to the Flag of the United States of America,
> and to the Republic for which it stands; one nation indivisible, with
> liberty and justice for all.

Strange people, the colored people, who through such scorn and rejection have clung so fiercely to the ideal of America. Strange country, that, careless of liberty and justice and indivisibility, yet raises a William Ragin to restore them to her, and gives to a small, spare man the heart to fight for justice, and defeats him in place after place, so that he may have a victory in Washington....

■

6.6. Septima Clark Recalls Her Firing over Membership in the NAACP (1963)

Septima Poinsett Clark (1898–1987) was a lifetime educator and civil rights worker referred to by Martin Luther King Jr., as the "Mother of the Movement." In the 1920s, while teaching at Charleston's Avery Normal Institute, Clark joined the local chapter of the NAACP. Her petitioning efforts were instrumental in the placement of black teachers in Charleston's black schools in 1920. By 1956, Clark was vice president of the Charleston NAACP; that same same year, the South Carolina legislature passed a law prohibiting city and state employees from being members of civil rights organizations. Clark refused to resign her membership and was accordingly fired by the Charleston City School Board. ::

I have worked long and hard with NAACP. I began working with this much-maligned organization . . . when I first went on the islands. I can remember the county supervisor coming to collect the dollar membership from us for the NAACP. Then when I later went to Columbia I worked with the NAACP and walked the streets recruiting memberships. In Charleston I was made a member of the education committee and then elected first vice president of the NAACP. And in Charleston as well as in the rest of South Carolina and the South—and other sections of the nation, I hasten to add—being a member of the NAACP makes one immediately suspect.

In fact, after the sensational 1954 opinion of the United States Supreme Court was handed down, in which segregation of public school children by race was held unconstitutional—and this decision, incidentally, was in a case which originated in South Carolina—school authorities in the country passed out questionnaires requiring among other things that we list organizations with which we were affiliated. I refused to overlook my membership in the NAACP, as some of the teachers had done, and listed it. In February 1956 after I was dismissed, I sent a registered letter to the superintendent asking for the reason why I had not been employed again but received only the signed card in return. I am of the opinion that the fact that I listed membership in the NAACP was not the only reason for my dismissal, but I believe it was the determining one. . . .

There were perhaps related reasons. In my civic work in Charleston and on Johns Island, where I had continued to work as the opportunity was provided me, and particularly in the relationship I had had with the Warings in seeking to better the conditions of the Negro teachers and the Negro citizenship in general, I had called attention to myself.

From Septima Poinsett Clark, *Echo in my Soul* (New York: Dutton, 1962), 111–18.

Too, in starting a Parent-Teacher group and in working consistently with it, I had become better known, particularly after we began developing a workshop course in which twenty-two communities were represented and some ninety persons participated. And when I asked Myles Horton[10] and his wife Zilphia to come down and take part in the workshop, I think that must have been the final straw. . . .

At the workshop we had handed out NAACP literature and also Highlander School announcements, and of course Myles and Zilphia and some others interested in Highlander had been on our programs. I had been completely outspoken in my talks and participation in the various discussions, though I was mindful of the fact that as a teacher in the public schools I would be vulnerable to criticism. I was not worried, however, and had no feelings of danger being imminent. I was trying to do what I felt was my duty; I was trying then as I had tried through the years before and have been trying in the years since to contribute something to the advancement of our southern community by helping elevate the lives of a large segment of it.

But the workshop . . . caused quite a commotion in Charleston. I remember that just after the workshop closed, a front page story in the newspaper reviewed the things we had done. It disclosed the fact—and we had in no way attempted to hide what we had been doing—that the pamphlets had been distributed and that these pamphlets advocated the desegregation of the public schools. The newspaper advanced the opinion that we were going a little too far. . . . So the publicity from our workshop activities created widespread discussion. And these various incidents and the attendant publicity contributed, I believe, to the situation that resulted in my dismissal in 1956. . . .

I was not nervous and not afraid . . . I felt then—and I feel now—that a kind Providence directs us when we strive to do what we think is right, and I have sought all the years since as an eighteen-year-old girl I went over on John's Island, to do what is right, not only for my own people but for all people.

■

6.7. Freedom Rider Remembers First Blood in South Carolina (1998)

Organized predominantly by the Congress of Racial Equality, the Freedom Riders were a racially mixed group of civil rights activists who rode interstate buses into the segregated South to protest the nonenforcement of Supreme Court decisions that ruled segregated public buses unconstitutional. After encountering only minor trouble in the Upper South, the riders suffered their first violent attack in Rock Hill, a precursor to the mob violence that awaited them further in the Deep South. John Lewis

From John Lewis, *Walking with the Wind: A Memoir of the Movement* (New York: Harcourt Brace, 1998), 142–43.

(born 1940), now a U.S. congressman from Georgia, was a budding civil rights activist that summer in 1961. ::

As Al Bigelow and I approached the "WHITE" waiting room in the Rock Hill Greyhound terminal, I noticed a large number of young white guys hanging around the pinball machines in the lobby. Two of these guys were leaning by the doorjamb to the waiting room. They wore leather jackets, had those duck-tail haircuts and were each smoking a cigarette.

"Other side, nigger," one of the two said, stepping in my way as I began to walk through the door. He pointed to a door down the way with a sign that said "COLORED."

I did not feel nervous at all. I really did not feel afraid.

"I have a right to go in here," I said, speaking carefully and clearly, "on the grounds of the Supreme Court decision in the *Boynton* case."

I don't think either of these guys had ever heard of the *Boynton* case. Not that it would have mattered.

"Shit on that," one of them said.

The next thing I knew, a fist smashed the right side of my head. Then another hit me square in the face. As I fell to the floor I could feel feet kicking me hard in the sides. I could taste blood in my mouth.

At that point Al Bigelow stepped in, placing his body between mine and these men, standing square, with his arms at his sides.

It had to look strange to these guys to see a big, strong white man putting himself in the middle of a fistfight like this, not looking at all as if he was ready to throw a punch, but not looking frightened either.

They hesitated for an instant. Then they attacked Bigelow, who did not raise a finger as these young men began punching him. It took several blows to drop him to one knee.

At that point several of the white guys by the pinball machines moved over to join in. Genevieve Hughes stepped in their way and was knocked to the floor.

That finally brought a reaction from a police officer who had stood by and witnessed the entire scene. He stepped in, pulled one guy off us and said, "All right, boys. Y'all've done about enough now. Get on home."

Within minutes more police arrived, including a sympathetic officer who asked if we wanted to press charges. I was back on my feet by then, woozy and feeling stabs of sharp pain above both eyes and in my ribs. My lower lip was bleeding pretty heavily. I've always had very sensitive lips. They cut easily.

We said no to the offer to press charges. This was simply another aspect of the Gandhian perspective. Our struggle was not against one person or against a small group of people like those who attacked us that morning. The struggle was against a *system*, the system that helped produce people like that. We didn't see these young guys who attacked us that day as the problem. We saw them as victims. The problem was much bigger, and to focus on these individuals would be nothing more than a distraction, a sideshow that would draw attention away from where it belonged, which in this case was the sanctioned system of segregation in the entire South.

The attack that day—the first time blood was drawn on the Freedom Ride—did exactly what we wanted it to do. It drew attention. The next morning's newspapers across the country carried a small story about the beating of these Freedom Riders in South Carolina. There's no telling, though, how many Americans paid attention to that little story, considering that the day's big headline was the flight of NASA's first manned rocket, which was circling the earth above us with an astronaut named Alan Shepard aboard.

I had no idea that history was being made up in space while I was being beaten in Rock Hill. It was only later that I learned about that. At the time, my entire world was framed by the windows of that Greyhound bus and by the towns and terminals we stepped into. Nothing else existed. Nothing else mattered. . . .

Later that day the other riders, who had left Charlotte two hours behind us, arrived in Rock Hill to find the Trailways terminal closed and locked. Their alarm turned to relief once we were reunited, but we all realized that morning was probably just the beginning, a warning shot of even worse to come. . . .

■

6.8. Demands of Black Charlestonians (1963)

The year 1963 was marked by violence and bloodshed in many Southern cities as the white establishment refused to abandon policies of segregation. However, in South Carolina, a summer-long civil disobedience campaign in Charleston led not to violent backlash but rather to progress, as black activists and whites committed to law and order quietly took steps to dismantle Jim Crow. ::

CHARLESTON, SOUTH CAROLINA

Under sponsorship of the NAACP branch in Charleston, South Carolina, Negro citizens have gained what is being hailed as the "most significant and productive break-through yet achieved as the result of desegregation demonstrations in the South.

Ninety King Street merchants in this old port city, where Civil War began 102 years ago, agreed on August 1 to meet the six demands put forth by the Charleston movement . . . led by youthful James Blake, Morehouse College student and member of the NAACP board of directors, and I. DeQuincey

The Crisis (August–September 1963): 413–14.

Newman,[11] NAACP field secretary for South Carolina. Five drug stores located in other parts of the city also agreed to desegregate their soda fountains. Negro leaders agreed to stop picketing the stores participating in the agreement and to call off the selective buying campaign.

In addition, the Francis Marion Hotel, Holiday Inn, two smaller motels, and four of the city's better restaurants have agreed to open their facilities to all irrespective of race or color.

During the demonstrations which covered a span of two months, more than 800 persons were arrested including Bishop D. Ward Nichols[12] of the AME Church, a native of Georgetown and an NAACP life member, Mr. Blake and Mr. Newman. The total arrests required the posting of bonds in excess of $1,000,000. Following the demonstration of July 16, Gov. Donald S. Russell ordered 125 state law enforcement officers into the city and alerted the National Guard.

Despite an injunction issued at the request of the City Council, Negroes continued the demonstrations. As a result, Newman and Blake were re-arrested, tried and found guilty of contempt of court and contributing to the delinquency of minors who participated in the demonstrations. They were each given suspended sentences of six months in prison. In addition they were ordered to jail for 10 days and fined $100.00.

State Circuit Court Judge Clarence E. Singletary has set August 9 for a hearing on their appeal from the judgment of the lower court. Meanwhile, both are now out on $15,000 bail for their leadership of the July 16 demonstration.

Meanwhile, negotiations for desegregation of all city-owned facilities continue with Mayor J. Palmer Gilliard. The Charleston County Library, the municipal golf course and city buses have already been desegregated. Negroes are seeking the desegregation of all city parks, playgrounds and swimming pools. Also employment of more Negro city workers in non-menial capacities.

The King Street merchants agreed in negotiations to meet the following six demands of the Negro citizens:

1. Equal job opportunity with appointment of Negro sales personnel.
2. Courtesy titles to all customers in conversation, accounts and correspondence.
3. Desegregation of lunch counters, sitting rooms, rest rooms, lounges, drinking fountains and other customer services.
4. Privilege of trying on hats, dresses and other clothing.
5. Serving customers in turn as they arrive, irrespective of race.
6. Equal pay and rank for Negro sales personnel.

The NAACP has agreed to help the merchants find men and women to fill the new job opportunities.

CHAPTER 7

"Common ground"

A NEW GENERATION OF
BLACK SOUTH CAROLINIANS

Isaiah DeQuincey Newman being sworn in by Lieutenant Governor
Mike Daniel as South Carolina's first African American state senator since
Reconstruction, October 25, 1983. From the Isaiah DeQuincey Newman Papers,
South Carolina Political Collections, University of South Carolina.

■

7.1. Keep Hope Alive (1988)

Jesse Jackson (born 1941) was born in Greenville, South Carolina. He became a prominent leader of the civil rights movement in the mid-1960s and achieved wide fame as a politician in the 1980s. He was twice a candidate for the Democratic nomination for president of the United States. His second-place showing in 1988 led to the following speech at the Democratic National Convention in Atlanta. ::

Tonight we pause and give praise and honor to God for being good enough to allow us to be at this place at this time. When I look out at this convention, I see the face of America, red, yellow, brown, black and white, we're all precious in God's sight—the real rainbow coalition.[1] . . .

My right and privilege to stand here before you has been won—in my lifetime—by the blood and sweat of the innocent. . . .

As a testament to the struggles of those who have gone before; as a legacy for those who will come after; as a tribute to the endurance, the patience, the courage of our forefathers and mothers; as an assurance that their prayers are being answered, their work has not been in vain, and hope is eternal—tomorrow night my name will go into nomination for the Presidency of the United States of America.

We meet tonight at a crossroads, a point of decision. Shall we expand, be inclusive, or suffer division and impotence? . . .

Tonight, I salute Governor Michael Dukakis.[2] He has run a well-managed and a dignified campaign. No matter how tired or how tried, he always resisted the temptation to stoop to demagoguery.

I've watched a good mind fast at work, with steel nerves, guiding his campaign out of the crowded field without appeal to the worst in us. I've watched his perspective grow as his environment expanded. I've seen his toughness and tenacity close-up. I know his commitment to public service.

Mike Dukakis's parents were a doctor and a teacher; my parents, a maid, a beautician and a janitor.

There is a great gap between Brookline, Massachusetts and Haney Street, the Fieldcrest Village housing project in Greenville, South Carolina. He studied law; I studied theology. There are differences of religion, region and race, differences in experiences and perspectives. But the genius of America is that out of the many, we become one.

Jesse Jackson, *Keep Hope Alive: Jesse Jackson's 1988 Presidential Campaign* (Boston: South End Press, 1989), 33–40.

Providence has enabled our paths to intersect. His foreparents came to America on immigrant ships; my foreparents on slave ships; we're in the same boat tonight. . . .

America's not a blanket woven from one thread, one color, one cloth. When I was a child growing up in Greenville, South Carolina, and grandmother could not afford a blanket, she didn't complain and we did not freeze. Instead, she took pieces of old cloth—patches, wool, silk, gabardine, crokersack, only patches—barely good enough to wipe your shoes with. But they didn't stay that way very long. With sturdy hands and a strong cord, she sewed them together into a quilt, a thing of beauty and power and culture.

Now, Democrats, we must build such a quilt. Farmers, you seek fair prices and you are right, but you cannot stand alone. Your patch is not big enough. Workers, you fight for fair wages. You are right. But your patch, labor, is not big enough. Women, you seek comparable worth and pay equity. You are right. But your patch is not big enough. Women, mothers, who seek Head Start and day care and prenatal care on the front side of life, rather than welfare and jail care on the back side of life, you're right, but your patch is not big enough.

Students, you seek scholarships. You are right. But your patch is not big enough. African Americans and Hispanics, when we fight for civil rights, we are right, but our patch is not big enough. Gays and lesbians, when you fight against discrimination and for a cure for AIDS, you are right, but your patch is not big enough. Conservatives and progressives, when you fight for what you believe, right-wing, left-wing, hawk, dove—you are right from your point of view, but your point of view is not enough.

But don't despair. Be as wise as my grandmamma. Pool the patches and the pieces together, bound by a common thread. When we form a great quilt of unity and common ground, we'll have the power to bring about health care and housing and jobs and education and hope to our nation. . . .

Don't surrender and don't give up. Why can I challenge you this way? Jesse Jackson, you don't understand my situation. You be on television. You don't understand. I see you with the big people. You don't understand my situation. I understand. You're seeing me on TV but you don't know what makes me me. They wonder why does Jesse run, because they see me running for the White House. They don't see the house I'm running from.

I have a story. I wasn't always on television. Writers were not always outside my door. When I was born late one afternoon, October 8th, in Greenville, South Carolina, no writers asked my mother her name. Nobody chose to write down our address. My mama was not supposed to make it. You see, I was born to a teenage mother who was born to a teenage mother.

I know abandonment and people being mean to you, and saying you're nothing and nobody, and can never be anything. I understand. Jesse Jackson is my third name. I'm adopted. When I had no name, my grandmother gave me her name. My name was Jesse Burns until I was 12. So I wouldn't have a blank space, she gave me a name to hold me over. I understand when you have no name. I understand.

I wasn't born in the hospital. Mama didn't have insurance. I was born in the bed at home. I really do understand. Born in a three-room house, bathroom in the backyard, slop jar by the bed, no hot and cold running water. I understand. Wallpaper used for decoration? No. For a windbreaker. I understand. I'm a working person's person, that's why I understand you whether you're African American or white. . . .

Hold your head high, stick your chest out. You can make it. It gets dark sometimes, but the morning comes. Don't you surrender. Suffering breeds character. Character breeds faith. In the end faith will not disappoint.

You must not surrender. You may or may not get there, but just know that you're qualified and you hold on and hold out. We must never surrender. America will get better and better. Keep hope alive. Keep hope alive. Keep hope alive. On tomorrow night and beyond, keep hope alive. . . .

■

7.2. Never Had It Made (1994)

Ernest Adolphus Finney Jr. (born 1931) earned a B.A. from Claflin College in 1952 and a law degree from South Carolina State College two years later. In 1961 he represented nine students who had staged one of the first sit-ins in South Carolina. He was elected to the General Assembly in 1972 and became the first African American to serve on the judiciary committee in the twentieth century. In 1983 Finney was named the state's first black circuit court judge. Two years after that, he became the first African American since Reconstruction to be elected to the South Carolina Supreme Court, and in 1994 he was named chief justice. His daughter Nikky Finney, who would go on to win the 2011 National Book Award in poetry, read the following poem at his investiture. ::

> Just a plain brown paper sack boy
> from a place and people
> who sweet fed him everything in double doses
> just in case his man size should ever
> wear a hole
> An ordinary brown corduroy boy
> from folk who never had it made
> but still managed to make

Nikky Finney, *Rice: Poems* (Evanston, Ill.: Northwestern University Press, 2013), 121–25.

whatever they were to be from scratch
A regular little fellow
whose mother never got to bathe or watch him grow
or even gaze him from the farmhouse window
where he loved to sit on a summertime box
of Virginia cured day dreams
umbrellaed by the big oak tree
and inbetween chores
and stare away at the longest dirt road
the only way in or out
to grandpop's farm
the same country road that all country boys
tried to stare down in their day
wondering what or who could ever be
at the end of all the dirt
watching it for signs of life
maybe somebody from the city might visit
some somebody from one of those shiny ready made
places
who could make magic
of a brown boy's country fried beginnings
Maybe one of those far away places
would take him just as homespun as he was
and grow him up to be something legal
maybe handsome
even dap debonair
and he might just become
the somebody who could easy talk
the most complicated of things
for the regulars
and for all others be
shiny as new money
From the first he was looking to be
one of those new Black men
who came visiting from the North
to talk pretty at the State College of South Carolina
one of those kinds
with the pocket chains and the shiny grey suits
with a hundred pounds of law books
under their arms
just like some kind of natural growth

stout with the law on their minds
devotees of justice
maybe he could be one of their kind
He never had it made
he only had a proud father and a circle of stubborn
arms and wiggling fingers
to keep his dying mama's promise
to raise the boy up at their sides
and not just anywheres
Don't let no strangers have him
knowing he would never have her there
to see to any of the raising herself
This one
that one there
had it sweetened and sifted
chewed up and spit back on his plate
he for sure had it prayed over
then chicken scratched around
in somebody's kitchen who loved him
through and through
over somebody's fire who pointed first to his
pantslegs
an then maybe a switch
whenever he was off his daily chalk straight line
And from beneath his granddaddy's wagon wheels
and form up under his people's stern tutelage
he was surely begun
but it wasn't nothing guaranteed
you know the ways I mean
all silver and engraved
He might'a had it boiled up every morning
explained and preached and on sunday gospelized
by an early rising grandmother
then a significant Claflin College
And I'm quite sure he soda jerked it back and forth
and baked his dreams in his own high hopes
to try and make sure it could so maybe happen
The good Lord willing and the creek don't rise
But he never had it brought out on some royal platter
never promised to him at his broken bones of a birth
the making of this man's silk deeds

came straight from polyester dreams
from tears and sea water sweat
from love and dirt work and the graciousness of his
God
all following him like a North star
He always loved the law
even in the middle of all those many years
when his own daughter argued history to him
poeting always what wasn't right fair or true
how he with the calm of a sailor
who had seen the ocean at its worst and then its best
with all the faith two eyes could keep safe for her
how he would always no matter say
"The law works, Girl."
And his own poetry has kept what was right right
and he has kept her and the law breathing
A steady drop of water
will wear a hole in a rock, Daughter.
Such are the vicissitudes of life, Son.
If you see me and the bear fighting,
you go and help the bear, my friend.
It's alright Babygirl, you win some and you lose some.
Just do the best you can with what you got everybody.
He is the justice man
and from his waiting tables as a young lawyer
for the white and the privileged
to this day here he has always believed
back then as boy with only a road
up here as man who never looks back
the law works Girl
Papa
Daddy
The Justice Man
you never had it made
but here you are making it
and all of us cross over with you
proud as peacocks in our brightest polyester
maybe that's what Pop
maybe that's what Mama Carlene
would say

∎

7.3. NAACP Boycott Resolution (1999)

Beginning in 1962, the Confederate battle flag was flown atop the dome of the South Carolina State House below the flags of the United States and South Carolina. Although the flag was ostensibly raised to commemorate the centennial of the Civil War, critics of the flag condemned it as a racist symbol placed atop the dome by conservative lawmakers in defiance of the civil rights movement. Though criticism and controversy escalated through the 1990s, lawmakers refused to address the issue, and in July 1999 black leaders in the state, with the support of the NAACP, called for a tourism boycott of South Carolina until the flag came down. In less than a year, the state lost at least $20 million in revenue, and legislators finally acquiesced with a compromise: the flag would be removed from the dome of the State House on July 1, 2000, and moved to a position beside the Confederate memorial on the capitol grounds. This was not a satisfactory arrangement to many African Americans and the NAACP, which vowed to maintain the boycott as long as the banner occupied any place of honor on the grounds. The NAACP Board of Directors voted to lift the 15 year boycott July 11, 2015, the day after the flag was finally removed. ::

1999 N.A.A.C.P. Emergency Resolution

ECONOMIC SANCTIONS FOR SOUTH CAROLINA

Whereas, the Confederate States of America came into being by way of secession from and war against the United States of America out of a desire to defend the right of individual states to maintain an economic system based on slave labor, and

Whereas, the Confederate Battle Flag was raised in the States that comprised the defunct Confederate States of America for the supposed celebration of the Centennial of the War Between the States and as an unspoken symbol of resistance to the battle for civil rights and equality in the early 1960's, and

Whereas, the Confederate Battle Flag has been embraced as the primary symbol for the numerous modern-day groups advocating white supremacy, and

Whereas, the placement of the Confederate Battle Flag at the South Carolina State House with the flags of two existing governments, the United States of America and the state of South Carolina, implies sovereignty and allegiance to a non-existent nation, and

Whereas, the Confederate Battle Flag in its present position of display makes a statement of public policy that continues to be an affront to the sensibilities and dignity of a majority of African Americans in the state of South Carolina, and

Whereas, the state of South Carolina possesses a unique linkage of heritage and family which makes South Carolina a prime destination for African American family reunions, resulting in tourism dollars that benefit the state of South Carolina, an estimated sixty-eight percent (68%) of all African American family reunions are held in South Carolina, and

Whereas, dollars spent on tourism, conventions and meetings by African Americans, other people of conscience and corporate entities serve to enrich the state of South Carolina, the "Mother State of Secession", which continues to fly the banner of secession

Now Be It Therefore Resolved, that the National Association for the Advancement of Colored People at its 1999 Annual Convention reaffirms its condemnation of the Confederate Battle Flag being flown over the South Carolina State Capitol and displayed within the South Carolina House and Senate Chambers, and renews its call for the removal and relocation of the Confederate Battle Flag to a place of historical rather than sovereign context.

Be It Further Resolved, that all units of the NAACP shall join in the South Carolina Conference of Branches in urging all families planning reunions in South Carolina to consider locations outside of the States as reunion sites until such time that the Confederate Battle Flag is removed from positions of sovereignty in the state of South Carolina.

Be It Further Resolved, that the National NAACP shall call upon other African American National Organizations, churches, and faith groups, businesses and corporations, and similar national entities of other cultural compositions that embrace freedom and justice to consider locations other than the state of South Carolina as convention or meeting sites, until such time that the Confederate Battle Flag is removed from positions of sovereignty in the state of South Carolina.

Be It Finally Resolved, that the National NAACP shall apply these economic sanctions against the state of South Carolina as well as any further measures as appropriate, commencing January 1, 2000, until such time that the Confederate Battle Flag is no longer displayed in positions of sovereignty in the state of South Carolina.

■

7.4. Race Is Still an Issue (2003)

James E. Clyburn (born 1940) was born in Sumter and was an active civil rights organizer while a student at South Carolina State College. In 1971 he became the

Source: James E. Clyburn, "Race is Still an Issue," Clyburn Congressional Page, "Capital Column," http://www.house.gov/apps/list/speech/sc06_clyburn030711raceanissue .html, accessed August 1, 2011.

Congressman James E.
Clyburn, official congressional photograph.

*first minority adviser to a South Carolina governor, and in 1992 he was elected as the
first African American member of South Carolina's congressional delegation in the
twentieth century. He became chairman of the House Democratic Caucus in 2006
and was elected majority whip in 2007.* ::

A few weeks ago various ceremonies were held around the nation commemo-
rating the 100th anniversary of the publication of, "Souls of Black Folks," W.E.B.
Dubois' 1903 treatise in which he intoned that this country's real challenge of
the 20th Century would be race. Recent events serve notice that he could have
included the 21st Century as well.

On Monday, June 23, the United States Supreme Court handed down a split
decision on Affirmative Action upholding the constitutionality of using race
as a consideration in admissions to the University of Michigan's Law school
while knocking down the point system the university used for admissions to its

undergraduate school.[3] On that same day life was snuffed out of Maynard Jackson,[4] arguably our nation's most successful practitioner of efforts to eliminate the current effects of past discrimination and level the playing field for future generations. . . .

I first met Maynard in April 1970 when he came to Charleston, South Carolina to keynote a banquet being held to launch my political career. The following morning I drove him to Columbia. His imposing physique left little room for me in the front seat of my 1969 non air-conditioned Mustang. And when he spoke, I found it necessary to keep the windows cracked, more to let out the decibels of his resonating voice than to let cool air in. He provided me with my first experience with surround sound.

A significant portion of Maynard's time and efforts during what turns out to be his final days were devoted to re-igniting the passions that in earlier times drove people of color to vote in record numbers. He had made that interest known in recent meetings of the Democratic National Committee.

As an African American, issues of race color my daily life. I experience them riding on elevators, getting on airplanes, and driving along the state's and nation's highways. And as the first such member of South Carolina's Congressional Delegation since post-Reconstruction (1897), racial issues occupy more than a fair amount of my congressional duties and responsibilities. But it often takes significant events to bring these issues into proper focus.

Three days after Maynard died, Senator Strom Thurmond passed away, and CNN requested an interview from me the following day. I consented, and met them at the Senator's monument on the south side of the Statehouse grounds prepared for an interview about the great statesman's life and legacy. Instead, I was led to the Confederate soldiers' monument on the north side of the Statehouse grounds, where the Confederate battle flag is prominently displayed. During the interview I was asked if I thought Thurmond's death meant South Carolina could now move beyond its preoccupation with racial issues.

In answering the reporter's query, I said simply, as long as the Confederate Battle flag flies in a place of honor and maintains a cloak of currency, lingering affects of our state's segregationist past will continue to infiltrate our daily lives and color our official conduct. That is why the United States Supreme Court affirmed the need to take affirmative action to level the playing field in college admissions. It is why I held Maynard in such high esteem. It is why every speaker at Senator Thurmond's funeral sought to affirm Thurmond's change of heart on issues of race. And it is why the ghost of W.E.B. DuBois still lingers in our judicial chambers and legislative halls.

■

7.5. We Stood There (2009)

Genealogical research during Barack Obama's 2008 presidential campaign revealed that his wife (and eventual First Lady), Michelle Obama, was descended from enslaved Gullah men and women who worked the rice fields at Friendfield Plantation near Georgetown, South Carolina. The poet Tracy Swinton Bailey, herself a descendant of Georgetown slaves, honored their shared roots in the celebratory verses reproduced here. ::

Dear Michelle,

We Stood There

As the mist rose off the surface of the great North Santee
With its twisted, mossy fingers straining toward dawn
You and I stood shoulder to shoulder on the banks
And watched them.
Dark men with strong backs and quick wit and gifted hands.
Mothers with high cheekbones and clouds of wooly hair
And the feeling of sweetgrass on their fingertips.
We stood there, we two, transported from another time, another day,
And watched as they carefully settled into their tiny boats
Stroke after measured stroke taking them to tend the rice
To hell
To the killing field
We gazed upon them, you and I, clamping our mouths shut with shaking
    hands
Fighting the urge to scream warnings of alligators.
Water moccasins,
Malaria moving mosquitoes.
But neither of us looked away,
Mesmerized by the beauty of their faces
And the new day turning blood red the mirror of the waters.
They stood there.
A cloud of witnesses; a million strong.
They stood there watching me, watching you

Tracy Swinton Bailey, "We Stood There," from *Go Tell Michelle: African American Women Write to the New First Lady*, ed. Barbara A. Seals Nevergold and Peggy Brooks-Bertram (Albany: SUNY Press, 2009), 79–80.

Watching over us all.
They stood behind your shoulder, to your right, one step behind
As you embraced him.
They whispered in your right ear as you whispered into his left.
And I heard a million whispers crescendo into a triumphant roar,
"Our daughter, we are O, so proud of you."

■

7.6. Barack Obama's South Carolina Primary Victory Speech (2008)

On January 26, 2008, South Carolina held its Democratic presidential primary, the first to be held that year in the South and the first in a state with a large African American population. Despite a bitter, racially charged contest, Obama marshaled a biracial coalition that swept him to victory. Black voters made up slightly more than half the Democratic electorate, but the future president also showed well among white voters. To some observers, Obama's victory signaled a shift to a postracial society. Though subsequent events have proved this suggestion premature, South Carolina had certainly entered into a new era of politics and race relations. ::

Thank you, South Carolina! [Cheers, applause.]
[Chants of "Yes, We Can! Yes, We Can!"]
Thank you. Thank you.
[Continued chants of "Yes, We Can!"]
Thank you, everybody. Thank you. Thank you, South Carolina. [Cheers, applause.] Thank you. Thank you, South Carolina. Thank you to the rock of my life, Michelle Obama. [Cheers, applause.]

Thank you to Malia and Sasha Obama, who haven't seen their daddy in a week. [Cheers, applause.] Thank you to Pete Skidmore[5] for his outstanding service to our country and being such a great supporter of this campaign. [Cheers, applause.]

You know, over two weeks ago we saw the people of Iowa proclaim that our time for change has come.[6] [Cheers, applause.] But there were those who doubted this country's desire for something new, who said Iowa was a fluke, not to be repeated again. Well, tonight the cynics who believed that what began in the snows of Iowa was just an illusion were told a different story by the good people of South Carolina. [Cheers, applause.]

After four great contests[7] in every corner of this country, we have the most

"Barack Obama's Victory Speech following the South Carolina Primary, January 26, 2008," in *Presidential Campaigns: Documents Decoded*, ed. Daniel M. Shea and Brian M. Harward (Santa Barbara, Calif.: ABC-CLIO, 2013), 233–38.

votes, the most delegates—[cheers, applause]—and the most diverse coalition of Americans that we've seen in a long, long time. [Cheers, applause.]

You can see it in the faces here tonight. There are young and old, rich and poor. They are black and white, Latino and Asian and Native American. [Cheers, applause.] They are Democrats from Des Moines and independents from Concord and, yes, some Republicans from rural Nevada. And we've got young people all across this country who've never had a reason to participate until now. [Cheers, applause.] . . .

But if there's anything, though, that we've been reminded of since Iowa, it's that the kind of change we seek will not come easy. Now, partly because we have fine candidates in this field, fierce competitors who are worthy of our respect and our admiration—[applause]—and as contentious as this campaign may get, we have to remember that this is a contest for the Democratic nomination and that all of us share an abiding desire to end the disastrous policies of the current administration. [Cheers, applause.]

But there are real differences between the candidates. We are looking for more than just a change of party in the White House. We're looking to fundamentally change the status quo in Washington. [Cheers, applause.] It's a status quo that extends beyond any particular party. And right now that status quo is fighting back with everything it's got, with the same old tactics that divide and distract us from solving the problems people face, whether those problems are health care that folks can't afford or a mortgage they cannot pay.

So this will not be easy. Make no mistake about what we're up against. . . . We're up against the idea that it's acceptable to say anything and do anything to win an election. But we know that this is exactly what's wrong with our politics. This is why people don't believe what their leaders say anymore. This is why they tune out. And this election is our chance to give the American people a reason to believe again. [Cheers, applause.]

But let me say this, South Carolina. What we've seen in these last weeks is that we're also up against forces that are not the fault of any one campaign but feed the habits that prevent us from being who we want to be as a nation.

It's a politics that uses religion as a wedge and patriotism as a bludgeon, a politics that tells us that we have to think, act, and even vote within the confines of the categories that supposedly define us, the assumption that young people are apathetic, the assumption that Republicans won't cross over, the assumption that the wealthy care nothing for the poor and that the poor don't vote, the assumption that African-Americans can't support the white candidate, whites can't support the African-American candidate, blacks and Latinos cannot come together.

We are here tonight to say that that is not the America we believe in. [Cheers, applause.]

[Chants of "Yes, We Can! Yes, We Can!"]

I did not travel around this state over the last year and see a white South Carolina or a black South Carolina. I saw South Carolina—[cheers, applause]—because in the end, we're not up just against the ingrained and destructive habits of Washington. We're also struggling with our own doubts, our own fears, our own cynicism. The change we seek has always required great struggle and great sacrifice. And so this is a battle in our own hearts and minds about what kind of country we want and how hard we're willing to work for it.

So let me remind you tonight that change will not be easy. Change will take time. There will be setbacks and false starts, and sometimes we'll make mistakes. But as hard as it may seem, we cannot lose hope, because there are people all across this great nation who are counting on us, who can't afford another four years without health care. [Cheers.] They can't afford another four years without good schools. [Cheers.] They can't afford another four years without decent wages because our leaders couldn't come together and get it done.

Theirs are the stories and voices we carry on from South Carolina—the mother who can't get Medicaid to cover all the needs of her sick child. She needs us to pass a health care plan that cuts costs and makes health care available and affordable for every single American. That's what she's looking for. [Cheers, applause.]

The teacher who works another shift at Dunkin' Donuts after school just to make ends meet—she needs us to reform our education system so that she gets better pay and more support and that students get the resources that they need to achieve their dreams. [Cheers, applause.]

The Maytag worker who's now competing with his own teenager for a $7-an-hour job at the local Wal-Mart because the factory he gave his life to shut its doors—he needs us to stop giving tax breaks to companies that ship our jobs overseas and start putting them in the pockets of working Americans who deserve it—[cheers, applause]—and put them in the pockets of struggling homeowners who are having a tough time, and looking after seniors who should retire with dignity and respect.

That woman who told me that she hasn't been able to breathe since the day her nephew left for Iraq, or the soldier who doesn't know his child because he's on his third or fourth or even fifth tour of duty—they need us to come together and put an end to a war that should have never been authorized and should have never been waged. [Cheers, applause.]

So understand this, South Carolina. The choice in this election is not between regions or religions or genders. It's not about rich versus poor, young versus old, and it is not about black versus white. [Cheers, applause.]

This election is about the past versus the future. [Cheers, applause.] It's about whether we settle for the same divisions and distractions and drama that passes for politics today or whether we reach for a politics of common sense and innovation, a politics of shared sacrifice and shared prosperity.

There are those who will continue to tell us that we can't do this, that we can't have what we're looking for, that we can't have what we want, that we're peddling false hopes. But here's what I know. I know that when people say we can't overcome all the big money and influence in Washington, I think of that elderly woman who sent me a contribution the other day, an envelope that had a money order for $3.01—[cheers, applause]—along with a verse of Scripture tucked inside the envelope. So don't tell us change isn't possible. That woman knows change is possible. [Cheers, applause.]

When I hear the cynical talk that blacks and whites and Latinos can't join together and work together, I'm reminded of the Latino brothers and sisters I organized with and stood with and fought with side by side for jobs and justice on the streets of Chicago. So don't tell us change can't happen. [Cheers, applause.]

When I hear that we'll never overcome the racial divide in our politics, I think about that Republican woman who used to work for Strom Thurmond, who's now devoted to educating inner-city children, and who went out into the streets of South Carolina and knocked on doors for this campaign. Don't tell me we can't change. [Cheers, applause.]

Yes, we can. Yes, we can change.

[Chants of "Yes, We Can! Yes, We Can!"]

Yes, we can.

[Continued chants of "Yes, We Can!"]

Yes, we can heal this nation. Yes, we can seize our future. And as we leave this great state with a new wind at our backs, and we take this journey across this great country, a country we love, with the message we've carried from the plains of Iowa to the hills of New Hampshire, from the Nevada desert to the South Carolina coast, the same message we had when we were up and when we were down, that out of many we are one, that while we breathe we will hope, and where we are met with cynicism and doubt and fear and those who tell us that we can't, we will respond with that timeless creed that sums up the spirit of the American people in three simple words: Yes, we can.

Thank you, South Carolina. I love you. [Cheers, applause.]

NOTES

Preface

1. Walter B. Edgar, *South Carolina, A History* (Columbia: University of South Carolina Press, 1997), 565.

Introduction

1. Walter B. Edgar, *South Carolina, A History* (Columbia: University of South Carolina Press, 1997), 21–22; Lawrence S. Rowland, Alexander Moore, and George C. Rodgers, *The History of Beaufort County, South Carolina*, vol. 1: *1514–1861* (Columbia: University of South Carolina Press, 1996), 18; Peter H. Wood, *Black Majority: Negroes in Colonial South Carolina from 1670 through the Stono Rebellion* (New York: Norton, 1974), 3–4.
2. Edgar, *South Carolina*, 22; Peter H. Wood, *Strange New Land: Africans in Colonial America* (New York: Oxford University Press, 1996), 3.
3. The phrase is from John Charles Chasteen's *Born in Blood and Fire: A Concise History of Latin America* (New York: Norton, 2001).
4. Wood, *Strange New Land*, 22; Jane Landers, *Black Society in Spanish Florida* (Urbana: University of Illinois Press, 1999), 13.
5. Wood, *Black Majority*, 6.
6. Edgar, *South Carolina*, 36; see also Jack P. Greene, "Colonial South Carolina and the Caribbean Connection," in *Imperatives, Behaviors, and Identities: Essays in Early American Cultural History*, ed. Jack P. Greene (Charlottesville: University of Virginia Press, 1992), 68–86.
7. Richard S. Dunn, *Sugar and Slaves: The Rise of the Planter Class in the English West Indies, 1624–1713* (New York: Norton, 1973), 71–74, 83, 225; Edgar, *South Carolina*, 37–38.
8. Dunn, *Sugar and Slaves*, 239.
9. Greene, "Colonial South Carolina," 69; Edgar, *South Carolina*, 36.
10. Wood, *Black Majority*, 15 n.4; Edgar, *South Carolina*, 41–42.
11. Edgar, *South Carolina*, 43–44; Robert K. Ackerman, *South Carolina Colonial Land Policies* (Columbia: University of South Carolina Press, 1977), 24; Peter A. Coclanis, *The Shadow of a Dream: Economic Life and Death in the South Carolina Lowcountry* (New York: Oxford University Press, 1989), 24–26.
12. Edgar, *South Carolina*, 48, 54–62; Rowland et al., *Beaufort County*, 63–65.
13. Wood, *Black Majority*, 13; Richard Waterhouse, *A New World Gentry: The Making*

of a Merchant and Planter Class in South Carolina, 1670–1770 (Charleston, S.C.: The History Press, 2005), 31; Edgar, *South Carolina*, 35, 48.

14. David Barry Gaspar, "A Dangerous Spirit of Liberty: Slave Rebellion in the West Indies in the 1730s," in *Origins of the Black Atlantic*, ed. Laurent DuBois and Julius S. Scott (New York: Routledge, 2013), 12.

15. Gregory E. O'Malley, *Final Passages: The Intercolonial Slave Trade of British America, 1619–1807* (Chapel Hill: University of North Carolina Press, 2014), 22; Edgar, *South Carolina*, 63.

16. Edgar, *South Carolina*, 67; Wood, *Black Majority*, xiv.

17. Edgar, *South Carolina*, 65; Daniel C. Littlefield, *Rice and Slaves: Ethnicity and the Slave Trade in Colonial South Carolina* (Urbana: University of Illinois Press, 1981), 8–32; Wood, *Black Majority*, 55–62.

18. Littlefield, *Rice and Slaves*, 118–21, 146–49.

19. Michael A. Gomez, *Exchanging Our Country Marks: The Transformation of African Identities in the Colonial and Antebellum South* (Chapel Hill: University of North Carolina Press, 1998), 154–58.

20. Ibid., 158–67; Marcus Rediker, *The Slave Ship: A Human History* (New York: Viking, 2007), 118.

21. Data from Voyages: The Trans-Atlantic Slave Trade Database, http://www.slave voyages.org/assessment/estimates (accessed December 18, 2015). The voyages database estimates that slaves on documented voyages represent four-fifths of the number actually transported.; Charles Spenser, *Edisto Island, 1663 to 1860: Wild Eden to Cotton Aristocracy* (Charleston, S.C.: The History Press, 2008), 55.

22. Edgar, *South Carolina*, 52–54; Robert L. Meriwether, *The Expansion of South Carolina, 1729–1765* (Kingsport, Tenn.: Southern Publishers, 1940), 19.

23. Quoted in Herbert Aptheker, *American Negro Slave Revolts* (New York: International Publishers, 1943), 171.

24. Wood, *Black Majority*, 218–68, 285–307.

25. Clayton E. Cramer, *Armed America: The Remarkable Story of How Guns Became as American as Apple Pie* (Nashville: Nelson Current, 2006), 33.

26. A. Leon Higginbotham, *In the Matter of Color: Race and the American Legal Process, the Colonial Period* (New York: Oxford University Press, 1980)), 167–68; Dunn, *Sugar and Slaves*, 239.

27. Steven J. Oatis, *A Colonial Complex: South Carolina's Frontiers in the Era of the Yamasee War, 1680–1730* (Lincoln: University of Nebraska Press, 2004), 34; Charles M. Christian, *Black Saga: The African American Experience: A Chronology* (New York: Civitas, 1999), 27–28.

28. John David Smith, *Slavery, Race, and American History: Historical Conflict, Trends, and Method, 1866–1953* (New York: M. E. Sharpe, 1999), 63; Edgar, *South Carolina*, 68–69.

29. Peter Kolchin, *American Slavery 1619–1877* (New York: Hill and Wang, 1993), 30; Edgar, *South Carolina*, 63, 66, 68–69; Coclanis, *Shadow of a Dream*, 64; Wood, *Black Majority*, 131–32.

30. Wood, *Black Majority*, 308–12.

31. Ibid., 309–14.

32. Jack Shuler, *Calling Out Liberty: The Stono Slave Rebellion and the Universal Struggle for Human Rights* (Jackson: University Press of Mississippi, 2009), 72.

33. Wood, *Black Majority*, 320–23.

34. Littlefield, *Rice and Slaves*, 160–61.

35. Edgar, *South Carolina*, 76; Robert M. Weir, *Colonial South Carolina, A History* (Columbia: University of South Carolina Press, 1997), 194; Wood, *Black Majority*, 323–26.

36. Edgar, *South Carolina*, 77.

37. Ibid., 131–32; Coclanis, *Shadow of a Dream*, 21–23, 50–51.

38. Greene, "Colonial South Carolina," 81; Edgar, *South Carolina*, 144; Judith A. Carney, *Black Rice: The African Origins of Rice Cultivation in the Americas* (Cambridge, Mass.: Harvard University Press, 2001), 78, 122.

39. Littlefield, *Rice and Slaves*, 92–98,105–9; Judith Carney and Richard Porcher, "Geographies of the Past: Rice, Slaves and Technological Transfer in South Carolina," *Southeastern Geographer* 33 (November 1993): 127–47.

40. Barbara Doyle, Mary Edna Sullivan, and Tracey Todd, *Beyond the Fields: Slavery at Middleton Place* (Columbia: University of South Carolina Press, 2008), 24.

41. Charles Joyner, *Down by the Riverside: A South Carolina Slave Community* (Urbana: University of Illinois Press, 1985), 127–30; Rowland et al., *Beaufort County*, 351–52, 362–63; Philip D. Morgan, "Work and Culture: The Task Syatem and the World of Lowcountry Blacks, 1700 to 1880," *The William and Mary Quarterly* 39 (October 1982): 563–99.

42. William S. Pollitzer, *The Gullah People and Their African Hertaige* (Athens: University of Georgia Press, 1999), 107–86; Ras Michael Brown, *African-Atlantic Cultures and the South Carolina Lowcountry* (New York: Cambridge University Press, 2012), passim; Gomez, *Exchanging Our Country Marks*, 244–90; Joyner, *Down by the Riverside*, passim.

43. Joseph E. Holloway, "The Sacred World of the Gullahs," in *Africanisms in American Culture*, ed. Joseph E. Holloway (Bloomington: Indiana University Press, 2005), 187–223; Rowland et al., *Beaufort County*, 134–36.

44. Gary B. Nash, *The Unknown American Revolution: The Unruly Birth of Democracy and the Struggle to Create America* (New York: Penguin Books, 2005), 60–61.

45. Quoted in *Niles Weekly Register*, July 15, 1820, 350.

46. Michael Lee Lanning, *African Americans in the Revolutionary War* (New York: Citadel Press, 2000), 146; Rudolph Alexander, *Racism, African Americans, and Social Justice* (Lanham, Md.: Rowman and Littlefield, 2005), 64–65; Edgar, *South Carolina*, 231.

47. Thomas Fleming, *The Perils of Peace: America's Struggle for Survival after Yorktown* (New York: HarperCollins, 2007), 254; Nash, *Unknown American Revolution*, 404–7.

48. Nash, *Unknown American Revolution*, 404–5.

49. Rowland et al., *Beaufort County*, 277–96.

50. Spenser, *Edisto Island*, 75; Edgar, *South Carolina*, 26; Joyce E. Chaplin, *An Anxious Pursuit: Agricultural Innovation and Modernity in the Lower South, 1730–1815* (Chapel Hill: University of North Carolina Press, 1996), 228–51; William L. Richter, *Historical Dictionary of the Old South* (Lanham, Md.: Scarecrow Press, 2013), 95.

51. Lacy K. Ford, *Origins of Southern Radicalism: The South Carolina Upcountry 1800–1860* (New York: Oxford University Press, 1988), 8–12; *Heads of Families, First Census of the United States: 1790, State of South Carolina* (Washington, D.C.: Government Printing Office, 1908), 29, 46, 102; Edgar, *South Carolina*, 309–10.

52. Edgar, *South Carolina*, 311; Ford, *Origins of Southern Radicalism*, 10–12, 84–88.

53. Edgar, *South Carolina*, 285–86; Steven Deyle, *Carry Me Back: The Domestic Slave Trade in American Life* (New York: Oxford University Press, 2005), 59–60.

54. Deyle, *Carry Me Back*, 41–62; Edgar, *South Carolina*, 275–76.

55. Edgar, *South Carolina*, 275–76; Edward E. Baptist, *The Half Has Never Been Told: Slavery and the Making of American Capitalism* (New York: Basic Books, 2014), 1–31.

56. Ira Berlin, *Generations of Captivity: A History of African American Slaves* (Cambridge, Mass.: Harvard University Press, 2003), 169.

57. Herbert G. Gutman, *The Black Family in Slavery and Freedom, 1750–1925* (New York: Vintage Books, 1976), 145–48.

58. See Baptist, *Half Has Never Been Told*, passim.

59. Lacy K. Ford, *Deliver Us from Evil: The Slavery Question in the Old South* (New York: Oxford University Press, 2009), 141–203; Edgar, *South Carolina*, 293; Janet Duitsman Cornelius, *When I Can Read My Title Clear: Literacy, Slavery, and Religion in the Antebellum South* (Columbia: University of South Carolina Press, 1992), 37–58; Bernard E. Powers, *Black Charlestonians: A Social History, 1822–1885* (Fayetteville: University of Arkansas Press, 1994), 17.

60. Edgar, *South Carolina*, 381; Stephanie McCurry, *Masters of Small Worlds: Yeoman Households, Gender Relations, and the Political Culture of the Antebellum South Carolina Low Country* (New York: Oxford University Press, 1995), 158–70.

61. J. Brent Morris, "'We are verily guilty concerning our brother': The Abolitionist Transformation of Planter William Henry Brisbane," *South Carolina Historical Magazine* 111, nos. 3–4 (July–October 2010): 118–25; James O. Farmer, *The Metaphysical Confederacy: James Henry Thorwell and the Synthesis of Southern Values* (Macon: Mercer University Press, 1986), 174–233; Rowland et al., *Beaufort County*, 411–12.

62. Barry Hankins, *The Second Great Awakening and the Transcendentalists* (Westport, Conn.: Greenwood, 2004), 69–70.

63. Albert J. Raboteau, *Slave Religion: The Invisible Institution in the Antebellum South* (New York: Oxford University Press, 1978), 215–322; Ira Berlin, "The Transformation of Slavery in the United States, 1800–1863," in *The Problem of Evil: Slavery, Freedom, and the Ambiguities of American Reform*, ed. Steven Mintz (Amherst: University of Massachusetts Press, 2007), 93–94.

64. Larry Koger, *Black Slaveowners: Free Black Slave Masters in South Carolina 1790–1860* (Jefferson, N.C.: McFarland, 1985), 34; Sherle L. Boone, *Meanings beneath the Skin: The Evolution of African Americans* (Lanham, Md.: Rowman and Littlefield, 2012), 108–14.

65. Marina Wikramanayake, *A World in Shadow: The Free Black in Antebellum South Carolina* (Columbia: University of South Carolina Press, 1973), 42–45; Michael P. Johnson and James L. Roarke, *Black Masters: A Free Family of Color in the South* (New York: Norton, 1984), 43–47; Powers, *Black Charlestonians*, 38–40.

66. Powers, *Black Charlestonians*, 55.

67. Edgar, *South Carolina*, 310; Koger, *Black Slaveowners*, 18–30, 227–30; Wikramanayake, *World in Shadow*, 45; Johnson and Roark, *Black Masters*, 63–64, 111–12, 280; Powers, *Black Charlestonians*, 47–50.

68. Powers, *Black Charlestonians*, 56–60; Edgar, *South Carolina*, 308–10.

69. Powers, *Black Charlestonians*, 64–67

70. Edgar, *South Carolina*, 327–8; John B. Boles, *Black Southerners, 1619–1869* (Lexington: University Press of Kentucky, 1984), 67.

71. See Douglas R. Egerton, *He Shall Go Out Free: The Lives of Denmark Vesey* (Madison: Madison House, 1999), 3–153.

72. Historians disagree about the extent to which the scope of the plot was exaggerated. See Robert L. Paquette, "From Rebellion to Revisionism: The Continuing Debate about the Denmark Vesey Affair," *Journal of the Historical Society* 4 (2004): 291–334.

73. Egerton, *He Shall Go Out Free*, 175–228.

74. Powers, *Black Charlestonians*, 21; William W. Freehling, *Prelude to Civil War: The Nullification Controversy in South Carolina, 1816–1836* (New York: Harper and Row, 1965), 111–15.

75. Aptheker, *American Negro Slave Revolts*, 279–86.

76. David Walker, *Walker's Appeal, in Four Articles* (Boston: David Walker, 1830), 44.

77. Egerton, *He Shall Go Out Free*, 213–14; Edgar, *South Carolina*, 339.

78. Aptheker, *American Negro Slave Revolts*, 310–11.

79. Daniel Walker Howe, *What Hath God Wrought: The Transformation of America, 1815–1848* (New York: Oxford University Press, 2007), 480–82, 509.

80. Ford, *Origins of Southern Radicalism*, 183–214, 338–74.

81. Steven A. Channing, *Crisis of Fear: Secession in South Carolina* (New York: Norton, 1974), 229–93.

82. Willie Lee Rose, *Rehearsal for Reconstruction: The Port Royal Experiment* (Indianapolis: Bobbs-Merrill, 1964), 13–31; Rowland et al., *Beaufort County*, 443–58.

83. Leon F. Litwack, *Been in the Storm So Long: The Aftermath of Slavery* (New York: Vintage, 1979), 3–63.

84. Augustin Taveau quoted in Eugene D. Genovese, *Roll Jordan Roll: The World the Slaves Made* (New York: Pantheon, 1974), 112.

85. George C. Rogers, *History of Georgetown County, South Carolina* (Columbia: University of South Carolina Press, 1970), 398–415.

86. Catherine Reef, *African Americans in the Military* (New York: Facts on File, 2010), 209–12.

87. See Martin H. Blatt, Thomas J. Brown, and Donald Yacovone, eds., *Hope and Glory: Essays on the Legacy of the 54th Massachusetts Regiment* (Amherst: University of Massachusetts Press, 2001), passim.

88. Morris, "We are verily guilty," 148–50.

89. *Frank Leslie's Illustrated Newspaper*, March 18, 1865.

90. *New York Daily Tribune*, April 4, 1865.

91. *New York Times*, April 14, 1865; Egerton, *He Shall Go Out Free*, xxiii.

92. Litwack, *Been in the Storm So Long*, 292–335.

93. Edgar, *South Carolina*, 379.

94. Joel Williamson, *After Slavery: The Negro in South Carolina during Reconstruction, 1861–1877* (New York: Norton, 1975), 33–63, 106–11; Litwack, *Been in the Storm So Long*, 387–449.

95. Litwack, *Been in the Storm So Long*, 387–449.

96. Edgar, *South Carolina*, 381–82; Wilbert L. Jenkins, *Seizing the Day: African Americans in Post–Civil War Charleston* (Bloomington: Indiana University Press, 1998), 111–32.

97. Edgar, *South Carolina*, 381; Eric Foner, *Reconstruction: America's Unfinished Revolution, 1863–1877* (New York: Harper and Row, 1988), 371.

98. William J. Cooper and Thomas E. Terrill, *The American South: A History*, vol. 2 (Lanham, Md.: Rowman and Littlefield, 2009), 451–52.

99. Cole Blease Graham, *The South Carolina State Constitution* (New York: Oxford University Press, 2011), 27–28.

100. *United States Congressional Serial Set* (Washington, D.C.: U.S. Government Printing Office, 1872), 260.

101. Daniel A. Novak, *Wheel of Servitude: Black Forced Labor after Slavery* (Lexington: University Press of Kentucky, 1978), 4–5; W.E.B. Du Bois, *Black Reconstruction in America: Toward a History of the Part Which Black Folk Played in the Attempt to Reconstruct Democracy in America, 1860–1880* (New York: Harcourt, Brace, 1935), 176.

102. Douglas R. Egerton, *The Wars of Reconstruction: The Brief, Violent History of America's Most Progressive Era* (New York: Bloomsbury Press, 2014), 216.

103. Foner, *Reconstruction*, 228–80.

104. Ibid., 5; Peggy Lamson, *The Glorious Failure: Black Congressman Robert Brown Elliot and the Reconstruction in South Carolina* (New York: Norton, 1973), 44.

105. Richard Zuczek, *State of Rebellion: Reconstruction in South Carolina* (Columbia: University of South Carolina Press, 2009), 50; Thomas C. Holt, "Negro Legislators in South Carolina," in *Southern Black Leaders in the Reconstruction Era*, ed. Howard N. Rabinowitz (Urbana: University of Illinois Press, 1982), 228; Thomas C. Holt, *Black over White: Negro Political Leadership in South Carolina during Reconstruction* (Urbana: University of Illinois Press, 1977), 225–42.

106. Edgar, *South Carolina*, 388; Holt, *Black over White*, 95.

107. Benjamin Ginsberg, *Moses of South Carolina: A Jewish Scalawag during Radical Reconstruction* (Baltimore: Johns Hopkins University Press, 2010), 124–27; Richard N. Current, *Those Terrible Carpetbaggers: A Reinterpretation* (New York: Oxford University Press, 1988), 214–35; Williamson, *After Slavery*, 331–35; J. Brent Morris, "No Peer in His Race: Robert Brown Elliott and the Radical Politics of Reconstruction Era South Carolina," in *Before Obama: A Reappraisal of Black Reconstruction Era Politicians*, ed. Matthew Lynch (Santa Barbara: Praeger, 2012), 18.

108. Edgar, *South Carolina*, 394–96.

109. Lou Faulkner Williams, *The Great South Carolina Ku Klux Klan Trials of 1871–1872* (Athens: University of Georgia Press, 1996), 1–39.

110. Ibid., 39.

111. Edgar, *South Carolina*, 401; Wyn Craig Wade, *The Fiery Cross: The Ku Klux Klan in America* (New York: Oxford University Press, 1998), 101–4.

112. Zuczek, *State of Rebellion*, 108.

113. Morris, "No Peer in His Race," 18–20.

114. Rod Andrew, *Wade Hampton: Confederate Warrior to Southern Redeemer* (Chapel Hill: University of North Carolina Press, 2008), 379.

115. Edgar, *South Carolina*, 403; Morris, "No Peer in His Race," 31–32.

116. Foner, *Reconstruction*, 575–86.

117. Morris, "No Peer in His Race," 34–35.

118. Edgar, *South Carolina*, 412–13; Andrew, *Wade Hampton*, 183–222.

119. Jack Bass and W. Scott Poole, *The Palmetto State: The Making of Modern South Carolina* (Columbia: University of South Carolina Press, 2009), 210; Edgar, *South Carolina*, 413.

120. George Brown Tindall, *South Carolina Negroes 1877–1900* (Columbia: University of South Carolina Press, 1952), 26–27.

121. Andrew, *Wade Hampton*, 225; Holt, *Black over White*, 217–18; James L. Underwood, *The Constitution of South Carolina: The Struggle for Political Equality* (Columbia: University of South Carolina Press, 1986), 36–40.

122. Edgar, *South Carolina*, 413–15.

123. Powers, *Black Charlestonians*, 264–65; Edgar, *South Carolina*, 417.

124. Edward L. Ayers, *The Promise of the New South: Life after Reconstruction* (New York: Oxford University Press, 1992), 257–58.

125. Ibid., 288; Underwood, *Constitution of South Carolina*, 42–43.

126. Ayers, *Promise of the New South*, 288–89.

127. Underwood, *Constitution of South Carolina*, 58–108.

128. Lynn Salsi, *Columbia: History of a Southern Capital* (Charleston, S.C.: Arcadia, 2003), 117; Christopher Waldrep, *The Many Faces of Judge Lynch: Extralegal Violence and Punishment in America* (New York: Palgrave Macmillan, 2002), 121.

129. Janet Hudson, *Entangled by White Supremacy: Reform in World War I-Era South Carolina* (Lexington: University Press of Kentucky, 2009), 11–40; Edgar, *South Carolina*, 469.

130. Ibid., 73–83.

131. Ibid., 83–100; Chad Williams, *Torchbearers of Democracy: African American Soldiers in the World War I Era* (Chapel Hill: University of North Carolina Press, 2010), 78–80.

132. Williams, *Torchbearers*, 138, 350–51; Reef, *African Americans in the Military*, 188–89.

133. Peter F. Lau, *Democracy Rising: South Carolina and the Fight for Black Equality since 1865* (Lexington: University Press of Kentucky, 2006), 56.

134. John Hammond Moore, *Columbia and Richland County: A South Carolina Community, 1740–1990* (Columbia: University of South Carolina Press, 1993), 379.

135. Williams, *Torchbearers*, 226.

136. Moore, *Columbia and Richland County*, 380.

137. Archie Vernon Huff, *Greenville: The History of the City and County in the South Carolina Piedmont* (Columbia: University of South Carolina Press, 1995), 323–25; Edgar, *South Carolina*, 483–86; Lau, *Democracy Rising*, 57–59.

138. Moore, *Columbia and Richland County*, 362.

139. Melissa Walker, *All We Knew Was to Farm: Rural Women in the Upcountry South, 1919–1941* (Baltimore: Johns Hopkins University Press, 2002), 243–48; Edgar, *South Carolina*, 484–85.

140. James C. Geisen, *Boll Weevil Blues: Cotton, Myth, and Power in the American South* (Chicago: University of Chicago Press, 2012), 34–35; Lau, *Democracy Rising*, 60–67; Edgar, *South Carolina*, 485–6; I. A. Newby, *Black Carolinians: A History of Blacks in South Carolina from 1895 to 1968* (Columbia: University of South Carolina Press, 1973), 200–201.

141. Edgar, *South Carolina*, 498.

142. Huff, *Greenville*, 333–73; Cheryl Lynn Greenberg, *To Ask for an Equal Chance: African Americans in the Great Depression* (Lanham, Md.: Rowman and Littlefield, 2009), 21–25; J. I. Hayes, *South Carolina and the New Deal* (Columbia: University of South Carolina Press, 2001), 158.

143. William E. Leuchtenburg, *The White House Looks South: Franklin D. Roosevelt, Harry S. Truman, Lyndon B. Johnson* (Baton Rouge: Louisiana State University Press, 2005), 61–65.

144. Hayes, *South Carolina and the New Deal*, 158–83.

145. Lau, *Democracy Rising*, 105, 129–30; Hayes, *South Carolina and the New Deal*, 171–75.

146. Lau, *Democracy Rising*, 219.

147. Underwood, *Constitution of South Carolina*, 158–74.

148. Ibid., 172–73; Lau, *Democracy Rising*, 140.

149. Hayes, *South Carolina and the New Deal*, 179–80.

150. Howard W. Odom, *Race and Rumors of Race: The American South in the Early Forties* (Baltimore: Johns Hopkins University Press, 2007), 92; Walter B. Edgar, *South Carolina in the Modern Age* (Columbia: University of South Carolina Press, 1992), 85.

151. Joseph Crespino, *Strom Thurmond's America* (New York: Macmillan, 2012), 51–55.

152. Kari A. Frederickson, *The Dixiecrat Revolt and the End of the Solid South, 1932–1968* (Chapel Hill: University of North Carolina Press, 2001), 58–66.

153. Marko Maunula, *Gutan Tag Y'all: Globalization and the South Carolina Peidmont, 1950–2000* (Athens: University of Georgia Press, 2010), 29.

154. Katherine Mellon Charron, *Freedom's Teacher: The Life of Septima Clark* (Chapel Hill: University of North Carolina Press, 2009), 150–67; Maunula, *Guten Tag Y'all*, 31.

155. Edgar, *South Carolina*, 519–20; Newby, *Black Carolinians*, 284–89.

156. Frederickson, *Dixiecrat Revolt*, 11–174, passim; Edgar, *South Carolina*, 521; John Egerton, *Speak Now against the Day: The Generation before the Civil Rights Movement in the South* (Chapel Hill: University of North Carolina Press, 1995), 499–501, 510.

157. Quoted in Kimberley Johnson, *Reforming Jim Crow: Southern Politics and State in the Age before* Brown (New York: Oxford University Press, 2010), 228.

158. Richard Kluger, *Simple Justice: The History of* Brown v. Board of Education *and Black America's Struggle for Equality* (New York: Knopf Doubleday, 2011), 334–35.

159. Septima Poinsett Clark, *Echo in My Soul* (New York: Dutton, 1962), 111–18; Edgar, *South Carolina*, 525–29; Numan V. Bartley, *The Rise of Massive Resistance: Race and Politics in the South in the 1950s* (Baton Rouge: Louisiana State University Press, 1999), 121.

160. Bartley, *Rise of Massive Resistance*, 116–17.

161. James L. Felder, *Civil Rights in South Carolina: From Peaceful Protests to Groundbreaking Rulings* (Charleston, S.C.: The History Press, 2012), 98–101; Bartley, *Rise of Massive Resistance*, 231; Moore, *Columbia and Richland County*, 419–20; Newby, *Black Carolinians*, 317–18; Raymond Arsenault, *Freedom Riders: 1961 and the Struggle for Racial Justice* (New York: Oxford University Press, 2006), 121–24.

162. Numan V. Bartley, *The New South: 1945–1980* (Baton Rouge: Louisiana State University Press, 1995), 298–306; Newby, *Black Carolinians*, 314–28; Baruch Whitehead, "We Shall Overcome: The Roles of Music in the US Civil Rights Movement," in *Music and Conflict Transformation: Harmonies and Dissonances in Geopolitics*, ed. Oliver Urbain (London: I. B. Tauris, 2008), 82–85.

163. Hartley, *New South*, 213; Edgar, *South Carolina*, 537–38.

164. Stephen O'Neill, "Memory, History, and the Desegregation of Greenville, South Carolina," in *Toward the Meeting of the Waters: Currents in the Civil Rights Movement of South Carolina during the Twentieth Century*, ed. Winifred B. Moore Jr. and Orville

Vernon Burton (Columbia: University of South Carolina Press, 2008), 286–99.

165. Dianne McWhorter, *Carry Me Home: Birmingham, Alabama, the Climactic Battle of the Civil Rights Revolution* (New York: Simon and Schuster, 2001), 311.

166. Bass and Poole, *Palmetto State*, 101.

167. Edgar, *South Carolina*, 538–39; Skip Eisiminger, ed., *Integration with Dignity: A Celebration of Harvey Gantt's Admission to Clemson* (Clemson: Clemson University Digital Press, 2003), passim; Newby, *Black Carolinians*, 332.

168. Philip G. Grose, *South Carolina at the Brink: Robert McNair and the Politics of Civil Rights* (Columbia: University of South Carolina Press, 2006), 13.

169. Edgar, *South Carolina*, 544.

170. Rebecca Bridges Watts, *Contemporary Southern Identity: Community through Controversy* (Jackson: University Press of Mississippi, 2007), 87–116.

171. Ibid., 107–8.

172. Edgar, *South Carolina*, xx.

173. William Lewis Burke and Belinda Gergel, *Matthew J. Perry: The Man, His Times, and His Legacy* (Columbia: University of South Carolina Press, 2004), 165; Edgar, *South Carolina*, 539–40.

174. Edgar, *South Carolina*, 538–39.

175. Walter J. Fraser, *Charleston! Charleston!: The History of a Southern City* (Columbia: University of South Carolina Press, 1990), 421–23.

176. Edgar, *South Carolina*, 541–42; Jack Bass and Walter DeVries, *The Transformation of Southern Politics: Social Change and Political Consequence since 1945* (Athens: University of Georgia Press, 1995), 260, 274–75; Orville Vernon Burton, "South Carolina," in *The Quiet Revolution: The Impact of the Voting Rights Act in the South, 1965–1990*, ed. Chandler Davidson and Bernard Grofman (Princeton: Princeton University Press, 1994), 191–232, 420–32.

177. Alton Hornsby, *Black America: A State by State Historical Encyclopedia* (Santa Barbara: ABC-CLIO, 2011), 757–58; Edgar, *South Carolina*, 562.

178. Charles E. Menifield, Stephen D. Shaffer, and Brandi J. Brassell, "An Overview of African American Representation in Other Southern States," in *Politics in the New South: Representation of African Americans in Southern State Legislatures*, ed. Charles E. Menifield and Stephen D. Shaffer (Albany: SUNY Press, 2005), 169.

179. Felder, *Civil Rights in South Carolina*, 134–35.

180. Crespino, *Strom Thurmond's America*, 250–51; Jack Bass and Marilyn W. Thompson, *Ol' Strom: An Unauthorized Biography of Strom Thurmond* (Columbia: University of South Carolina Press, 2002), 253–56.

181. Bass and Poole, *Palmetto State*, 135–36; Crespino, *Strom Thurmond's America*, 296.

182. Bass and De Vries, *Transformation of Southern Politics*, 269–70.

183. Glenn Feldman, "The Status Quo Society, the Rope of Religion, and the New Racism," in *Politics and Religion in the White South*, ed. Glenn Feldman (Lexington: University Press of Kentucky, 2005), 307–8.

184. Edgar, *South Carolina*, 560.

185. Felder, *Civil Rights in South Carolina*, 128.

186. John M. Coski, *The Confederate Battle Flag: America's Most Embattled Emblem* (Cambridge, Mass.: Harvard University Press, 2009), 250; K. Michael Prince, *Rally 'Round the Flag, Boys!: South Carolina and the Confederate Flag* (Columbia: University of South Carolina Press, 2004), 179–86.

187. "Sanford issues apology for Orangeburg Massacre," *The State*, February 9, 2003, http://goo.gl/kpCIti (accessed May 1, 2014).

188. "Sanford Attends NAACP Forum in Georgia without Challenger," http://www.goupstate.com/article/20061013/NEWS/610130348, (accessed May 1, 2014).

189. "South Carolina Boycott Still On!," *The Crisis* (May–June 2000): 52.

190. Quoted in Lau, *Democracy Rising*, 230.

191. Citing State unemployment rates, by race/ethnicity and overall, 2015Q1, EPI analysis of Bureau of Labor Statistics Local Area Unemployment Statistics (LAUS) data and Current Population Survey (CPS) data, Economic Policy Institute, http://goo.gl/Tu5ipV, accessed January 13, 2016.

192. 2008–2012 American Community Survey 5-Year Estimates, Table B19301, South Carolina Review and Fiscal Affairs Office, http://abstract.sc.gov/chapter13/income4.html accessed January 13, 2016.

193. 2009–2013 American Community Survey Single-Year Estimates, Table S1701, South Carolina Revenue and Fiscal Affairs Office, http://abstract.sc.gov/chapter13/income14.html accessed January 13, 2016.

194. Bass and Poole, *Palmetto State*, 196.

195. Walter B. Edgar, "Beyond the Tumult and the Shouting: Black and White South Carolina in the 1990s," in *The Southern State of Mind*, ed. Jan Nordby Gretland (Columbia: University of South Carolina Press, 1999), 98.

196. Sellers and Gantt quoted in Bass and Poole, *Palmetto State*, 202, 204.

197. "Obama Wins Big Victory in South Carolina Primary," January 26, 2008, http://www.nbcnews.com/id/22854377/ns/politics-decision_08/t/obama-wins-big-victory-sc-primary/ (accessed May 1, 2014).

198. "Obama's Sweep in South Carolina Sets Up Super Tuesday Face-Off," *Jet*, February 11, 2008, 6.

199. "Obama Wins S.C. by Wide Margin," *Boston Globe*, January 27, 2008, http://www.boston.com/news/nation/articles/2008/01/27/obama_wins_sc_by_wide_margin/?page=full (accessed May 2, 2014).

200. "Obama on Shoulders of Men Like Charlotte's Harvey Gantt," September 6, 2012, http://thegrio.com/2012/09/06/obama-on-shoulders-of-men-like-charlottes-harvey-gantt/ (accessed May 2, 2014).

201. Simeon Booker, *Shocking the Conscience: A Reporter's Account of the Civil Rights Movement* (Jackson: University Press of Mississippi, 2013), 220.

202. "President Obama: Harvey Gantt Helped Set Course for Young Black Leaders," http://www.charlotteobserver.com/2012/09/05/3503596/architect-served-as-a-building.html (accessed May 1, 2014).

203. Tony Leon Powell, *North Carolina: Race of the Century* (Minneapolis: Ambassador Press, 2006), 45; "President Obama: Harvey Gantt Helped Set Course for Young Black Leaders."

204. Quoted in Bass and Poole, *Palmetto State*, 202.

Chapter 1: "The people commonly called Negroes"

1. Historians debate the location of this river, offering as possibilities the Spanish Punta de Santa Elena (modern Port Royal), a location near Wynyah Bay, or further south near the mouth of the Savannah River.

2. Ayllón.

3. San Felipe Puerto de Plata, Dominican Republic.

4. A seine is a fishing net that hangs vertically in relatively shallow water with its base held down by weights and its topic held at the surface by floats.

5. An area ruled by a hereditary nobleman possessing special quasi-royal prerogatives. The Lords Proprietors, though swearing allegiance to King Charles II, were granted the power to rule Carolina largely independent of the king.

6. From the Spanish *cacique*. Originally a title derived from the Taino for pre-Columbian chiefs of the Caribbean, in this context the title referred to influential landholding leaders in the colony.

7. Yards, a spar on a ship's mast from which sails are set.

8. See the 1690 "An Act for the Better Ordering of Slaves," *The Statutes at Large of South Carolina*, vol. 7 (Columbia: A. S. Johnson, 1840), 343–47.

9. A gallows-type structure from which dead bodies were hung for public display.

10. Pentecost.

11. Castrated.

12. A writ similar to bail directed to an officer of the law commanding him to take sureties for a prisoner's appearance and then to set him at large.

Chapter 2: "De bless fa true, dem wa da wok haad"

1. Prior to the mid-1730s, slave owners in South Carolina held more Native American slaves than did slave owners in any other colony. The population was drawn largely from raids on enemy tribes or supplied by Native American groups that were in alliance with colonial authorities.

2. Charles Towne was the capital of colonial South Carolina.

3. South Carolina had passed laws in 1724 and 1739 requiring whites to bring their guns with them to church on Sundays, since this was the only day slaves were not busy working and thus presented the most likely window for slave rebellion.

4. The Stono rebels had famously used drums during their revolt in attempts to call more slaves to arms.

5. John Laurens (1754–1782), lieutenant colonel in the Continental Army. As a member of the South Carolina General Assembly in 1779, 1780, and 1782, he introduced unsuccessful plans to recruit an African American regiment. He was killed in battle on August 27, 1782.

6. Isaac Huger (1743–1797) was a wealthy South Carolina planter and a brigadier general in the Continental Army.

7. "... is natural law."

8. William H. Seward (1801–1872), American antislavery politician who served as governor of New York, U.S. senator, and secretary of state under Abraham Lincoln and Andrew Johnson.

9. John 12:8.

10. Song of Solomon 6:10.

Chapter 3: "A jubilee of freedom"

1. The British captured Charlestown, South Carolina, in May 1780.

2. Waters was a Charles Town carpenter to whom King had been apprenticed at age sixteen.

3. A smallpox epidemic had gripped North America during the war, and more people died from the disease than in combat-related injuries.

4. The base of the British commander Lord Cornwallis in Camden, South Carolina.

5. Captain Lewes was commander of the Rocky Mount Militia Regiment, a Loyalist American militia.

6. Lightly armed cavalry.

7. The British vacated their post at Nelson's Ferry, located on the Santee River near present-day Eutawville, in May 1781.

8. Perth Amboy, New Jersey, then under the control of the Patriots.

9. The Treaty of Paris required the British to withdraw "without causing any *Destruction*, or carrying away any *Negroes* or other *Property* of the American Inhabitants." British commanders interpreted this to mean that slaves freed before ratification of the treaty would remain enslaved thereafter.

10. Birchtown, six miles from Shelburne, Nova Scotia, became the largest settlement of free blacks in North America.

11. Liele (1750–1828) was the slave of a Baptist deacon near Savannah, Georgia, and was licensed as an exhorter in 1773. He was ordained as a missionary to the region's slaves in 1775 and later became the first African American missionary to Jamaica.

12. Matthew 11:28.

13. Waite Palmer (1722–1795) was a white minister, born in Connecticut. With Liele, Palmer converted and baptized the original African Americans members of the church. Following Lord Dunmore's Proclamation, white ministers were prohibited from preaching to slaves, "lest they should furnish . . . too much knowledge," and Palmer passed responsibility of his flock to David George.

14. George Galphin (1700–1780) was a wealthy trader and diplomat and owner of David George at the time of the American Revolution. Palmer's children taught George to read using the Bible, and the Silver Bluff Church initially met in a barn on his property.

15. The British captured Savannah on December 29, 1779, and held it until May 1781.

16. Ebenezer, Georgia, was severely damaged in the Revolutionary War, though it served as the temporary capital of the state in 1782.

17. George Whitefield (1714–1770) was an Anglican preacher who is often credited with having sparked the First Great Awakening in America. He arrived in the colonies in 1738 and in 1740 began an extended preaching circuit from New York to South Carolina. Though a slave owner himself, he often criticized abuses within the institution and preached of God's salvation to slaves and slaveholders alike.

18. Amos 4:12.

19. Marrant had been apprenticed to a Charleston musician, and, after mastering the violin and the French horn, he played for the students at his master's music school and was regularly hired to play for balls and events in the community.

20. This witness was not identified. His testimony was given upon the guarantee that he would not be prosecuted or named in the record.

21. Revelation 22:11.

22. Matthew 28:18–20.

23. King's Highway, U.S. 271.

24. Charles T. Trowbridge (1835–1907) was captain of Company A, First South Carolina Volunteers, and later lieutenant colonel of the Thirty-third USCT. He remained in South Carolina after the war as an agent of the Freedman's Bureau.

25. David Hunter (1802–1886), Union general during the Civil War and commander

of the Department of the South from March to September 1862 and from January to June 1863. Hunter ordered the emancipation of the slaves of South Carolina, Georgia, and Florida in May 1862, but the unauthorized order was immediately rescinded by Abraham Lincoln.

26. This was actually Hunter's order of May 8, 1862, to enlist two regiments of African American soldiers.

27. Rufus Saxton (1824–1908), Union Army brigadier general during the Civil War and military governor of the Department of the South from 1862 to 1865. After the war, he serves as assistant commissioner of the Freedman's Bureau for the states of South Carolina, Georgia, and Florida.

28. On the night of April 27, 1862, fifteen slaves rowed a Confederate barge to the Union blockade fleet.

29. Congress authorized the distribution of half the *Planter*'s appraised value among the crew. Smalls's share was $1,500.

30. Samuel Francis DuPont (1803–1865), US Navy rear admiral, had been ordered to attack Charleston with a fleet of ironclads at the time of Smalls's arrival.

31. Robert Gould Shaw (1837–1863) was the son of a wealthy Boston abolitionist family and was appointed commanding officer of the Fifty-fourth Massachusetts Infantry Regiment. He was killed in the Second Battle of Fort Wagner and was buried in a mass grave with his black troops.

32. Frazier was sixty-seven years old at the time of the meeting and had been a Baptist minister for thirty-five years. He had been born a slave in North Carolina but purchased his and his wife's freedom in 1857.

33. Emancipation Proclamation.

34. The act of July 4, 1864. permitted agents from Northern states to recruit soldiers among African Americans in the Confederate states and to credit them against the draft quotas of the Northern states.

35. The Twenty-first USCT, organized from the understaffed Third, Fourth, and Fifth South Carolina Colored Infantry, had arrived in Charleston on February 18, 1865, to begin guard duty.

36. Stewart L. Woodford (1835–1913), Colonel of the 103rd USCT.

37. John Porter Hatch (1822–1901), military commander of Charleston from February through August 1865.

Chapter 4: "All men are born free and equal"

1. Richard H. Cain (1825–1887) was born free in Virginia and was educated at Wilberforce University. After the Civil War, Cain moved to Charleston as missionary superintendent for the AME church. He was active in politics and served two terms in Congress as a representative from South Carolina during Reconstruction.

2. The South Carolina Constitutional Convention of 1865 was dominated by the antebellum elite, did not allow African Americans the right to vote, and retained racial qualifications for the legislature.

3. This line is from a 1795 poem by the Scottish poet Robert Burns, "Is There for Honest Poverty," which is famous for its egalitarian ideas of society

4. Delegate Benjamin Franklin Whittemore (1824–1894) had been a chaplain in the Union Army before moving to South Carolina. He was elected as a Republican to Congress in 1868.

5. Alexander Stephens (1812–1883) of Georgia was vice president of the Confederacy. In 1873, he was elected to Congress, where he had served from 1843 to 1859.
6. The Slaughter-House Cases, 83 U.S. 36 (1873), were the first Supreme Court interpretation of the Fourteenth Amendment. The decision interpreted the Amendment as protecting the privileges and immunities conferred by U.S. citizenship but not those incident to citizenship of a state.
7. James B. Beck (1822–1890), U.S. Congressman from Kentucky from 1867 to 1875.
8. Elliott refers here to *Dred Scott vs. Sanford*, 60 U.S. 393 (1857).
9. This refers to Stephens's "Cornerstone Speech" of March 21, 1861, in which he explained the fundamental differences between the constitutions of the Confederacy and the United States, laid out the Confederate causes for civil war, and defended slavery by asserting that "Our new Government is founded upon exactly the opposite ideas; its foundations are laid, its cornerstone rests, upon the great truth that the negro is not equal to the white man; that slavery, subordination to the superior race, is his natural and normal condition."
10. John T. Harris (1823–1899), Democratic congressman from Virginia from 1859 to 1861 and from 1871 to 1881.
11. *Dred Scott vs. Sanford* (1857).
12. Ellenton, near present Barnwell, South Carolina, was annexed as part of the Savannah River nuclear site in 1950.
13. Anthony Pickens Butler led a band of white troops to Ellenton from Aiken, South Carolina.
14. African American state legislator from Barnwell County.

Chapter 5: "Each tomorrow will find us farther than today"

1. Benjamin Tillman.
2. James Aldrich (1850–1910), protégé of James Henry Hammond and successful defender of the white Ellenton rioters.
3. John L. McLauren (1860–1934) served as a U.S. senator from South Carolina from 1897 to 1903.
4. Junkers were the landed nobility in nineteenth-century Prussia. They controlled vast estates that were maintained by servants, who had few rights.
5. Shaw Memorial School employed two black teachers, but only because of the requirement set by the school's founding benefactor, Robert Gould Shaw, that the school have "some" black educators.
6. Thomas Ezekiel Miller (1849–1938) was born free but was raised by slaves in Ferebeeville, South Carolina. He served in the South Carolina Legislature from 1874 to 1882 and in the U.S. Congress from 1890 to 1892. He was later appointed the first president of South Carolina State University.
7. Proverbs 22:7.
8. Galatians 6:9.
9. Olin D. Johnson (1896–1965) was governor of South Carolina from 1935 to 1939 and from 1943 to 1945. He also served as a U.S. senator from 1945 to 1965.
10. NAACP.
11. In New York City.

Chapter 6: "We Shall Overcome"

1. Osceola E. McKaine (1892–1955) was a Sumter native and a World War II veteran, who, upon his return after the war, became a civil rights advocate and co-founder of the Progressive Democratic Party. He ran as the PDP candidate for the U.S. Senate in 1944, the first African American candidate for elected office in South Carolina since Reconstruction.
2. The Southern Negro Youth Conference was founded in Richmond in 1937 by young people who had attended the National Negro Congress the year before. At its peak, twelve years later, the group had expanded to ten chapters and eleven thousand members.
3. Founded in 1938, the Southern Conference for Human Welfare was a Birmingham-based civil rights organization committed to expanding voting rights among African Americans in the South.
4. Founded as the Commission on Interracial Cooperation in 1919, the Southern Regional Council was created to avoid racial violence and to promote racial equality in the south.
5. The Civil Rights Congress was formed in 1946 at a national conference for radicals. Until 1956, it used litigation and demonstrations to call attention to racial injustice in the United States.
6. In *Smith v. Allwright,* 321 U.S. 649 (1944), the Supreme Court declared unconstitutional a Texas state law that authorized the Democratic Party to set its own internal rules, including regarding the use of all-white primaries.
7. 321 U.S. 649 (1944), a U.S. Supreme Court ruling that declared the all-white Democratic primaries in Texas unconstitutional.
8. *Brown v. Board of Education* (1954).
9. Joseph A. DeLaine (1898–1974) was a Methodist minister and civil rights reformer from Clarendon County, South Carolina. He was instrumental in working with the NAACP on the *Briggs v. Elliott* case, which became one of the five cases consolidated into the U.S. Supreme Court case *Brown v. Board of Education.*
10. Myles Horton was a cofounder of the Highlander Folk School in Newmarket, Tennessee, a social justice leadership training school famous for its role in educating activists during the civil rights movement. His wife, Zilphia, was a constant collaborator until her death in 1956.
11. Isaiah Dequincey Newman (1911–1985) was a Methodist minister and civil rights leader. He served as NAACP field director for South Carolina from 1960 to 1969. In 1983, Newman won election to the South Carolina State Senate, becoming the first African American to serve in that body since 1887.
12. Decatur Nichols (1900–2005) was born in Georgetown, South Carolina. He became the fifty-ninth bishop of the AME Church in 1940 and was active in the civil rights movement.

Chapter 7: "Common ground"

1. Jackson founded the National Rainbow Coalition in 1984 as a political organization to seek equal rights for all Americans and to demand social programs, protection of voting rights, and affirmative action for minority groups that had suffered under the economic policies of President Ronald Reagan.

2. Michael Dukakis (born 1933) was twice governor of Massachusetts and was the 1988 Democratic nominee for president of the United States.

3. *Grutter v. Bollinger,* 539 U.S. 306 (2003).

4. Maynard Jackson (1938–2003) was the first African American mayor of Atlanta.

5. Skidmore, an Iraq war vet, traveled with Obama through his South Carolina campaign tour and introduced him at various rallies.

6. Obama won the Democratic Iowa caucuses, which took place on January 3, 2008.

7. Iowa, New Hampshire, Nevada, and Michigan.

INDEX